Adam as

Adam as Israel

Genesis 1–3 as the Introduction to the Torah and Tanakh

SETH D. POSTELL

PICKWICK *Publications* · Eugene, Oregon

ADAM AS ISRAEL
Genesis 1–3 as the Introduction to the Torah and Tanakh

This study is based on the Hebrew Scriptures, with versification keyed to the Biblica Hebraica Stuttgartensia (which does not always coincide with English versification). Unless stated otherwise, all verses have been translated directly from the Hebrew by the author.

Information and tables by Tvi Erlich, "The Story of the Garden of Eden in Comparison to the Position of Mount Sinai and the Tabernacle," *Alon Shvut for Graduates of the Har Eztion Yeshiva* 11 (1998) 17–35, reproduced by permission.

Pickwick Publications
An Imprint of Wipf and Stock Publishers
199 W. 8th Ave., Suite 3
Eugene, OR 97401

www.wipfandstock.com

ISBN 13: 978-1-61097-176-8

Cataloging-in-Publication data:

Postell, Seth D.

    Adam as Israel : Genesis 1–3 as the introduction to the Torah and Tanakh / Seth D. Postell.

    xii + 204 p. ; 23 cm. Including bibliographical references and indexes.

    ISBN 13: 978-1-61097-176-8

    1. Bible. O.T. Genesis I–III—Criticism, interpretation, etc.. 2 Bible. O.T. Pentateuch—Criticism, interpretation, etc. 3. Eden. I. Title.

BS561 P575 2011

Manufactured in the U.S.A.

*I lovingly dedicate this book to Murray Postell,
my father, fishing partner, and friend.*

Contents

Tables and Figures

Acknowledgments

THE LION'S PORTION OF thanks goes to my wife, Ling, and to my three children, Yael, Nadav, and Yoav, for their loving support and encouragement throughout the research and writing of this book (Prov 31:10; Ps 127:3). I wish to acknowledge my beloved mentor and dear friend, Dr. John H. Sailhamer. He has been the single most positive influence on my life as a follower of Yeshua. And he, more than any other person I know, has stimulated within me an unquenchable love for the Hebrew Bible. I regard my time as his PhD student as one of the greatest honors and privileges of my life. Dr. John Goldingay and Dr. David Howard deserve acknowledgement for their willingness to carefully interact with my research and also for their thoughtful comments and clarifying questions.

I also want to thank Helen Breger, Holocaust survivor and friend, who spent many hours helping me polish up my German translations. I thank Dr. Bob Cole for his encouragement to publish this manuscript and for his kind endorsement. Janet Reese also deserves special mention for her tireless efforts to ensure that I had all the resources necessary to complete my research. I also want to thank Dr. Richard Hays for pointing me to some helpful resources on the topic of intertextuality. I want to extend a special word of thanks to Carol Barr, without whom this book would likely never have been published. Thank you, Carol, for your willingness to edit the manuscript and for your passion for details. A special word of thanks goes to my editor, Robin Parry, for poring over every detail of my manuscript. His questions and comments resulted in greater clarity in my own thinking and writing.

Finally, I wish to thank the following individuals for helping me overcome the many challenges involved with writing and completing this book: Nicole Anderson, David Brewer, Daniel Ezell, Jenni and Zhava Glaser, Gregg Hagg, You-lim Hahn, Karol Joseph, Marcie Linares, Dr. Rick Melick, John Milton, Jhan Moskowitz, Tim North, Jennifer Rodgers, Brian

Sandifer, Barbara Stahl, Yohanan Stanfield, Jeff Swank, Wes Taber, Ryan Walcott, and Dr. Gregg Watson.

Above all, I wish to praise my God and King for graciously answering many prayers from start to finish.

Abbreviations

ANE	Ancient Near East
BHS	*Biblia Hebraica Stuttgartensia*
Bib	*Biblica*
CBQ	*Catholic Biblical Quarterly*
CG DD	*Cairo Geniza Targumic Fragment: MS DD*
E	Elohist Source
ERT	*Evangelical Review of Theology*
Frg. Tg. P	Fragment Targum, Recension P
Frg. Tg. VNL	Fragment Targum, Recension VNL
Gen. Rab.	*Genesis Rabbah*
GKC	*Gesenius' Hebrew Grammar*
J	Yahwist Source
JBL	*Journal of Biblical Literature*
JETS	*Journal of the Evangelical Theological Society*
JTS	*Journal of Theological Studies*
JSOT	*Journal for the Study of the Old Testament*
JSOTSup	Journal for the Study of the Old Testament Supplement Series
LXX	Septuagint
MT	Masoretic Text
P	Priestly Source
Q	Qumran
SJT	*Scottish Journal of Theology*
Tg. Neof.	Targum Neofiti
Tg. Onq.	Targum Onqelos
Tg. Ps.-J.	Targum Pseudo-Jonathan
Tanakh	The Torah, the Prophets, and the Writings
TynBul	*Tyndale Bulletin*

VT	*Vetus Testamentum*
VTSup	Vetus Testamentum Supplement Series
Vulg.	Vulgate
ZAW	*Zeitschrift für die alttestamentliche Wissenschaft*

1

Introduction

Pre-critical Christian scholars interpreted Genesis 1–3 as the fountainhead for all biblical theology and the basis for God's ultimate act of redemption through the provision of the Seed of the woman in the person of the Messiah.[1] These scholars also accepted without question the continuity between the intentionality of Torah or Book of Moses (in its canonical or final form) and the NT interpretation of it (see John 5:46–47). In essence, Moses (the man and the book) was regarded as a faithful witness of the future Messianic realities (see Heb 3:5), and the compositional intentionality of the Pentateuch was tightly moored to the hope of the new covenant. The rise of critical scholarship, however, brought in its wake not only the rejection of the literary unity of Genesis 1–3, but also a whole new understanding of the compositional history and intentionality of the Pentateuch in its final form. Genesis 1–3 was deemed to be composed of two mutually contradicting creation accounts from differing time periods and with differing theologies. Eventually, Gen 2:4b—3:24 was attributed to an earlier prophetic source ("J"), and 1:1—2:4a was attributed to a final post-exilic priestly layer ("P"). Likewise, the intentionality of the Pentateuch (or Hexateuch/ Tetrateuch) was tightly bound to the agenda of the post-exilic priestly circles: namely, Second Temple Judaism.

Recent trends in modern Pentateuchal scholarship in particular, and biblical studies in general, have called into question both the notion of the disunity of Genesis 1–3 (and the Pentateuch as a whole) as well as the assumption that the intentionality of the final form (canonical) Pentateuch is bound up with the priestly agenda of Second Temple Judaism. Although the climate of Pentateuchal studies is changing, there have been relatively few attempts to interpret Genesis 1–3 as a coherent

---

1. See the history of interpretation in chapter 2.

unity, and as a literarily strategic introduction to the Law, the Prophets, and the Writings (Tanakh) as a whole.

PURPOSE

The primary purpose of this book is to apply a text-centered, compositional analysis to Genesis 1–3 in order to discern the relationship between these chapters and the remainder of the Torah. In addition, the function of Genesis 1–3 in the canonical Tanakh is investigated. Studies of the first three chapters of Genesis have generally focused on the exposition of the content of the individual hypothetical sources,[2] ANE parallels,[3] scientific and ecological issues;[4] ethical issues of gender, sexuality, and marriage;[5] and theological issues pertaining to the image of God and the doctrine of the Trinity.[6] Although there have been many literary analyses applied to Genesis 1–3,[7] to date there have been relatively few

2. Bauks, "Genesis 1 als Programmschrift," 333–45; Bechtel, "Rethinking," 77–117; Bechtel, "Genesis "2.4b—3.24," 3–26; Begrich, "Paradieserzählung" 93–116; Engnell, "'Knowledge' and 'Life,'" 103–19; Firmage, "Genesis 1" 97–114; Hurowitz, "P—Understanding the Priestly Source," 30–37, 44–47; Kutsch, "Paradieserzählung," 9–24; Levin, "Redaktion RJP," 15–34; Lohfink, "Erzählung von Sündenfall," 81–101; Schüle, "Würde," 440–54; Vervenne, "Genesis 1,1—2,4," 35–79; Weimar, "Struktur und Komposition," 803–43.

3. Atwell, "Egyptian Source," 441–77; Harris, "Symbolism in Creation." Hurowitz, "Genesis of Genesis," 36–48, 52–54; Johnston, "Genesis 1," 178–94; Sparks, "Enuma Elish," 625–48; Walton, "Creation in Genesis 1:1—2:3," 48–63; Walton, Lost World of Genesis One.

4. Bozung, "Evaluation," 406–23; Elbert, "Genesis 1," 23–72; Greenspoon, "From Dominion to Stewardship?" 159–83; McConnell, "In His Image" 114–27; Raj, "Yahweh's Earth," 40–60; Ronan, "Stewardship Model," 18–19; Zimmer, "Creation Story," 77–92; Zimmer, "Creation of Man," 16–26; Zimmer, "Genesis 1 as Sign," 172–80.

5. Claassens, "Moon Spoke Up: Genesis 1," 325–42; D'Angelo, "Gender Refusers," 149–73; Jastram and Weinrich, "Man" 3–96; Jervis, "Story," 265–79; Magnuson, "Marriage," 26–42; Scotchmer, "Lessons from Paradise," 80–85; Stark, "Augustine on Women," 215–41; Tarwater, "Covenantal Nature of Marriage"; Valiyapparambil, "Power of the Powerless," 163–64.

6. Auld, "Imago Dei in Genesis" 259–62; Baker, "The Image of God," 97–109; Grenz, "Social God," 87–100; Jenson, "Bible and Trinity," 329–39; MacDonald, "Imago Dei and Election," 303–27; Mays, "Self in Psalms," 27–43; McConnell, "In His Image," 114–27; Packer, "Reflected Glory," 56; Towner, "Clones of God," 341–56; Wall, "Imitatio Creatoris," 21–42.

7. Collins, "What Happened?" 12–44; Collins, Genesis 1–4; Culley, "Action Sequences," 25–33; Hess, "Genesis 1–2," 143–53; Jobling, "Myth Semantics," 41–49; Kovacs, "Structure," 139–47; Levine, "Curse and Blessing," 189–99; Lim, Grace. Ouro,

text-centered attempts to interpret Genesis 1–3 as the introduction to the Pentateuch.[8] Furthermore, text-centered studies that have attempted to interpret Genesis 1–3 as the introduction of the Pentateuch are by no means exhaustive. It is the contention of this book that Genesis 1–3 merits further investigation, not only in terms of its relationship to the rest of the Pentateuch, but also in terms of its significance for discerning the overall redactional concerns behind the formation and shaping of the Tanakh.[9]

THESIS

In this book the following thesis is argued: when understood as the introduction to the Torah and to the Tanakh as a whole, Genesis 1–3 intentionally foreshadows Israel's failure to keep the Sinai Covenant as well as their exile from the Promised Land in order to point the reader to a future work of God in the "last days." Adam's failure to "conquer" (Gen 1:28) the seditious inhabitant of the land (the serpent), his temptation and violation of the commandments, and his exile from the garden is Israel's story *en nuce*.[10] The certitude of failure in the introduction to the Pentateuch anticipates the conclusion (Deut 28:69 [29:1, English versions]—34:12). Just as it was in the beginning, under the best of circumstances, so also it will be in the end. In the conclusion to the Pentateuch, Moses presents Israel's future apostasy and exile as a certainty (see Deut 30:1–10; 31:28–29). Thus, the Pentateuch is framed with a prophetic awareness[11] of Israel's exile due to their failure to keep the Sinai Covenant both in the present and in the future (see for example Deut 32:1–43) because of the evil "inclination" (יצר) of their heart (compare Gen 6:5; 8:21 with Deut 31:21). This *inclusio* of pessimism at both ends of the Pentateuch with respect to human abilities to "do this and live," not only supplies the contextual framework for interpreting the Sinai Narrative, but also provides

"Linguistic and Thematic Parallels" 44–54; Ouro, "Garden of Eden Account," 219–43; Parker and Patte, "Structural Exegesis," 141–59; Patte, "Genesis 2 and 3," 1–164; Shea, "Unity of Creation Account," 9–39; Trimpe, *Von der Schöpfung*.

8. Notable exceptions include Collins, *Genesis 1–4*; Sailhamer, *Pentateuch as Narrative*; Toews, "Genesis 1–4," 38–52.

9. The Law, the Prophets, and the Writings.

10. See Bovell, "Genesis 3:21?" 361–66.

11. For the notion of a "prophetic" Pentateuch—in contradistinction to a "priestly" Pentateuch as is commonly assumed—see Sailhamer, *Meaning of Pentateuch*, 248–49.

the rationale for the need of a new work in the "last days," whereby God would rectify the human inclination by means of a circumcised heart (Deut 30:6). Moreover, the groundwork is also laid for the expectation of another "Adam" (another priest-king) to arise from among the people of Israel who will ultimately fulfill the creation mandate in the "last days." In other words, Genesis 1–3, when read as integrally related to the Pentateuch and the Tanakh as a whole, *is not meant to encourage Israel to keep Sinai*; rather, it forthrightly admits that Israel did not (and will not) keep it, and therefore prepares the reader to wait expectantly in exile for a new work of God in the last days (just as Jacob and Moses did).

2

History of Interpretation

A S WILL BE SEEN in this brief history of the interpretation of Genesis 1–3, the pre-critical scholars, both Jewish and Christian, presumed the unity of the Pentateuch based on the belief that the Scriptures of Israel were divinely inspired. For Christian Pentateuchal scholarship, Julius Wellhausen marks an important turning point in the ways in which Christians understood Genesis 1–3 in particular, and the Pentateuch in general. Recent trends in biblical scholarship have resulted in fundamental alterations in the conceptualization of the compositional history of the Pentateuch as well as a new appreciation for the compositional structure of the final canonical form of the text.

PRE-CRITICAL APPROACH

Jewish Interpretation

Although it is frequently assumed that Jewish midrashic interpretation is not concerned with authorial intent,[1] Isac Leo Seeligmann demonstrated that many of the associations of midrashic exegesis are part and parcel of the inner-biblical interpretation of the Hebrew Bible itself.[2] For a long time Jewish scholars have noticed "associations" between the early chapters of Genesis and Israel's history as it unfolds in the Pentateuch, as well as in the rest of the Hebrew Bible. Jewish exegetes noted textual (and historical) patterns from Genesis 1–3 replicated elsewhere in the Tanakh (Israel's biblically recorded history). According to Paul Morris,

> A pattern is forged linking the precise details of the creation of
> the world and the creation of Israel based on "associated" bibli-

---

1. By authorial intent, I am referring to the intentions of the individual(s) responsible for the final form of any given biblical composition.

2. Seeligmann, "Voraussetzungen," 150–81.

cal readings (for example, of the word "created") to establish that Israel (like the Torah) was pre-existent and that the world was created only for Israel and Torah (*Gen Rab.* 1.4, 10). This pattern generates a series of parallels between the "textual/historical" and the "natural." The very structures of creation are reflected and repeated in the patterns of Israel's history, *and* human history, the creation of the natural world and Jewish religious life, sin and punishment, and creation and redemption.[3]

Associations are drawn between the creation of the world and the creation of Israel: thus, the "gathered waters" in Gen 1:6 foreshadow the gathered waters of the Flood and the parted waters of the Red Sea (*Gen Rab.* 5.5). Parallels are drawn between Adam and Abraham (*Gen Rab.* 14.6; 15.5 on Gen 2:7; *Gen Rab.* 12.9 on Gen 2:4; *Gen Rab.* 24.5).[4] Adam's violation of the divine commandment and his punishment (curse and exile) foreshadow Israel's subsequent failure to keep the Torah and their punishment (curses and exile). Perhaps this is most clearly expressed in *Gen Rab.* 19.9:

> And the Lord God called to the man, how were you yesterday of my opinion, but now of the opinion of the serpent, yesterday from the end of the world and until its end, and now in the midst of the trees of the garden? Rabbi Avihu said in the name of Rabbi Hanina, it is written (Hos 6): "And they transgressed the covenant like Adam," they are like the first man. What of the first man? I brought him into the midst of the Garden of Eden and I commanded him, and he transgressed the commandment. And I judged him with sending away and casting out.[5] And I mourned for him, "How?"[6] I brought him into the midst of the Garden of Eden, of which it is said, "I brought him [ויניחהו] into the Garden of Eden" and I commanded him, of which it is said, "And the Lord God commanded Adam." And he transgressed the

---

3. Morris, "Exiled from Eden," 122.

4. Ibid., 151 n. 16, 17.

5. The words used here for sending away and casting out (שלוחין and גרושין) are the same terms used for the disannulment of a marital covenant (divorce). It is not clear if *Gen Rab.* 19 intentionally depicts the man and woman's exile from the garden as a divorce.

6. By using the term "mourned" (קונן) here, the Midrash is drawing a connection between God's question to Adam ("where are you?") and the book of *'ēchâ* (Lamentations), both of which are spelled with the same consonants, איכה. God's "mourning" over Adam for breaking the "covenant" foreshadows Lamentations, a book mourning Israel's broken covenant.

commandment, of which it is said, "Did you eat from the tree concerning which I commanded you not to eat from it?" And I judged him with the sending away, of which it is said, "And the Lord God sent him from the Garden of Eden." And I judged him with the casting out, which is written, "And he cast out the man." And I mourned for him, "How?" of which it is said, "And the Lord God called to the man and he said to him, "Where are you [אַיֶּכָּה]?"" איכה is written, [for] his sons whom I also brought into the land of Israel, I commanded them and they transgressed the commandment. I judged them with the sending out and the casting out and I mourned for them, "How [אֵיכָה]?" those whom I brought to the land of Israel, of whom it is said (Jer 2), "And I brought you to the land of the gardens [כרמל]" and I commanded them, of which it is said (Exod 26), "And you must command the sons of Israel." And they transgressed the commandment, of which it is said (Dan 9): "And all Israel transgressed your Torah." I judged them with the sending out, of which it is said (Jer 15), "I am sending them from before my face and they shall go out." I judged them with casting out, of which it is said (Hos 8), "I cast them out from my house." I mourned for them, "How? [אֵיכָה];" of which it is said (Lam 1:1), "How does she sit?"[7]

It is important to note that Jewish exegetes regard the giving of the Torah and the observance of its commandments as the ultimate remedy of Adam's sin and the restoration of God's creation purposes. Morris writes: "Finally, there is the related theme of the eventual redemption of Israel as the ultimate overcoming of the sin of Adam (*Gen. Rab.* 21.1). While Adam was given but one commandment but failed to observe it, Israel has been given the 613 commandments of the Torah and keeps them. While Adam consigned his descendants to the "flaming sword" (Gen 3:24, identified with Gehenna) and was denied from the Tree of Life, the Torah will "save" Adam's descendants and enable them to participate in the eternal life of the final redemption (*Gen Rab.* 21.9)."[8]

Jerome

Jerome was unique among the early church fathers in his knowledge of the Hebrew language; in essence, he was the prototypical Christian

---

7. Kantrowitz, *Judaic Classics Library*, (translation my own).
8. Morris, "Exiled from Eden," 125.

Hebraist.[9] Jerome's knowledge of Hebrew and the Jewish interpretations led him, in some instances, to depart from the Messianic interpretations of certain texts accepted as such by the church.[10] It is clear throughout Jerome's treatment of Genesis 1–3 that his primary interests were of a philological and text-critical nature.[11] Of interest is Jerome's preference for what would become identified by Jews and Christian scholars as the literal meaning, the *peshaṭ*.[12] Jerome shows no signs of awareness of, or burden to interact with, the midrashic interpretations of Genesis 1–3 (already noted above in *Genesis Rabbah*).

Nicholas of Lyra (c. 1270–1349)

Nicholas of Lyra was a medieval Hebraist who was profoundly influenced by the medieval exegetes, most notably Rashi, Rabbi Shlomo ben Isaac.[13] Even the title of Lyra's magnum opus, *Postilla litteralis super totam Bibliam*, "The Literal Postilla on the Entire Bible," evidences the extent to which the Franciscan scholar embraced Rashi's *pashaṭ*, or literal sense. Although Lyra does not mention any connections between Adam and Israel in his commentary on Genesis 1–3, his comments on Genesis 2:8b reflect an awareness of a key theme in Israel's story developed later in the Pentateuch. Noting the fact that Adam was not native to paradise, Lyra writes, "By this he shows that Adam was formed outside the garden, in order to show that that place is not owed in itself out of nature, but out of grace."[14] God graciously brings Adam to this special garden

9. For an insightful history of the Christian Hebraists, see Hailperin, *Rashi and the Christian Scholars*.

10. Jerome, *Saint Jerome's Hebrew Questions on Genesis*, 30. This is clear, for instance, in the Vulgate's reading of Num 24:7 as "Agag" (see MT), rather than "Gog" (see Q, LXX, Aquila, Symmachus, Theodotion) and also in his rejection of the christological reading of Gen 1:1, namely, "In the Firstborn Son, God made the heavens and the earth."

11. Ibid., 31, 33. Jerome raises key text-critical issues for the interpretation of Genesis 1–3, such as the meaning of קדם ("aforetime" [see Aquila, Symmachus, Theodotion, Vulg.] or "east" [LXX]?) in 2:8 and the original reading of 3:17 (Is it "because of you," בעבורך [MT; Aquila], "your deed," בעבודך [LXX, Vulg.], or "because of your transgression," from עברה or עון [Theodotion, Jerome's Hebrew manuscript]?).

12. Compare Jerome's insistence on the "literal" meaning of בראשית with *Gen Rab.* 1.1, where the meaning of בראשית is being informed by Prov 8:21–31, and is identified as the Torah ("wisdom").

13. Hailperin, *Rashi*, 138; Merrill, "Rashi," 70.

14. "Per hoc ostendit quod Adam fuit formatus extra paradisum. Ad ostendendum quod ille locus non debebatur sibi ex natura sed ex gratia." Lyra, *Postilla super totam*

from another place, much the same way he graciously brings Israel out of Egypt in order to place them in the Promised Land (see Deut 7:8). Thus, Lyra's interpretation of Genesis 2:8 is not only quite sensitive to the text, but also anticipates the eventual recognition by modern scholars of the covenantal nature of God's relationship with Adam, such that it parallels the theology of Deuteronomy.

John Calvin

Calvin's comments suggest that the reformer already saw all the major themes of Scripture introduced in Genesis 1–3. His holistic reading of these chapters led him to the following conclusions regarding their intended purpose. In Genesis 1, (1) mankind was placed into a world intended to display the beneficence and majesty of God in order to elicit their adoration; (2) in return for God's provision of the created world for man's use, mankind was obligated to obey their creator; and (3) the image endowed humanity with understanding and reason above the beasts whereby they might live in pensive reverence toward God.[15] In light of God's beneficence and man's special intelligence, the Fall in chapter 3 not only reinforces man's folly and culpability, but also "represents man as devoid of all good, blinded in understanding, perverse in heart, vitiated in every part, and under sentence of eternal death."[16] To be clear, Calvin perceived the *intention* (what Moses really meant) of Genesis 1–3 to point to the coming of the redemption provided by Christ, by underscoring man's totally depraved nature (see Gen 6:5; 8:21; see also Jer 17:9).[17] It is obvious from these views that Calvin's perception of the intentionality of the Pentateuch was primarily in agreement with the "prophets" and also the NT, and not, as Wellhausen argued, a document whose message is antithetical and antagonistic to the prophets and the NT.

Bibliam. Translation my own. I wish to acknowledge Jenni Glaser for her help to ensure the accuracy of this, as well as subsequent, Latin translations.

15. Calvin, *Commentaries*, 64–65.

16. Ibid., 65.

17. Ibid., 64–65.

Johannes Coccejus

Coccejus' comments suggest that he is drawing from a wide array of
scholarship (past and present) on Genesis, both Jewish[18] and Christian.
In his interpretation of Genesis 1–3, Coccejus' exegetical method presumes the unity of the Pentateuch and its prophetic intentionality. This
is evident in the following ways: (1) Coccejus' attempt to argue that רוח
(breath/wind/spirit) in Genesis 1:2 is "Spirit" rather than "wind" on the
basis of its usage elsewhere in the Pentateuch;[19] (2) his explanation of

18. Coccejus, *Opera omina theologica,* 8: "Adhuc semel utitur Moses ea parabola,
Deut 32:11 . . . Ex. Breischith Ketanna . . . Quae parabola intelligi non postest, nisi ei, cui
hoc verbum attribuitur isto modo, attribuas studium, voluntatem, curem, quae videtur
in aquila esse, quum se libret & vibrat super pullis suis." Translation: "Thus far Moses
uses this parable once, Deut 32:11 . . . from *Berayshit Kettana* . . . A parable, which cannot be understood, unless by the one to whom this word is attributed. In that way, you
attribute (that) zeal, will, (and) care, which are seen in the eagle, which flies and flutters
over its chicks."

19. Ibid.: "Et porro Moses de *Spiritu Dei* non aliter loquitur, quam ut misso a Deo
hominibusque donato, & in eis habitante, & in eis operante sanctificationem & pru-
dentiam, & scientiam, & omne opus, & imprimis elocutionem verbi divini cum omni
fidelitate. Vide Num 24:2. *Et venit super ipso Spiritus Dei.* Bileam. Deut 34:9. Josua
plenus Spiritu sapientiae. Confer Num 11:17. *Seponam de Spiritu, qui est super te.* Ubi
etiamsi metonymia sit effecti pro causa, nihilominus significatur ipsa causa donorum
impertiendorum. Sic v. 25. ubi dicitur *Spiritus super eis quievisse* (בנוח עליהם רוח).
Quae phrasis quasi idem insinuat, quod רחיפה. Quid enim est ferri alis instar aqui-
lae super aliquo, nisi quod per *dari super aliquo, venire super aliquo, quiescere super
aliquo,* & similes formulas significari potest: quae in שכינה (ανακεφαλειν). Etiam
dicit: *Implebo illum Spiritu Dei.* Exod 31:3. 35:31. Neque aliter potest intelligi *Spiritus
Sapientiae,* Exod 28:3. Deut 34:9. quam personae Divinae hoc nomen posit esse. Nam
si est qualitas hominis, quomodo efficit eas qualitates? Si est potentia, quamodo etiam
deliberat? Genes. 6:3: *Non* ידון *disceptabit Spiritus meus de homine. Ventus* non solet
ita appellari. Tantum Psalmo 147:18. est ישב רוחו *facit flare ventum suum.* & sic Targ.
ורוחא מן יי מנשבא *ventus a Domino flabat.* Sed haec facile distinguuntur. Aliud est
רוח נושבת aliud רוח אלהים מרחפת. Hoc non potest dici de vento: quamadmodum illud
non dicitur de Spiritu Sancto. Etiam Joh 3:8 in eodem versiculo facile est distinguere
notionem venti & Spiritus."

Translation: "And moreover, Moses speaks about the Spirit of God not otherwise
than about it being sent by God and given to men, and dwelling in them, and effect-
ing in them sanctification and prudence and knowledge and every work, and foremost
the utterance of the divine word with all faithfulness. See Num 24:2. *And the Spirit of
God came upon him* (Balaam). Deut 34:9. *Joshua [was] filled with the Spirit of wisdom.*
Compare Num 11:17. *I will set apart from the Spirit, which is over you.* When, although
metonymy has been affected for the case, nonetheless it is signified for the sake of the
gifts that must be shared. Thus v. 25, where the *Spirit is said to have rested upon them.*
A saying which somehow implies the same thing as "hover." From what is to be born
on the wings of an eagle over someone, except that *to be given upon someone, to come*

2:4b as a transition from the history of creation to the history of man, rather than two sources with conflicting creation accounts;[20] (3) his understanding of the change in the divine names in Genesis 1–3;[21] and (4) his awareness of a link between the cherubs in Genesis 3:24 and the tabernacle.[22] Although Coccejus refers to the Jewish commentators throughout his treatment of Genesis 1–3,[23] he does not mention possible parallels between Genesis 1–3 and subsequent Pentateuchal (and biblical historical) narratives.

Matthew Poole's Synopsis Criticorum

Matthew Poole's *Synopsis Criticorum* represents a synopsis of interpretations from the leading biblical scholars of the seventeenth century. Poole's comments on the unity of Scripture and the importance of allowing Scripture to elucidate Scripture clearly reflect the pre-critical period in which he lived and worked. He writes, "Our work hath been only to give thee the plain sense of the Scripture, and to reconcile seeming contradictions where they occurred, and as far as we were able to open Scripture by Scripture, which is its own best interpreter, comparing things spiritual with spiritual, 'that thy faith might not stand in the wisdom of men, but in the wisdom and power of God.'"[24] It is also clear that Poole understood the book of Genesis in its larger canonical context, a

---

upon someone, *to rest upon someone,* and similar formulas can be signified: which are in "dwelling" (to summarize). He also says: *I will fill him with the Spirit of God.* Exod 31:3; 35:31. Nor is it possible that the *Spirit of wisdom* could be understood otherwise. Exod 28:3; Deut 34:9; since this name can be of a divine person. For if the quality is of a human, how does he affect these qualities? If there is potential, to what extent does he also deliberate? Gen 6:3. *My Spirit will not contend with men.* The wind is not customarily called this. It is only in Ps 147:18: *He makes his wind blow.* And thus in the Targums: *and the wind was blowing from the Lord.* But these things are easily distinguished. The one is "the wind is blowing [נושבת]," the other "the Spirit of God is hovering [מרחפת]." This cannot be said about the wind: just as that is not said about the Holy Spirit. Even John 3:8 is easily able to distinguish the notion of wind and Spirit in the same verse."

20. Ibid., 19.

21. Ibid., 29.

22. Ibid., 61.

23. Ibid., 8. Another example is his reference to *Baal Turim* where it is argued on the basis of the numerical worth (gematria) of מרחפת that the Spirit of God is the Spirit of the Messiah.

24. Poole, *Exegetical Labors*, 63; see also 18, 42.

book looking forward to the remedy of human transgression by means of the promise of a savior through the loins of Abraham.[25]

In terms of the relationship of Genesis 1–3 to the rest of the Pentateuch, Poole draws on numerous scholars who note the following connections: the ten-fold use of "and God said" in Genesis 1 and the "Ten Words" (Decalogue);[26] the significance of עבד ("to work") and שמר ("to keep") in Gen 2:15 as it relates to the Torah (Sinai) and its worship elsewhere in the Pentateuch;[27] the parallel structures of the commandments given to the man and woman (see Gen 3:3) and the commandments given to Israel (Exod 20:4, 5; Lev 26:1): לא + *yiqtol* (second, masculine, plural).[28] Poole also points to the connection between the "voice walking" in the garden and the "voice walking" at Sinai (Gen 3:8; Exod 19:19), thereby inferring a connection between the Lord's appearance in the garden and his appearance on Mount Sinai.[29] The immediacy of the serpent's curse is paralleled to the immediacy of the curse pronounced on those who would incite others to idolatry.[30] While not an explicit parallel to Israel, Poole's reference to Adam being brought into paradise (Gen 2:15) may be an implicit parallel. "From this place and from Genesis 3:23, it is clear that he was created outside of Paradise, so that he might understand that he is not the son of Paradise, but a settler; so that he might attribute it, not to his own nature, but to the grace of God (Lapide)."[31]

Moreover, Poole's reference to Jeremiah 15:1 in the context of his interpretation of Genesis 3:23 intimates a connection between Adam and Eve's punishment and Israel's exile.[32] Poole regards Genesis 49:17 as an inner-textual[33] allusion to Genesis 3 and an elucidation of the subtlety of the serpent.[34] Poole refers to the Jewish interpretation linking the de-

---

25. Ibid., 67.

26. Ibid., 80.

27. Ibid., 157–58.

28. Ibid., 184–85.

29. Ibid., 192.

30. Ibid., 200.

31. Ibid., 157.

32. Ibid., 230.

33. By "*inner-textual*" I mean allusions to and citations of texts that are located within the same composition (e.g., Gen 49:10 and Num 24:9).

34. Poole, *Exegetical Labors*, 179–80, 208, 216.

ceit of the serpent with the deceit of the Gibeonites,[35] thereby drawing a parallel between the serpent and the Canaanites.[36]

CRITICAL APPROACHES

Although critical approaches to the Bible started during the Enlightenment,[37] the seeds of biblical criticism were sown during the period of the Reformation. According to R. K. Harrison, the Mosaic authorship of the Pentateuch was first challenged by Andreas Rudolf Budenstein's (1480–1541) observation that Moses could not have authored his own obituary (see Deut 34).[38] Initially, however, these scholars did not doubt Mosaic authorship nor did they reject inspiration. Rather, there was an acknowledgment that Moses had composed the Pentateuch from ancient sources.[39] Jean Astruc (1684–1766) is an important scholar whose views paved the way for the documentary hypothesis.[40] To be clear, Astruc, like Campegius Vitringa before him, did not doubt Mosaic authorship. Rather, he appears to be among the first biblical scholars who shifted his attention away from the final *product* (the canonical text) to the *process* of the production of the text from earlier sources. Based on such criteria as the use of the divine names and doublets, Astruc attempted to disassemble Genesis into four columns. Astruc's source analysis led to the eventual perceived fragmentation of Genesis into an accumulation of redactions and additions throughout a complex and lengthy compositional history.

35. Ibid., 200–201: "The Hebrews say, *in the age to come, all things will receive healing and restoration, except the serpent and the Gibeonites.* By the *Gibeonites,* they understand the hypocrites, for by deceit they forced themselves upon the Israelite people." This is taken from *Gen Rab.* 20.5 where the Gibeonites are mentioned in the context of God's punishment of the serpent (Gen 3:14). Important to note, *Gen Rab.* comes to this conclusion on the basis of Isa 65:25, a clear allusion to the curse in Gen 3:14.

36. This association may not be fortuitous when one considers the fact that both the serpent and the Gibeonites are portrayed as "shrewd" (ערמה/ערום) inhabitants of the land who are immediately cursed ([ים]ארור) for their treachery (Gen 3:1, 14; Josh 9:4, 23).

37. Barton, *Reading Old Testament*, 24. According to Barton, the European Enlightenment rejected the doctrine of inspiration and regarded the biblical books as merely "texts from the past." See also Keiser, "Genesis 1–11," 1.

38. Harrison, *Introduction to Old Testament*, 8.

39. Ibid., 11–12. Campegius Vitringa (seventeenth century) believed that Moses composed Genesis from ancient sources from the Patriarchal period.

40. Astruc, *Conjectures sur la Genèse*.

Since many surveys of the history of critical scholarship have been written,[41] it is sufficient here to note that critical studies in Genesis paved the way for the search for source-critical analyses embracing the entire Pentateuch. This search eventually resulted in the identification of at least four hypothetical sources, and each source was identified on the basis of criteria such as similar vocabulary and distinctive theological and ideological emphases.

Three consequences ensued. First, the interpretation of the final form of the Pentateuch was no longer the goal for biblical interpretation.[42] Second, biblical history, which had been taken at face value by all pre-critical scholars,[43] was dropped in favor of critically reconstructed histories of Israel based on the dating and theologies of the individual sources. Third, attempts to identify and string together homogenous textual strata resulted in a redefining and questioning of the actual parameters of the Pentateuch itself: Genesis–Numbers (Tetrateuch), Genesis–Deuteronomy (Pentateuch), or Genesis–Joshua (Hexateuch). Although there have been recent attempts by critical scholars to treat the Pentateuch as a literary unity, as Ernest Nicholson remarks, this assumption can no longer be taken for granted.[44] The result: it was no longer possible to read Genesis 1–3 as a coherent text introducing a coherent composition (the Pentateuch).[45]

41. See for example, Alexander, *From Paradise to Promised Land*, 7–30; Harrison, *Introduction to Old Testament*, 19–61; Nicholson, *Pentateuch in Twentieth Century*; Whybray, *Making of Pentateuch*.

42. Von Rad, "Form Critical Problem," 1, writes, "On almost all sides the final form of the Hexateuch has come to be regarded as a starting-point barely worthy of discussion, from which the debate should move away as rapidly as possible in order to reach the real problems underlying it."

43. Hans W. Frei, *Eclipse of Biblical Narrative*.

44. Nicholson, *Pentateuch in Twentieth Century*, 256.

45. Von Rad, *Genesis*, 72: "Ever since the advent of critical science in theology, the story of Paradise and the Fall has repeatedly been the subject for thorough analysis. The results of this research, recorded in many monographs and articles, were complex, to be sure, and often mutually contradictory; but they agreed, nevertheless, on one point: that they vigorously contradicted the traditional exposition of the church. Above all, there were an increasing number of irregularities, doublets, and other offences which struck the exegetes schooled in criticism, and raised serious doubts about the unity and inner compactness of the text." John Barton (*Reading Old Testament*, 28) concurs when he writes, "The case which argues that Genesis 1:1—2:4a and 2:4b–25 formed originally separate accounts of the creation is an exceedingly difficult one to refute or even to weaken."

At this point it would be helpful to see how critical scholars have approached Genesis 1–3.[46] Astruc identified two different sources on the basis of the use of divine names Elohim (1:1—2:4a) and Yahweh (2:4b—3:24). Later critical studies concurred with Astruc's findings: Genesis 1–3 represented two distinct literary sources. Careful attention to these sources revealed two mutually contradicting creation accounts.[47] Eduard König mentions two primary reasons behind the acceptance of differing literary sources in the book of Genesis: (1) linguistic arguments, such as the alternate uses of the divine names (Elohim in 1:1—2:3, YHWH in 2:4—3.24); and (2) formal idiosyncrasies concerning the content of the hypothetical sources.[48]

König represents a fairly typical critical assessment of Genesis 1–3: he attributes Genesis 1:1—2:3 to "P," 2:4–25 to a "J" redactor, and 3:1–24 to "J." König proposes a number of solutions to the literary relationship between Gen 1:1—2:3 and 2:4—3:24, but in the end deems them to be either impossible or unlikely.[49] He concludes that both sections represent differing conceptions of the creation arising from two differing Pentateuchal sources that have found expression in Israel's tradition.[50]

Hermann Gunkel marked a decisive turn away from a focus on hypothetical source documents to the tradition-history behind the literary sources. Gunkel, however, assumed Wellhausen's sources and their dating to a certain degree. He rejected the idea of single authors—rather, the sources came from schools of narrators or collectors who were bound to transmit their inherited materials faithfully—of the earlier source materials (e.g., "J" and "E") and regarded "P" as the only genuine author *per se*.[51] It is also clear from the arrangement of Gunkel's commentary—Genesis 1–3 is treated according to the order of the critical dating of "J" and "P"—that Gunkel thought little of the possibility of a compositional

---

46. For an excellent synopsis of the history of critical approaches to Genesis 1–3, see Ska, "Genesi 2–3," 1–6.

47. König, *Genesis,* 54: "Gleich die Schöpfungsdarstellung 1 1–2 3 weicht von 2 4 b ff. ab. Denn um hier nur einen einzigen Punkt herauszuheben, in 1 1–2 3 liegt die Menschenschöpfung hinter der Pfanzenschöpfung, aber nach 2 4 b ff. ist das Verhältnis umgedreht."

48. Ibid., 39–83.

49. Ibid., 221–23.

50. Ibid., 223, 225.

51. Gunkel, *Legends of Genesis,* 130, 153.

strategy behind the final form of the text.[52] According to Joel Rosenberg, scholarly attention from the time of Gunkel on moved from source questions—deemed more or less settled—to the preliterary development behind the documents.[53]

Gerhard von Rad also assumed Wellhausen's sources and their dating,[54] but understood them in terms of a long traditio-historical pre-literary development.[55] Like Gunkel, Von Rad's commentary isolates and treats the "P" and "J" material, not in terms of their canonical form, but in a critically reconstructed conglomeration of sources. As for his treatment of Genesis 1:1—2:4a, Von Rad argues that this text represents priestly doctrine that is "intended to hold true entirely and exactly as it stands."[56] By this, Von Rad means there is nothing "symbolic" or figuratively poetic about the "P" creation narrative. Von Rad is equally convinced that the priestly account of creation does not represent the work of a single author, but embodies the sacred knowledge handed down by many generations of priests.[57] Concerning the "Fall Narrative," Von Rad contends that Genesis 3 is "conspicuously isolated in the Old Testament." In his words, "No prophet, psalm, or narrator makes any recognizable reference to the story of the Fall."[58] Von Rad did not regard Genesis 1–3 as a cohesive introduction to the Pentateuch, nor did he find any significant literary connections to Genesis 1–3 elsewhere in the Old Testament.

CHALLENGES TO CRITICAL APPROACHES

Of Priests or Prophets?

A major tenet of Wellhausen's documentary hypothesis is the priority of "J" to the other sources, particularly "D" and "P."[59] Recent critical

---

52. Gunkel, *Genesis übersetzt*. Gunkel analyzes the "J" Paradise Narrative first, and only afterwards deals with the "P" Creation Narrative (beginning on page 89).

53. Rosenberg, *King and Kin*, 2.

54. Von Rad, *Genesis*, 23.

55. Ibid., 72.

56. Ibid., 45.

57. Ibid., 61.

58. Ibid., 98.

59. In a recent analysis of Genesis 2–3, Ska ("Genesi 2–3," 20) concludes there are no sufficient grounds to identify Genesis 2–3 as two stories, or even an older story reworked into a later one. Rather, with the exception of some editorial additions (e.g., Gen 2:10–14), the text is essentially unified. His findings challenge one of the most

studies of Genesis 2–3 (classically assigned by critical scholars to the "J" author[60]), however, have resulted in a questioning of the date of "J" due to the pervasive presence of wisdom themes as well as elements attributed to late Deuteronomistic covenant theology.[61] Eckart Otto, for example, maintains that Genesis 2–3 contains a mixture of wisdom and late Deuteronomistic material and that it even presupposes the existence of "P".[62] In his words, "Gen 2:4—3:24, therefore, thoroughly presupposes the Priestly Document and leads a dialogue with the priestly account of creation."[63] Otto goes so far as to argue that the "P" account of the creation of mankind (Gen 1:26–27) is lacking essential details that only Genesis 2:7 provides. He writes,

> Not only is Genesis 2:7 terminologically tied to Genesis 1. Genesis 1:27 contains the "fact" of the creation of man, whereas following up on Genesis 2:7 the "how" is developed. This connection is underlined by means of another peculiarity of this verse. Genesis 2:7b leaves the narrative layer and states the creation of man with the words "and the man became a living being." This phrase is tied to the confirmation of execution of the priestly formula of completion "and it was so" in Genesis 1:3, 7, 9, 11, 15, 24, 30. In the creation of man in the priestly document such an expected formula behind Genesis 1:26 is lacking.[64]

---

influential works on Genesis 2–3 since the late nineteenth century: Karl Budde, *Die biblische Urgeschichte: Gen 1—12, 5.* See also Stordalen, *Echoes of Eden,* 194.

60. See for example König, *Genesis,* 67.

61. Otto, "Paradieserzählung Genesis 2–3"; Schökel, "Motivos Sapienciales," 295–316; Witte, *Biblische Urgeschichte.* Ska ("Genesi 2–3," 24) argues that Genesis 1 and 2–3 are contemporaneous.

62. Otto, "Paradieserzählung Genesis 2–3," 183–84. For example, נפש חיה, in Gen 2:7, 19 is only found elsewhere in Gen 1:20, 21, 24, 30; 9:10, 12, 15, 16; Lev 11:10, 46 (all attributed to "P") and Ezek 47:9. In a subsequent chapter I also discuss parallels between the Garden of Eden and the Tabernacle and correlations between Genesis 3 and the purity laws. The evidence strongly suggests that the author of the "J" account presupposed the "P" material (e.g., Sinai and its legislation).

63. "Gen 2,4—3,24 setzt also durchgängig die Priesterschrift voraus und führt einen Dialog mit dem priesterschriftlichen Schöpfungsbericht." Ibid., 188:

64. "Nicht nur terminologisch wird Gen 2,7 an Gen 1 angeknüpft. Gen 1,27 beinhaltet das 'Daß' der Schöpfung des Menschen, während daran anknüpfend Gen 2,7 das 'Wie' entfaltet. Dieser Zusammenhang wird durch eine weitere Eigentümlichkeit dieser Verse unterstrichen. Gen 2,7b verläßt die Erzählebene und konstatiert die Schöpfung des Menschen mit den Worten *wajᵉhî hāʾādām lᵉnœš ḥajjāh.* Diese Formulierung knüpft an die Vollzugbestätigung der priesterschriftlichen Geschehensformel *wajᵉhî ken* in Gen 1,3.7.9.11.15.24.30 an. Bei der Menschenschöpfung der Priesterschrift fehlt eine derartige hinter Gen 1,26 zu erwartende Formel." Ibid., 183–84.

Otto's words point to overriding compositional intentions that go beyond any putative and contradictory sources. Moreover, the fact that Genesis 2–3 is aware of the "priestly" materials and even includes vocabulary classically assigned to "P" undermines Wellhausen's theory both in terms of his understanding of the chronological relationship of "J" to "P" and in terms of the notion of clearly identifiable and distinguishable literary criteria used to distinguish one hypothetical source from another.

Joseph Blenkinsopp and Gordon Wenham have also argued for the priority of "P" over "J" in Genesis 1–11 on the basis of a careful literary analysis.[65] Blenkinsopp concludes that the "J" additions to the "P" material consistently reinforce the notion of human sinfulness in a spirit akin to the later prophets, namely Jeremiah and Ezekiel.[66] The purpose here is not to argue for the existence or the priority of one hypothetical source over another. Rather, these findings suggest that the endeavor to interpret Genesis 1–3 by means of the classic documentary hypothesis is becoming more and more untenable. As noted, Genesis 2–3 represents a mixture of vocabulary and themes attributed to a gamut of diversely dated sources.[67]

A Prophetic Redaction of the Pentateuch

In addition, questions regarding the chronological relationship of the sources have important implications for one's understanding of the intentionality of the final Pentateuch.[68] Wellhausen's newer documentary hypothesis championed the idea that the priestly writers were the finalizers of the Pentateuch, and consequently, the Pentateuch in its final

---

65. Blenkinsopp, "P and J," 1–15; Wenham, "The Priority of P," 240–58.

66. Blenkinsopp, "P and J," 15: "The sense that the author is attempting to come to terms with an experience of spiritual and moral failure suggests familiarity with later prophecy, especially Jeremiah and Ezekiel." Although he apparently does not question the literary relationship of "J" and "P," Witte (*Biblische Urgeschichte*, 248) reaches similar conclusions with respect to a strong emphasis on human sin in the final redaction of Genesis 1–11: "Durch die endredaktionelle Einlage der 'Sünden(fall)erzählungen' in 6,1–4; 9,20–27 und 11,1–9 kennzeichnet der Charakter der 'jahwistischen' Urgeschichte als seiner 'narrativen Hamartiologie' die gesamte Urgeschichte." Translation: "By means of the final redactional insertation of fall narratives in 6:1–4, 9:20–27, and 11:1–9, the character of the 'Yahwistic' Primeval History characterizes the entire Primeval History as his 'Narrative Hamartiology.'

67. See Witte, *Biblische Urgeschichte*, 325 n. 1.

68. See Hans-Christoph Schmitt, "Spätdeuteronomistische Geschichtswerk," 264.

form represented the priestly agenda of Second Temple Judaism.[69] As Wellhausen conceived the compositional evolution of the Pentateuch, earlier prophetic sources (such as "J" and "E") were gradually supplemented and supplanted by the intentions of the priestly writers. In other words, the Pentateuch evolved from earlier prophetic kernels to a document representing priestly intentions: namely, the legitimization of post-exilic Judaism. This hypothesis regarding the development of the Pentateuch profoundly affects the manner in which one interprets Genesis 1–3. Not only do these three chapters represent conflicting sources from differing periods; but also, the primitive anthropology and hamartiology of Genesis 2–3 is suppressed by the more optimistic anthropology of Genesis 1 with respect to human ability to keep the law. In effect, Wellhausen's theory undermines the classic Christian doctrine of human depravity and inability to keep the law by affording Genesis 1:1—2:4a the last word on human ability in the final Pentateuch.

Wellhausen's understanding of the compositional history of the Pentateuch, however, differed markedly from earlier critical scholars such as Heinrich Ewald.[70] According to Ewald, the *Grundshrift* (or the Book of Origins, later identified by Wellhausen as "P") was the foundational document of the Pentateuch. Subsequent prophetic narrators (editors), however, supplemented the *Grundschrift* in light of Israel's ongoing failures to keep the stipulations of the covenant. According to Ewald, the Pentateuch moved from a document primarily concerned with Israel and the law toward an increasingly eschatological document with a messianic universalism embracing all nations into the plan of God.[71] In essence, developments in Israel's religious history reflected by the additions of the subsequent prophets resulted in a compositional

---

69. Wellhausen, *Prolegomena*.

70. Ewald, *History of Israel*.

71. "If we then regard closer the truths which are here forced upon us, we shall have to confess that they flow from a height of prophetic activity and advanced national culture totally foreign to the Book of Origins. The developed Messianic expectations, the truth of the infinite all-surpassing grace of Jahve beside the deep sinfulness and corruption of the earthly (or natural) man, the similar truths of the non-causal origin of the wicked principle in man—these are such illustrious thoughts, which the sun of these ages was the first to elicit from the sacred soil" (ibid., 101–2:). Ewald argues that passages such as Gen 3; 8:21; 18:1—19:28; Exod 32–34 were later prophetic additions to the "Book of Origins," all of which serve to reinforce the need for the eschatological hope as represented in the person of the Messiah.

evolution whose final development was moving closer and closer toward the NT faith.[72]

Although Wellhausen's hypothesis regarding the priestly intentions of the final Pentateuch continues to represent the consensus view among critical scholars, I have already noted that the priority of the hypothetical prophetic sources ("J" and "P") can no longer and should no longer merely be assumed by critical scholars. Moreover, there is a growing trend among biblical scholars to attribute the final elements of the Pentateuch to prophetic redactors:[73] in essence, a return to Ewald's (and W. M. L. de Wette's[74]) understanding of the compositional movement of the Pentateuch from a legal document towards a prophetic-eschatologically oriented final form.

Hans-Christoph Schmitt, for example, attempts to analyze the extent to which the writing prophets (*Schriftprophetie*) influenced the final form of the Pentateuch (*Endgestalt des Pentateuch*).[75] By means of a redactional-historical analysis, Schmitt investigates redactional clues reflected in the structure of the present shape of the Pentateuch, whereby large tradition-complexes have been brought together into a larger

---

72. Schmitt, "Redaktion des Pentateuch," 171. Schmitt's attempt to discern the influence of the prophets on the final redaction of the Pentateuch apparently brings Ewald's pre-Wellhausian perspective on the final Pentateuch back to life: "Zwar wird man heute nicht ohne weiteres über Wellhausen hinweg wider an Schraders und de Wettes Pentateuchtheorien anknüpfen können, dennoch stellt sich angesichts der neuesten Forschungsbeiträge zum literarischen Problem des Pentateuch die Frage, ob wir nicht doch mit einem wesentlich stärkeren Einwirken der Schriftprophetie auf die Endgestalt des Pentateuch rechnen müssen, als dies das Ergebnis der Untersuchung Zimmerlis vermuten läßt." Translation: "Although today one cannot easily resist Wellhausen for Schrader and de Wette's theories of the Pentateuch, nevertheless the question is raised in light of recent research contributions to the literary problem of the Pentateuch, whether or not we should reckon a much greater influence of the writing prophets on the final form of the Pentateuch, as the result of Zimmerli's investigation suggests."

73. See for example, Horbury, *Jewish Messianism*, 25–31.

74. Schmitt, "Redaktion des Pentateuch," 170–71.

75. Ibid., 171. See also Schmitt, "Spätdeuteronomistische Geschichtswerk," 261–79. Here Schmitt extends his argument regarding a prophetic redaction of the Tetrateuch to embrace Deuteronomy as well as the so-called Deuteronomistic History (Josh 1—2 Kgs 25). For a thorough treatment of Schmitt's work and its implications for one's understanding of the compositional intentions of the Pentateuch, see Sailhamer, *Pentateuch as Narrative*, 60–62.

whole—this method is akin to M. Noth's analysis of the Deuteronomistic History.[76]

Looking at the four major tradition complexes of the Tetrateuch (the Patriarchal Narratives, the Exodus Narratives, the Sinai Narratives, and the Wilderness Narratives), Schmitt observes that in compositionally strategic positions in each complex there exists a tight relationship between the initial element of "promise" (*Verheißung*) and the appropriate response of faith, or what he calls the "faith theme" (*Glaubens Thematik*). Schmitt notes that the entire Exodus Narrative Complex is framed by the notion of believing in the Lord and in his prophetic mediator of the promise (see Exod 4:31; 14:31).[77] The "faith theme" of the Exodus Narratives is also repeated in the commencement of the Sinai Narrative (Exod 19:9a) and in a central place in the Patriarchal Narratives, namely Genesis 15, whereby "believing" (v. 6) is strategically sandwiched between the promise of an offspring and the promise of the land.[78] Finally, the "faith theme" appears in the Wilderness Narrative, where it is reported that Israel and Moses' failure to "believe" results in their falling short of reaping the blessings of the land "promise."[79] Schmitt finds that in all these cases, the "faith theme" and its concomitant themes (such as Moses' plea for mercy on the basis of God's reputation in Numbers 14, the correlation of "faith" and "signs," the prophetic depictions of Abraham and Moses, an exilic situation, etc.) find their closest parallels to writings of the later prophets (see Isa 7:1–17; Ezek 20).[80] Finally, Schmitt addresses the literary relationship of this "prophetic" redaction to the "priestly" layer and concludes that, in every case, it involves a "post-priestly" redaction.[81]

Schmitt's concluding remarks are particularly relevant for my purposes. Schmitt argues that these post-priestly prophetic redactions picture Moses, not primarily as a transmitter of the divine regulations, but as a prophetic herald of the divine promise.[82] Moreover, the prophetic

76. Schmitt, "Redaktion des Pentateuch," 172–73.

77. Ibid., 175.

78. Ibid., 178.

79. Ibid., 178–81.

80. Ibid., 175, 179.

81. Ibid., 181–85.

82. "So steht am Ende der Pentateuchentstehung nicht die Abschließung in ein Ordnungsdenken Charakters. Vielmehr geht es hier darum, in prophetischem Geiste die

influence on the final redaction of the Pentateuch strongly suggests that the final stage of the Pentateuchal redaction does not orient itself towards the regulations of a theocracy emanating from priestly circles—contrary to the vast consensus of OT scholars since Wellhausen—but rather, it is preeminently concerned with the same eschatology reflected in the growth of the prophetic books.[83] He writes, "So at the end of the development of the Pentateuch the conclusion does not stand in a manner of thinking oriented to regulations of a theocratic character. Rather, the point here is to preserve the openness for a new act of God in a prophetic spirit and in this context with the concept of 'faith' taken out of the prophetic tradition to emphasize a mindset that also later the New Testament regards as central for the relationship with God."[84]

Schmitt's findings clearly parallel and support Blenkinsopp and Wenham's argument for a prophetic author of Genesis 1–11 whose theology is akin to the later prophets. In my opinion, these findings ought to influence significantly one's understanding of the function of Genesis 1–3 in the Pentateuch, and in particular, how these chapters reflect upon the Sinai Covenant and its portrayal of Israel's history as one of failure under that covenant. In other words, even where certain approaches to Genesis 1–3 may acknowledge its function as the introduction to the Pentateuch, all too often it is assumed that its intentionality is bound up with the propagation of the Sinai Covenant.

Literary or Final Form Approaches

In addition to the growing trend of critical scholars questioning the traditional relationship of the hypothetical sources, other scholars analyzing the Bible by focusing on the final form of the text and its literary artistry

---

Offenheit für ein neues Handeln Gottes zu waren und in diesem Zusammenhang mit dem aus der prophetischen Tradition entnommenen Begriff des 'Glaubens' eine Haltung herauszustellen, die später auch das Neue Testament als für das Gottesverhältnis zentral ansieht." Ibid., 188. Translation: "So at the end of the development of the Pentateuch the conclusion does not stand in a manner of thining oriented to regulations of a theocratic character. Rather, the goal here is to preserve the openness for a new act of God in a prophetic spirit and in this context with the concept of 'faith' taken from the prophetic tradition to emphasize a mindset that also later the New Testament regards as central for the relationship with God."

83. Ibid.

84. Ibid., 188–89.

have questioned the existence of the hypothetical sources altogether.[85] According to Keiser, the second half of the twentieth century marked two significant shifts in the treatment of Genesis 1–11. First, whereas critical studies of Genesis prior to this time focused primarily on the "becoming" of the text and/or the utilization of the various sources to discern the development of Israel's religion and traditions, "developments in biblical studies resulted in an increased concern with the literary presentation and authorial intent," and consequently, "scholars began to focus more on the creative aspects of text formulation, regardless of original writing or redaction and their employment for the purpose of conveying an intended message."[86] Second, there was a renewed appreciation for and emphasis on the interpretation of the final form of the biblical text in its canonical context.[87]

Important figures in this movement away from a historical emphasis toward an appreciation for the literary artistry, rhetoric, and coherency of the final form of the text, and a text-centered orientation to the interpretation of the Hebrew Bible include James Muilenburg, Hans Frei, J. P. Fokkelman, Robert Alter, Meir Sternberg, and Shimeon Bar-Efrat.[88] According to Johnson T. K. Lim, the rejection of atomistic approaches to Pentateuchal scholarship and the focus on the final form of the text is radically changing the scholarly field: "Today, the landscape in biblical studies has changed significantly and drastically. The tide has changed with the twentieth century making a 180-degree turn to reading the Bible holistically in its final form as a text with impetus from Brevard Childs, Robert Alter and others . . . The edifice of the old historical paradigm marked by the Wellhausen Documentary Hypothesis, which seemed to serve its generation well, is being modified and slowly making way for new interpretive paradigms."[89]

85. Commenting on Genesis 2–3 Stordalen (*Echoes of Eden*, 194) writes, "As is becoming increasingly clear, conventional criteria for determining textual incoherence are hardly convincing." As a result, Stordalen (ibid., 197) notes a shift to the "final text" since around the middle of the previous century.

86. Keiser, "Genesis 1–11," 1–2.

87. Ibid., 2.

88. Muilenburg, "Form Criticism," 1–18; Frei, *Eclipse of Biblical Narrative*; Fokkelman, *Reading Biblical Narrative*; Alter, *Art of Biblical Narrative*; Sternberg, *Poetics*; Bar-Efrat, *Narrative Art*.

89. Lim, *Grace*.

Alter, rejecting earlier compositional models, describes the process of biblical composition in terms akin to the production of a movie, whereby a biblical author makes a text by "editing and splicing and artful montage of antecedent literary materials," resulting in a "multifaceted truth by setting in sequence two different versions that brought into focus two different dimensions of his subject."[90] Worth quoting is Sergei Eisenstein's description of both the process and the effect of montage in the making of movies. Eisenstein writes,

> The basic fact was true, and remains true to this day, that the juxtaposition of two separate shots by splicing them together resembles not so much a simple sum of one shot plus one shot—as it does a *creation*. It resembles a creation—rather than a sum of its parts—from the circumstance that in every juxtaposition *the result is qualitatively* distinguishable from each component element viewed separately . . . What is essentially involved in such an understanding of montage? In such a case, each montage piece exists no longer as something unrelated, but as a given *particular representation* of the general theme that in equal measure penetrates *all* the shot-pieces. The juxtaposition of these partial details in a given montage construction calls to life and forces into the light that *general* quality in which each detail has participated and which binds together all the details into a *whole*, namely, into that generalized *image*, wherein the creation, followed by the spectator, experiences them.[91]

Along these lines, Alter argues that the very beginning of the Hebrew Bible opens with the montage-like juxtaposition of two different creation stories. While Alter does not deny that these accounts represent two very different, and even contradictory[92] sources, he differs markedly from critical scholars in several important ways. First, Alter's focus on the final form leads him to regard the one responsible for this production as the author of Genesis, rather than merely one of its many redactors.[93] Second, and corollary to the first, by identifying the one responsible for the composite text as an "author," Alter presents this person as an individual fully in command of all his source materials (and not merely a redactor who is bound to preserve, in spite of

90. Alter, *Art of Biblical Narrative*, 140.

91. Sergei Eisenstein, *The Film Sense*, 7–8, 11; italics original.

92. Alter, *Art of Biblical Narrative*, 141.

93. Ibid.

contradictions, all the inherited materials).[94] Third, as a composer with complete command of his source material, he intentionally chose not to modify or harmonize his sources.[95] Fourth, and finally, the acceptance of these three compositional presuppositions results in Alter's attempt to identify the compositional strategy (or authorial intent) behind the composite artistry, whereby he does not explain away or harmonize the tensions in the text, nor does he pit one source against the other; rather, he attempts to explain the authorial intention of the text in its final form. In Alter's own words, "[T]he text we have of the creation story has a coherence and significant form which we can examine, and I would argue that there were compelling literary reasons for the Genesis author to take advantage of both documents at his disposal—perhaps also rejecting others about which we do not know—and to take advantage as well of the contradictions between his sources."[96]

In Alter's brief analysis of the creation accounts, he argues that the author intentionally juxtaposed these two versions to present a complementary picture of how the world came into being, the coherence and complexities of creation, divine order and human choice, and the tensions between what women were originally created to be and what they actually are in Israelite society.[97]

Joel Rosenberg, like Alter, also focuses on the final form of the text of Genesis 2–3. Rosenberg is primarily concerned with the intentions of the final redactor rather than the sources behind the text.[98] And like Alter, his understanding of authorship is analogous to the production of a film ("documentary movie"). Rosenberg even goes so far as to suggest that Genesis 1–3 serves "to define the movements" of the entire

---

94. Ibid., 147, 141, respectively.

95. Ibid.

96. Ibid., 142.

97. Ibid., 141–47.

98. Rosenberg, *King and Kin*, 50: "I stress here, as well, that I intend no literary-historical hypotheses as such. For present purposes, 'received text,' 'composition,' and 'redaction' are all more or less synonymous. I retain the last term primarily as a way of indicating that the author of the story's finished structure was, after all, a traditionary collector, limited by the obligation to preserve the character and uniqueness (if not the actual verbatim formation) of each inherited element while simultaneously seeking an arrangement of elements that would make a statement of its own. This is a type of 'authorship' obviously quite different from that in the modern sense of the term, although it does resemble, in certain respects, the techniques of a documentary movie."

Pentateuch as well as the Deuteronomistic History.[99] Along these lines, Rosenberg narrows Genesis 2–3 down to a three-fold function: "(1) to make clear the genesis of the motivation in the *individual* to cooperate with his successor generations; (2) to account for the *cultural* origins of generational continuity . . . and (3) to justify the particular *religious* pre-occupation of Israelite society with the formation of a *tradition*, seen as a chain of 'generations' acting in cooperation to ensure the transmission of the values, laws and insights (believed to be God-given) that enable life to survive on earth."[100]

Rosenberg believes these to be the principal themes throughout the rest of Genesis–Kings.[101] Although I differ markedly from Rosenberg with respect to the principal themes, I concur with his thesis regarding the importance of Genesis 1–3.

Thus we see in this new focus on the final form of the text a willingness to accept the possibility of a literary coherence and authorial strategy of the final form of the text.

99. Ibid.

100. Ibid., 65.

101. Ibid., 66.

3

Recent Studies

S EVERAL RECENT STUDIES (SINCE 1990) have significant correlations with this book. In what follows I review studies that have attempted to discern the meaning of Genesis 1–3 as a coherent literary unit within the Pentateuch, as well as studies focused on the relationship between the early chapters of Genesis and Israel's history as it is portrayed in the Deuteronomistic History (Josh 1—2 Kgs 25).

THOMAS KEISER

Thomas Keiser's recent dissertation argues for the literary and theological coherence of Genesis 1–11. He devotes considerable attention to Genesis 1 and 2. According to Keiser these two chapters represent "probably the highest profile issue related to the unity of the Primeval History," because critical scholarship has regarded Genesis 1 and 2 as "two separate, and often apparently contradicting, creation accounts."[1] Keiser argues for the unity of Genesis 1–2 by offering diachronic and synchronic evidence, rhetorical features present in the text, and by looking at the Hebrew accenting in the discourse structure (discourse analysis).[2]

After a thorough literary analysis, Keiser devotes the final chapter to the relationship of Genesis 1–11 to the Pentateuch as a whole. Keiser argues, like Terence Fretheim, that the relationship between the introduction and the conclusion of the Pentateuch are key to understanding its overall strategy.[3] Keiser's appraisal of the introduction and conclusion

---

1. Keiser, "Genesis 1–11," 28.

2. Ibid., 29–34. For more diachronic evidence, see Blenkinsopp, *Pentateuch: Introduction*, 62–63; Shea, "Unity of Creation Account," 9–39. On discourse structure, see Lode, "Two Creation Stories," 1–52.

3. Keiser, "Genesis 1–11," 194. See especially Fretheim, *Pentateuch*, 53–63.

of the Pentateuch are of a more general nature, however,[4] and so his argument for the importance of the introduction and the conclusion of the Pentateuch remain largely unexplored.[5]

ANDRÉ SOUSAN

André Sousan's dissertation applies a rhetorical critical analysis to Genesis 2–3.[6] He discusses important literary features[7] and difficult exegetical issues related to the exegesis of the chapters.[8] He also notes possible literary parallels between Adam and Abram[9] as well as Adam and Israel. Further, he devotes a considerable amount of attention to the correlations between Genesis 2–3 and the Primary History. Among the parallels he notes is the bringing of Adam/Israel from a desert land into a luscious land of plenty. Sousan writes, "[T]he interpretation of God's benevolence in transporting Adam from a desertic world to a paradisia-cal garden, in exchange of which Adam is commanded to take care of the garden and not eat from one tree, has a covenantal character that

4. Keiser, "Genesis 1–11," 198–201.

5. For instance, Keiser does not analyze the significance of the large clusters of terminology found only in the introduction and conclusion to the Pentateuch. Thus, Keiser's observations are, for the most part, not grounded in the text. As I shall argue in a subsequent chapter, these lexical inclusions are important evidence for evaluating both the meaning of Genesis 1–3 and, in turn, the overall intentions of the Pentateuch in its final form.

6. Sousan, "Woman in Eden," 89. Sousan's rhetorical-critical methodology is guided by J. Muilenburg's rhetorical criticism and Roland Barthes' five codes of textual analysis. Barthes' five codes are (1) the hermeneutic code, (2) the proairetic code, (3) the semic code, (4) the cultural code, and (5) the symbolic code (Sousan, "Woman in Eden," 103–5).

7. Ibid., 109–12. For example, Sousan argues that the word employed for the creation of woman in 2:22, namely to "build" (בנה), is intentionally assonantal with the Hebrew word for "building" a family (see Gen 16:2; Ruth 4:11; Jer 31:3–4) through sons (בנים). He also calls attention to numerous word plays in Gen 2–3, including "Adam," "ground," and "mist" (אדם, אדמה, אד), "man" and "woman" (איש, אישה), "naked," "shrewd/prudent," and "skin" (עור, ערום, ערומים), "pain," "plants," and "tree" (עץ, עשב , עצבון), to "stretch out" (שלח, qal) and to "send out" (שלח, piel), and a possible metathesis of "cherub" (כרוב) and "bless" (ברך).

8. Ibid., 144. For example, the relationship between the "tree of the knowledge of good and evil" and the "tree of life," both of which are described as being "in the midst of the garden."

9. Ibid., 125. Sousan argues for the existence of an intentional link between Adam's sleep in 2:21 and Abram's sleep in 15:12—note the use of the root נפל ("to fall") and תרדמה ("sleep") in both passages. This is discussed in a subsequent chapter.

recalls the transport of Israel from a desert to the promised land under the terms of the Covenant at Sinai."[10]

Sousan's contribution to the discussion of Genesis 2–3 comes by way of his understanding of Genesis 2–3 as an intentional metaphor of the prophets' interpretation of the Sinai Covenant as a marriage between God and his people:[11] Adam corresponds to the people of Israel (a collective group of males and females) and Eve corresponds to the wife of God or the Royal City.[12] According to Sousan, the "*ādām*" represents generic humanity, and the woman represents the *s̆egullâ* (סגולה; see Exod 19:5), or, God's special choice personified. Sousan equates Adam's inability to find a partner among the animals (Gen 2:20) with his volitional decision to keep the covenant (Gen 2:16–25) rather than choosing to live like an animal. Eve's creation, therefore, is a direct response to man's declaration of obedience to the covenant. She becomes the means through which God's covenant with the man is ratified. Sousan sees in Genesis 2–3 strong parallels to the narrative in Exodus 19–24, where Israel willingly accepts the conditions of the covenant (see Exod 19:8), and, as a result, the covenant is then ratified (Exod 24:5–6). The ratification of the covenant enables Israel to become God's "special treasure," *s̆egullâ* (Exod 19:5).[13] Sousan finds numerous parallels between the formulations of God's "covenant" with Adam and with Israel. To quote him at length:

> The respective formulations of the covenant with Adam and the Covenant at Sinai then become identical, making the former a metaphor for the latter:
>
> (1) two parties, of which one is the divine witness, respectively God and Adam, and God and the people of Israel;
> (2) a prologue of past benefactions, respectively the transport of Adam to the garden and the Exodus from Egypt;
> (3) the obligations specified by God, respectively the duties and commandments given to Adam, and the Ten Commandments;
> (4) the declarations of obedience of Adam and the people of Israel;

10. Ibid., 176.
11. Ibid., 241–42.
12. Ibid., 203.
13. Ibid., 184.

(5) God's ratification of the declaration of obedience, respec-
     tively by the creation of the woman and by the creation of
     the *šᵉgūllâ*.[14]

In light of the alleged parallels, Sousan concludes that Genesis 2–3
teaches that the divine purpose for the creation of humanity is to perpetuate life through the gift of covenants.[15] Sousan attempts to substantiate his thesis by means of tracing the inner-biblical effective history of
Genesis 2–3 throughout the remainder of the Tanakh, particularly the
Prophets and Canticles.

JOHNSON TENG KOK LIM

Johnson Teng Kok Lim, in his recent study of Genesis 1–11, advocates
what he calls a "reader responsible reading," by which he means "reading
a text in accordance with its genre and exercising some kind of hermeneutical humility as we engage the text." Thus, his goal is to understand
the text rather than undermining it.[16] Lim identifies the theme of Genesis
1–11 (from Eden to Babylon) as "grace in the midst of judgment," a title
echoing Paul's statement in Romans, "where sin abounds, grace much
more abounds."[17] Lim argues that this theme not only connects with the
rest of Genesis, but also with the remainder of the Pentateuch, particularly as this relates to Moses and Israel as recipients of grace in spite of
their sin and rebellion.[18] Moreover, Lim argues that Genesis 1–11 are
pivotal chapters in the rest of the OT, whereby subsequent biblical authors pick up on its themes of creation, blessing, sin, and mercy.[19]

C. JOHN COLLINS

C. John Collins, like Lim, focuses on the final form of Genesis 1–4 (he
proposes a discourse-oriented literary approach[20]) as part of the final
edition (form) of the Pentateuch.[21] Although Collins argues that the real

---

14. Ibid., 185.
15. Ibid.
16. Lim, *Grace*, vii.
17. Ibid., 192.
18. Ibid., 193.
19. Ibid., 194.
20. Collins, *Genesis 1–4*, 5–32.
21. Ibid., 33.

author is the person responsible for the final form of the text, the implied author is Moses (see Josh 1:7–8, 1 Kgs 8:53, Mal 4:4, Dan 9:11, etc.), and so, in terms of a reading strategy, the Pentateuch is best understood when interpreted *as if* it is Moses' words to Israel.[22] According to Collins, no argument is necessary to show that the Pentateuch is about the Mosaic Covenant.[23] Moreover, Collins contends that the Mosaic Covenant is the realization of the covenants and promises previously made to the Patriarchs, and not their replacement. It is from within this context that Collins interprets Gen 1:1—4:26: "Genesis 1–11 sets the stage for this mission of Israel to live as God's treasured people and thereby to be the vehicle of blessing to the rest of the world."[24] Genesis 1 introduces the one God who enters into a relationship with the first human beings (representatives of the universal character of God's plan); and although that relationship is broken (Gen 2–3), God mercifully persists in restoring his universal plan for creation through a particular nation by means of the Mosaic Covenant.[25] Thus, for Collins, Genesis 1–3 sets the universal stage upon which a particular covenant (Mosaic) is introduced. This is particularly clear when Collins discusses environmental ethics in the context of the creation mandate to "dominate" and "subdue" the "earth" (Gen 1:26, 28).[26] Collins argues on the basis of commandments and conditions that Genesis 2:15–17 is to be understood as a covenant between God and Adam (see Hos 6:7; also Sir 14:17),[27] and Adam is to be understood as one who acts on behalf of his future posterity.[28] Collins does not develop parallels between Adam's reception and violation of the "covenant" and Israel's reception and violation of the covenant. Rather, he argues that the purpose of Genesis 1–4 is intended to undergird the religion of the Pentateuch (the Mosaic Covenant) by (1) introducing God as the Creator who provided a world divinely suited for his covenant partners; and (2) pointing to the human need for redemption through the fulfillment of covenant ordinances (Sinai's sacrifices) as a means of returning

22. Ibid., 36–37.
23. Ibid., 33.
24. Ibid., 35.
25. Ibid.
26. Ibid., 68–69.
27. Ibid., 112–14.
28. Ibid., 114.

to "Eden."[29] It should be noted at this point that Collins' interpretation of Genesis 1–4 as an endorsement of the Mosaic Covenant is contrary to the one taken in this book: yet, his focus on the final form of Genesis 1–4 within the context of the final form of the Pentateuch is shared.

GENESIS 1–3, THE PENTATEUCH,
AND THE HISTORY OF ISRAEL

Several other studies elaborate the importance of Genesis 1–3 as the introduction to the Pentateuch, and include parallels between the opening chapters and Deuteronomic theology, as well as the remainder of the so-called "Primary History" (Gen 1:1—2 Kgs 25:30). Alonso Schökel was among the first scholars[30] to call attention to parallels between the opening chapters of Genesis[31] and the *historia salutis* ("the history of salvation" or "salvation history"). He also pointed out a constellation of terms found almost exclusively in wisdom literature.[32] Schökel noticed connections between Genesis 2–3, not only with key passages in the Pentateuch, but also with later events in the biblical history. Parallels noted by Schökel include (1) the narrative depiction of Adam's covenantal relationship to God in Genesis 2–3 and Israel's covenantal relationship to God in Exodus 19–34 (covenant-sin-punishment-reconciliation); (2) the depiction of Adam's being taking from outside the garden and placed ("rested") inside it and Israel's being brought from outside the land of Canaan and being placed inside it (see Gen 2:15; Deut 3:20; 30:3–4; Josh 1:13, 15; Jer 27:11; Ezek 36:34; 37:14, 21; Isa 14:1); (3) Adam's downfall following his "cleaving" to a woman and the downfall of Israel at Baal Peor and also the downfall of Israel's subsequent kings due to their having cleaved to seductive women; (4) the apodictic laws of the

29. Ibid., 244–45.

30. According to Sousan ("Woman in Eden," 178–81), Karl Barth also noticed this connection. See Barth, *Church Dogmatics*, 273.

31. It would appear that Schökel excluded Gen 1:1—2:4a from his range of investigation for source critical reasons. As I already argued, attempts to interpret Gen 2–3 in isolation from Gen 1 seriously undermine an exegetical vantage point only appreciated by means of a holistic reading of these chapters.

32. Schökel ("Motivos Sapienciales" 302–3) perceptively notes parallels between Adam and Solomon, such as wisdom concerning the animal world and downfalls connected with women. He fails to factor in the royal overtones of Gen 1:26–28 into his analysis of the parallels between Adam and Solomon (this is more thoroughly treated in a subsequent chapter).

garden and the apodictic laws of Sinai; and (5) the covenantal style of the consequence of disobedience in the garden and the consequence of disobedience to Sinai.

Several scholars concur with Schökel's findings with respect to the relationship of Genesis 1 and 2–3, Deuteronomic theology, and Israel's biblical history.[33] The following is a list of these scholars with abbreviated summaries of their findings in the footnotes: Joseph Blenkinsopp,[34] Carlos R. Bovell,[35] Martin Emmrich,[36] Brian G. Toews,[37] William J. Dumbrell,[38] and Terence Fretheim.[39]

33. For a recent history of interpretation of Gen 2–3 see Gillingham, *Image*, 10–44; Stordalen, *Echoes of Eden*, 305–17.

34. Blenkinsopp, *Pentateuch Introduction*, 66. So also, for example, Gardner ("Genesis 2:4b—3," 15), who writes, "Genesis 3 can be viewed as a mythological interpretation of Israelite religious history from the time of the settlement." Gardner draws parallels between Eve's duplicity in Adam's downfall with subsequent women in the Deuteronomistic History (see 1 Kgs 11:4–13; 16:31–33) and the garden with the Promised Land. For the conviction of a redactional effort to link the Tetrateuch and Deueteronomy with the Deuteronomistic History, see Schmitt, "Spätdeuteronomistische Geschichtswerk," 261–79.

35. Bovell, "Genesis 3:21?" 361–66. Bovell draws parallels between the serpent and the Canaanites, and Adam's mandate to conquer the land and Israel's mandate to do the same. Bovell's primary thesis is that Gen 3:21 (the provision of the garments of skin) represents an attempt on the part of the exilic writers of the final composition of the Pentateuch to explain the exile to current and/or subsequent readers that Israel had in fact become just like the inhabitants of Canaan (Adam and Eve are now dressed like the animals of the land), they had not kept the Torah, and therefore they were no longer worthy of the land.

36. Martin Emmrich, "Temptation Narrative," 3–20. Emmrich's work provides a rare attempt to understand the temptation narrative as part of the Pentateuch, and in terms of its contribution to the Primary History. Emmrich sees parallels between the gift of the garden and the gift of the Promised Land, the two trees (representing life and death) and the Torah, the serpent and the false prophets (Deut 13:1–3), and the woman of the garden and the women who would later instigate Israel's apostasy from the Lord.

37. Toews, "Genesis 1–4," 38–52. Toews' argument is broader than that of Bovell and Emmrich. He argues that Gen 1–4 is the introduction proper to the entire OT and its theology. In addition to finding parallels between Gen 1–3 and Israel's history, Toews attempts to trace archetypical patterns introduced in Gen 1–4 throughout the rest of the tripartite Hebrew canon. With respect to the relationship between Gen 1–4 and the Pentateuch, Toews sees parallels between the dividing of the waters of creation and the dividing of the Red Sea, the Garden of Eden and the Tabernacle, and the covenant theology of Gen 2–3 and the book of Deuteronomy (e.g., exile due to disobedience).

38. Dumbrell, "Genesis 2:1–3," 219–30; see also, Dumbrell, *Faith of Israel*. Dumbrell notes that both Adam and Israel share royal-priestly roles (see especially Gen 1:26, 28; Exod 19:4–6), both enjoy the conditional provision of a divinely prepared land, and both lose access to the divine space due to their transgression and exile.

39. Fretheim, *Pentateuch*. Although he does not deny the existence of different

From within another faith tradition, Tvi Erlich, an Israeli scholar writing in Modern Hebrew, also finds numerous links between the story of the Garden of Eden and the story of Israel's sojourn at Mount Sinai.[40] On the basis of numerous innertextual links between these two narratives, Erlich argues that Sinai and the tabernacle (and a return from exile to a special land prepared by God) are depicted as the solution to Adam's sin, or as he describes it, תיקון חטא הקדמון. Although Erlich discusses the similarities between Eden and Sinai, he argues that the distinctions between these two narratives are the key for one's interpretation and assessment of the theological import of Sinai within the Pentateuch. Although both narratives recount sin and retreat (חטא ונסיגה), a careful comparison reveals important and exegetically significant differences. At this point it would be helpful to reproduce a portion of Erlich's charts highlighting the similarities and key differences between the two narratives.[41]

sources underlying Gen 1–3, Fretheim's commitments lie with the final form of the text (ibid., 72). His desire to understand Gen 1–3 as part of the Pentateuch leads him to the conclusion that the two trees, the giving of commandments, and the choices of life and death in the garden anticipate the giving of the law at Sinai (Deut 30:15–20) (ibid., 75). Fretheim argues that the juxtaposition of the very good creation with the subsequent entrance of sin "dramatically portrays the need for a reclamation of creation" and demonstrates God's "commitment to stay with the world, come what may in the wake of human sinfulness" (ibid., 72).

40. Erlich, "Story of Garden," 17–35 [Modern Hebrew].
41. Ibid., 20–34; translation from Modern Hebrew my own.

TABLE 1: Similarities between the Garden of Eden and the Sinai Narrative (Erlich)[42]

Garden of Eden	Position of Mount Sinai
God gives commandments directly to Adam, who in turn communicates them to his wife.	God gives commandments directly to Moses, who in turn communicates them to Israel.
The woman sins, Adam is dragged after her, and both of them are distanced from the Lord.	The people sin, but Moses is not dragged after them,[43] and therefore, he causes the rectification of the sin and renewed approach to the Lord.
The one who does not take heed (שמר) and transgresses the Lord's commandment will surely die (מות ימות) (Gen 2:15–17).	The one who does not take heed (שמר) and transgresses the Lord's commandment will surely die (מות ימות) (Exod 19:12–13).
The woman added to the prohibition not to touch (נגע), although this was not commanded, and as a consequence, subtracted from the commandment in the end (Gen 3:2–3).	The prohibition of touching (נגע) was included in the Lord's commandment in order to prevent a serious sin of ascending the mountain without permission (Exod 19:12–13).
Commandments of do and commandments of do not do, concerning which the man will transgress in the continuation of the narrative (Gen 2:16–17).	Commandments of do and commandments of do not do, concerning which the people will transgress in the continuation of the narrative (Exod 20:2–3).
After the sin, the man was unable to hear the voice (שמע קול) of the Lord and to stand before the *Shekinah*, and therefore he fearfully[44] (ירא) hides from the presence of the Lord (Gen 3:8, 10).	Similar to the first man's reaction, the people of Israel are unable to directly hear the voice (שמע קול) of the Lord and to stand near the *Shekinah*. Therefore, they fearfully (ירא) stand at a distance from it, and request Moses to intercede to the Lord on their behalf (Exod 20:14–15; Deut 5:19–20).
After the sin, Adam enters into a situation in which he is prevented from drawing near to life (חיים) (Gen 3:24).	Due to the sin of the first man, the people of Israel are unable to stand in the presence of the revelation of the living (חיים) God (Deut 5:22).

42. *Source:* Tvi Erlich, "The Story of the Garden of Eden in Comparison to the Position of Mount Sinai and the Tabernacle," *Alon Shvut for Graduates of the Har Eztion Yeshiva* 11 (1998) 20–34. Used by permission.

43. Elsewhere, however, Moses follows the people in their unbelief (Num 20:12; see 14:11), and like Adam (and Israel), he dies in exile.

Garden of Eden	Position of Mount Sinai
The chosen man of humanity is cast out from the presence of God (Gen 3:23–24).	The chosen man of humanity is called into a close encounter with the Lord (Exod 24:12, 18).
The woman influences the man to sin and, consequently, to lose connection with the Lord (Gen 3:17, 23).	Since Eve influenced Adam to sin, when Israel wants to draw close to the Lord it is incumbent upon them to separate themselves from women (Exod 19:15).
The man in the Garden of Eden aspired to reach an imaginary good (טוב), but when he transgressed the Lord's commandment, God guarded (שמר) the way to life (הדרך לחיים) from him (Gen 3:24).	Keeping (שמר) the commandments of the Lord leads the people of Israel on the way (דרך) that leads to the true good (טוב) and to the true life (חיים) (Deut 20:14–15).
The man goes away from the place of the *Shekina* and cherubim are caused to dwell (שכן) at the entrance to the garden with the flaming sword (Gen 3:24).	The people of Israel are privileged to draw near to the *Shekina* and the glory of God dwells (שכן) on Mount Sinai before the eyes of Israel (Exod 24:16–17).
The man's return to the dust of the ground (אדמה) constitutes part of his atonement for his sin (Gen 3:17).	The ground (אדמה) from which the man was fashioned atones for his sins (Exod 20:24).
The sin obligates the man to cover his nakedness (ערותו) (Gen 3:21).	The location of the textual portion after the Ten Commandments is apparently not entirely understood. But if this portion is tied to the Garden of Eden, then the matter is understood that also on Mount Sinai it is commanded concerning atonement of the ground for the sin of the first man, and it is essential to even point out the maintenance of modesty in attire because it comes out of the original sin (Exod 20:22).

44. Erlich does not use the word "fearfully" in his explanation but underlines this term as an innertextual link between both passages in the body of his paper. I have added this word to the chart in order to bring out an important element in his observations.

Erlich also finds numerous parallels between the Fall in Genesis 3 and the Golden Calf Narrative. It will be helpful to reproduce a portion of his chart:

TABLE 2: Parallels between Genesis 3 and the Golden Calf Narrative (Exod 32:1–6)[45]

The Sin in the Garden	The Sin of the Calf
The description of Adam and Eve just prior to their sin (יתבששו) (Gen 2:25)	Even the word בשש from the root בוש is reminiscent of the story of the Garden of Eden in the sense of the shame in the nakedness and even at Mount Sinai in the context of Moses' delay. It is essential to notice that the use of the *polal/hithpolal* with this root only appears in these two places (Exod 32:1).
Transgression of the commandment do-not-do which was thrown upon the man was done by means of eating (Gen 3:6).	Transgression of the first commandment do-not-do in the Ten Commandments: "Do not make for yourselves a carved image" combines the act of eating with the sin (Exod 32:3–6).
The Lord's inquiry of the sin (Gen 3:13)	Moses' inquiry, who did not sin, of the one who catalyzed the sin (Exod 32:21)
Adam is condemned to death in his sin and the sword guards the tree of life from the sinful man (Gen 3:19, 24).	The people of Israel rectify their sin by putting to death the sinners with the sword (Exod 32:27)
The man is sent out (שלח) and cast out (גרש) from the Garden of Eden and from the presence of the Lord and he is not able to go in the way (דרך) of life (Gen 3:23–24).	God minimizes the level of his connection with the people and now it is not the Lord himself who leads them but he sends (שלח) his angel who casts out (גרש) the peoples of Canaan, lest the Lord destroy Israel who is going on the way (דרך) (Exod 33:2–3).

Again, the key to evaluating the theology of Sinai within the Pentateuch, according to Erlich, lies in the differences between the accounts of the Fall of Adam and the Fall of Israel (the golden calf). Erlich makes much of the fact that though the people (corresponding to Eve)

45. *Source:* Tvi Erlich, "The Story of the Garden of Eden in Comparison to the Position of Mount Sinai and the Tabernacle," *Alon Shvut for Graduates of the Har Eztion Yeshiva* 11 (1998): 20–34. Used by permission.

sinned, Moses (corresponding to Adam) did not. In fact, on the basis of Moses' intercession God consents not to destroy Israel and to abide with the people in their conquest of the land (Exod 33:15–17). Moses also participates in the atoning process by investigating—God was the investigator in the garden—the events concerning the golden calf, destroying the idol, making the people drink of its ashes, and then commanding the Levites to slay the offenders.[46] Erlich also argues on the basis of the parallels and differences between the position of Mount Sinai and the tabernacle, and between the tabernacle and the Garden of Eden, that, although Israel failed (like Eve), Moses (unlike Adam) successfully mediates for the provision of God's lasting presence and closeness (unlike the garden) with the people of Israel.[47]

Unique to Erlich, moreover, is his comparison of the sin in the garden and the sin of Nadab and Abihu. Both sins involve taking (לקח), giving (נתן), and violating what God commanded (צוה) (Gen 3:6, 11; Lev 10:1); both sins involve *lex talionis* of death (Gen 2:17; Lev 10:2); both sins result in a bodily removal from the presence of the *Shekinah* (Gen 3:23–24; Lev 10:3); in both cases the tunics (כתנות) of the violators (Gen 3:21; 10:5) are mentioned. Yet, Erlich argues that this parallel is not an exact repetition of Adam's total failure because the punishment was meted out on the individuals responsible and not on all of Israel (unlike the garden) and access to the presence of God remained after Nadab and Abihu's sin (unlike the garden).[48] Erlich concludes his article, however, by noting that Israel's entrance into the Promised Land and the building of the temple was the divinely intended means of rectifying the sin in the garden. Yet, Israel's violation of the commandments again resulted in the expulsion from the chosen place. In essence, Adam's sin was repeated again.[49]

At this point, it is worth pointing out an important distinction between Erlich's analysis of Genesis 1–3 and its connections to the Sinai Narrative and those of many others. Erlich's thesis is rooted in the conviction that innertextual links between the garden and Sinai are intended to provide an exegetical framework for a theological assessment of the

46. Ibid., 27–28.

47. Ibid., 29–33. Erlich acknowledges, however, that fear resulting from the first sin (Gen 3:10) remains as an abiding testimony to conditions after the Fall.

48. Ibid., 33–35.

49. Ibid., 35.

significance of the Sinai Covenant within the Pentateuch. While I completely agree with Erlich's thesis, my interpretation of the Pentateuch's theological assessment of the Sinai Covenant differs markedly from his.

JOHN SAILHAMER

To date, John Sailhamer's *The Pentateuch as Narrative* represents the only full-scale attempt to apply a text-centered compositional analysis to the Pentateuch.[50] According to Sailhamer, the key to discerning the compositional strategy of the Pentateuch is the presence of three macrostructural junctures where the author has inserted large blocks of poetry into structurally strategic locations.[51] Sailhamer notes that in each of these poems a key figure (Jacob, Balaam, and Moses) proclaims what will take place in the "last days" (see Gen 49:1; Num 24:14; Deut 31:39).[52] On this basis, Sailhamer argues that eschatology is primary to the compositional concerns of the Pentateuchal author. Since the Pentateuch spans from the "beginning" (Gen 1:1) to the "end," Sailhamer suggests that "one of the central concerns lying behind the final shape of the Pentateuch is an attempt to uncover an inherent relationship between the past and the future."[53] By recognizing the "inherent relationship between the past and the future" the reader discovers a vital hermeneutical key for unlocking the purpose of the Pentateuchal narratives: many of the narratives assume a narrative-typological significance. "Earlier events foreshadow and anticipate later events. Later events are written to remind the reader of past narratives."[54] If Sailhamer is correct, one would expect to find "narrative typology" in the early chapters of Genesis as well.

Before looking at his interpretation of Genesis 1–3, it is essential to note that Sailhamer, like Erlich, views the covenant between God and Israel at Mount Sinai as the central concern of the Pentateuch. However, unlike many Pentateuchal scholars, Sailhamer makes a careful distinction between the Sinai Covenant and the Pentateuch as a whole. Thus,

---

50. For an explication of compositional analysis or composition criticism, see Fohrer et al., *Exegese des Alten Testaments*, 139–42.

51. Sailhamer, *Pentateuch as Narrative*, 36.

52. Ibid.

53. Ibid., 37.

54. Ibid., 37–41. Sailhamer argues, for instance, that Gen 12:10–20 foreshadows Gen 41—Exod 12, and the spread of sin in Gen 1–11 parallels the defilement of the camp in Lev 11–16.

the Pentateuch is an evaluation of the Sinai Covenant, but not the covenant itself.[55] The Pentateuch's perspective on the Sinai Covenant is summarized in three points: (1) the covenant of Sinai is presented as God's means of restoring God's original plans to bless humanity (Gen 1:26–28; 12:1–3; Exod 2:24); (2) the Sinai Covenant failed to restore the creation blessing because of Israel's failure to trust and obey God; (3) God's plan to restore the creation blessing will one day succeed when God gives Israel a circumcised heart to trust and obey (Deut 30:1–10).[56] Thus, the overall thrust of the Pentateuch is oriented toward the future, and encourages the reader to wait on God to fulfill his promises.

Turning to Genesis 1–3, Sailhamer argues that Gen 1:1—2:4a (a literarily cohesive unit) serves as the introduction to the Pentateuch.[57] Based on his sense of the overall intentions of the Pentateuch and the importance of the Sinai Covenant, Sailhamer argues that 1:1—2:4a introduces three central themes of the Pentateuch: God the Creator, human beings, and the land.[58] Sailhamer entitles Gen 1:2—2:3 the "preparation of the Land." The dividing of the waters of creation and the gift of the land are seen as parallels to the dividing of the waters of the Red Sea and God's gift of the land to the people of Israel.[59] Sailhamer also notes the fact that the poem of Deuteronomy 32 draws a connection between the creation account and God's covenant with Israel, using the same terminology found in Genesis 1.[60] The dividing of the waters on the third day (1:9–13) parallels the Flood (Gen 6–9) and the parting of the Red Sea (Exod 14–15): and, in all three places water is an obstacle for human enjoyment of the land.[61]

Sailhamer regards Genesis 2:4–24 as the gift of the land, and understands the Garden of Eden as a prototypical tabernacle (Exod 25–31, 35–40). Based on the geographical descriptions (2:8–14), Sailhamer posits that the location of Eden is closely aligned with the land promised to Abraham and his descendants (see Gen 15:18).[62] Sailhamer also

---

55. Ibid., 27.

56. Ibid.

57. Ibid., 26.

58. Ibid., 28–29.

59. Ibid., 84.

60. Ibid.

61. Ibid., 91.

62. Ibid., 97–100. Several parallels between Gen 2–3 and 15–16 (Adam and

contends that the terminology used to describe Adam's occupation in the garden (2:15) depicts the first man as a priest who is called to worship and obey God. Moreover, as in the remainder of the Torah, Adam's enjoyment of the land, like Israel's, is contingent upon his obedience to the commandments (Deut 30:15–18)[63]

Finally, Sailhamer entitles Genesis 2:25—4:26, "the land and the exile."[64] According to Sailhamer, the "sound" of the Lord and Adam's retreat foreshadow the Lord's appearance on Mount Sinai and Israel's retreat (Exod 20:18–21): thus, Adam and Eve's sin in the garden foreshadows Israel's sin at Mount Sinai. Also noted by Sailhamer in the Fall Narrative is the author's interest in eating, a concern later elaborated on in the Torah (Lev 11; Deut 14). The covering provided for Adam's nakedness (Gen 3:21) anticipates the covering provided for the nakedness of the priests (Exod 28:42–43). Sailhamer argues that Adam's exile from the garden is intended to parallel the casting out of a ritually impure individual from the midst of the people (Exod 31:14), thereby portraying the Fall as akin to ritual contamination (see Lev 13:1—14:57). Finally, the cherubim standing guard to the access of the Tree of Life foreshadow the Torah's presence in the Ark of the Covenant (also protected by cherubim; Exod 25:10–22; Deut 31:24–26).

CONCLUSION

In the history of interpretation, I called attention to an emerging return to certain assumptions governing the pre-critical Christian interpretation of Genesis 1–3. First, I noted a return to the acceptance of the unity of Genesis 1–3, albeit for reasons clearly differing from those maintained by pre-critical scholars. Second, I pointed to a return to the conviction of a prophetic orientation of the canonical Pentateuch. Finally, I discussed a growing number of scholars who seek to understand Genesis 1–3 as an integral part of the Pentateuch. I also referred to scholars who find parallels between Genesis 1–3 and Israel's biblical history.

There is more work to be done, however. To some extent, the diversity of interpretations are piecemeal, with no concerted effort to connect the dots leading from the Pentateuch to the Primary History, and

---

Abraham), which are discussed in a subsequent chapter, lend credence to this association between Eden and the Promised Land.

63. Ibid., 100–101.
64. Ibid., 102–16.

from the Primary History to the canonical Tanakh. This book represents an attempt to meet this need by means of a more thorough analysis of Genesis 1–3 and its relationship to the Pentateuch, to the Primary History, and finally, to the tri-partite canon or Tanakh.

4

Methodology

INTRODUCTION TO THE TEXT-CENTERED APPROACH

THERE ARE NO UNIFORM definitions of a "text-centered" approach to the Hebrew Bible. More than ten years ago, John Barton pointed out the presence of "two quite distinct types of 'text-immanent' approach[es]," one known as "structural" or "structuralist" exegesis, and the other, the "canonical method."[1] John Sailhamer and others have also proposed another uniquely evangelical form of "text-centered," or "text-immanent" exegesis.[2]

This chapter makes explicit the working assumptions upon which subsequent chapters are grounded. The first part of this chapter clarifies what I mean by "text-centered" by discussing what is *not* entailed in my "text-centered" approach. The following section spells out the focus of a "text-centered" approach and the implications of the textuality of a text for biblical exegesis and interpretation. In this section intertextuality and the criteria for identifying intertextuality are discussed. The third section explains one particular text-centered approach known as "composition criticism" or "compositional analysis."

Approaches to the interpretation of the OT[3] are categorized along three axes of focus: the author, the text, or the reader. Text-centered approaches have typically been associated with a focus on the text and/ or the reader with little or no regard for the intentions of the historical author. The text-centered approach advocated in this book, however,

1. Barton, *Reading Old Testament*, 2; Patte, "Genesis 2 and 3." *Semeia* devotes an entire journal volume to structural analyses of Gen 2–3.

2. Sailhamer, Introduction. See also Wong, Text-Centered Approach.

3. I am using the term OT here, rather than Tanakh or Hebrew Bible, as a more general term, since Tanakh refers to a specific order of the OT.

maintains that a text in its final form embodies the intentionality of a historical author.

It is important to understand that by "author" I mean the individual or individuals responsible for the *final form* of a given text, in this case, the Pentateuch. As a conservative Old Testament scholar, I affirm the existence of an essentially Mosaic Torah (i.e., the Mosaic authorship of a pre-canonical Torah as stated in Josh 1:8). But in this book my concern is to understand the intentionality of the individual (author) responsible for the Torah in its *final* form. As I make clear in the remainder of this chapter, I understand the final form Torah to be an accurate ("inspired") interpretation of its pre-canonical form, although I make no attempt to defend the existence of a Mosaic Torah. Since the goal of my exegetical labors is to interpret the Torah in its final form, the affirmation or denial of an essentially Mosaic Torah is inconsequential to my argument as a whole. Henceforth, when I refer to the "author" of the Pentaeuch, I mean the individual(s) responsible for the Pentateuch in its final form.

TEXT-CENTERED APPROACH

What It Is Not

It Is Not Ahistorical

Han's Frei's *Eclipse of Biblical Narrative* has had a profound influence upon Biblical Studies. Frei argued that certain assumptions rooted in the ideas of the Enlightenment resulted in a shift in focus from the pursuit of the meaning of a biblical text to the search for meaning either in *events depicted by* a biblical text or by *ideas derived from* a biblical text. According to Frei, this hermeneutical shift from the interpretation of the verbal meaning of biblical texts to the exposition of the events and ideas behind the text led to the eventual *eclipse of the biblical narrative*. To be clear, pre-critical scholars did not make a distinction between the meaning of the biblical texts and the events described by those texts. Rather, for these scholars the biblical narratives described what had taken place in the real world. For many biblical scholars, however, the critical investigation of the Bible, with its focus on the events described by the narratives, resulted in the eventual denial of the veracity of the biblical text. In response to this growing threat against biblical truth, conservative Christians wedded the interpretation of the verbal meaning of the Bible with an explication of the events described by the Bible in their attempts to defend the veracity of the biblical text (apologetics) against the onslaught of critical methodologies. Frei's intention was not to deny or to defend the historicity of the "history-like" biblical narratives. Rather, his primary purpose was to expose the hermeneutical eclipse of biblical narrative in order to bring scholarly attention back to the interpretation of the verbal meaning of the biblical narratives themselves.

Frei's observations had important implications for biblical scholars across the conservative-critical spectrum since they brought to the fore a reevaluation of the locus of meaning in biblical interpretation. Left unanswered in Frei's approach, however, is the relationship between the "history-like" narratives and "actual history" itself. Frei appears to be ambivalent towards historical referentiality.[4] Carl F. H. Henry, in his critique of Frei on this point, writes, "Narrative theology in the broader sense offers us a hermeneutical theory that affirms the comprehensive authority of Scripture yet suspends the question of its ontological truth and historical factuality."[5]

With the advent of literary approaches since the time of Frei came a growing recognition of sophisticated literary techniques present in the biblical text. This resulted in a further questioning of the referentiality of the biblical text. As a result, many text-centered approaches tend to be ahistorical.[6]

A text-centered approach, however, need not entail ambivalence to (or rejection of) the referentiality of the text or the importance of historical studies.[7] Sailhamer, for example, affirms Frei's understanding

4. Frei, Review of *Eclipse of Biblical Narrative*, 239: "[C]an the question of historical truth be bypassed in the manner which Frei's hermeneutic requires? Could not a realistic narrative be both moving and meaningful, and yet be historically false?" See also Borsch, "Eclipse of Biblical Narrative," 572; Henry, "Narrative Theology," 3–19; and Barton's critique of Frei's non-referential theory of biblical narrative, in Barton, *Reading Old Testament*, 160–67. In his response to Henry, however, Frei explicitly states that he does not deny referentiality, nor does he deny the historical reality of Christ's death and resurrection (although he encloses *historical reality* in quotations marks) (Frei, "Response," 21–24).

5. Henry, "Narrative Theology," 19.

6. White, "Value of Speech Act Theory," 53: "The developing 'literary' approaches to the biblical text have generally not carried forward the concern of the new hermeneutic with language and history, but have relied on various 'new critical' and formalist methods which perpetuate the theoretical cleavage between the historical and aesthetic dimensions of the text."

7. On the relationship of synchronic and diachronic studies, and for a rejection of an ahistorical text-centered approach, see Talstra, "From 'Eclipse' to 'Art,'" 15.

of the relationship between text and meaning, yet takes issue with Frei's premise that biblical authors only intended their narratives to be "history like" rather than "real history."[8] V. Philips Long demonstrates that the mere presence of literary artistry in biblical narrative does not *ipso facto* relegate a narrative to the genre of historical fiction.[9] There are, according to Long, no formal distinctions between a historical narrative and a historical fiction.[10] Historical fiction and fiction-like history can only be distinguished in many cases on the basis of the intentionality of the author. That is, did the author intend to "represent" events or to "create" them? While it is not always possible to determine an author's intentionality, evidence suggests the biblical writers intended to depict real events and were also constrained by their subject matter (referentiality).[11]

Moreover, it would be self-defeating for a biblical author to depict fictitious redemptive acts for the purposes of eliciting faith in the God of Israel.[12] In Henry's words, "The notion that the narrative simply as narrative adequately nurtures faith independently of all objective historical concerns sponsors a split in the relationships of faith to reason and to history that would in principle encourage skepticism and cloud historical referents in obscurity."[13]

Described in terms of speech-act theory, testifying (illocution) about Yahweh's fictitious deeds in order to evoke faith (perlocution) in the reality of God's power and goodness would be infelicitous.[14] While faith certainly involves an element of the unverifiable, it is difficult to understand how a description of fictitious events (such as the splitting

---

8. Sailhamer, *Introduction*, 73 n. 121. According to Sailhamer, 55, "It can also be said today with confidence that there is reasonable evidence that the biblical narratives recount reliable historical events."

9. Long, "History and Fiction," 232–54.

10. This is also corroborated by inconclusive attempts within the realm of speech act theory to establish definitive criteria for distinguishing fiction from real speech acts in literary texts. See White, "Introduction: Speech Act Theory," 14.

11. Long, "History and Fiction," 243. See also Japhet, "Periodization," 504–5; Kofoed, *Text and History*.

12. The "faith theme" in the Pentateuch strongly suggests that a primary compositional motivation for its composition was to evoke a faith response from its readers. See Schmitt, "Redaktion des Pentateuch."

13. Henry, "Narrative Theology," 11.

14. See Austin, *How to Do Things*, 12–24; see also Searle, *Speech Acts*; Searle and Vanderveken, *Foundations of Illocutionary Logic*.

of the Red Sea in Exod 14:31) procures the kinds of faith-responses in Yahweh intended by the biblical authors.

In terms of the historicity of Genesis 1–3, the challenges are obvious. Two comments, however, are in order. First, there are textual reasons for suggesting that the author of the final form of Genesis 1–3 *intended* to represent real historical events.[15] Second, subsequent biblical authors apparently understood Genesis 1–3 to be about real historical events.[16] Therefore, regardless of where a modern reader's faith commitments lie, it seems best to suspend historical judgment in order to appreciate authorial intention and to understand the text on its own terms. In Meir Sternberg's words, "To make sense of the Bible in terms of its own conventions, one need not believe in either [inspiration or history], but one must postulate both."[17]

It Is Not Divorced from Authorial Intentionality

Many literary approaches to the Bible are based on theories stemming from "New Criticism."[18] They are frequently associated with a disregard for authorial intention and *the* meaning of a text. Daniel Patte is clear on this point when he writes, "So as to dispel the illusion that a narrative is a monolithic meaning entity, literary studies emphasize the multiplicity of its potential meanings."[19] An influential essay emanating from the circles of New Criticism was written by W. K. Wimsatt and M. C. Beardsley (1946). These authors challenged the romantic assumption that, to understand a literary work, it is necessary to know the author's thoughts and feelings at the time of writing.[20] Although Wimsatt and Beardsley

---

15. The genealogical lists linking Adam to Abraham (see Gen 5:1ff.), for example, strongly suggest that the author regarded Adam as a real historical figure. In fact, there are no indications that any of the subsequent biblical authors, either OT or NT, regarded Gen 1–3 as a myth.

16. For example, the author of Chronicles begins his genealogical list of real historical figures with Adam (1 Chr 1:1).

17. Sternberg, *Poetics*, 81. (Words in brackets provided.) Later (ibid., 82) he writes, "With God postulated as double author, the biblical narrator can enjoy the privileges of art without renouncing his historical titles."

18. According to Barton (*Reading Old Testament*, 144), three primary theses of New Criticism are (1) literary texts are artifacts, (2) authorial intention is a fallacy, and (3) the meaning of a text is determined by the canon of literature in which it is located.

19. Patte, "One Text," 4.

20. Wimsatt and Beardsley, "Intentional Fallacy," 468–88. For a detailed analysis of

did not deny a designing intellect (intention) behind the production of a literary work, they rejected this as the standard by which it must be interpreted.[21] The meaning of a literary work is loosened from the intention of the author at the moment of its conception; its meaning is intrinsic to the work itself (a text is an artifact).[22] Any attempt to interpret a literary work in terms of its author's intentions is dubbed the "intentional fallacy." It is important to note that some literary approaches to the Bible (such as structuralism) have incorrectly understood Wimsatt and Beardsley's "intentional fallacy" as a denial that a text means what the historical author meant it to mean, thereby dubbing any discussion of authorial intent a fallacy.[23]

I also reject the view that it is necessary to recover the intentions of the historical author outside of the text or to reconstruct the author's inner thoughts and feelings at the time of writing in order to understand the text itself. Yet it is problematic to divorce a text from the intentions of its historical author (personality[24]). Only by regarding the text as the embodiment of a historical author's intention is there a possibility of adjudicating between mutually exclusive interpretations.[25] Daniel Patte's comments on intention in the context of speech act theory are helpful:[26]

---

the assumptions of romantic hermeneutics, see Gadamer, *Wahrheit und Methode*, or *Truth and Method*.

21. See Hays, *Echoes*, 201 n. 90.

22. Wimsatt and Beardsley, "Intentional Fallacy," 477: "The evaluation of the work of art remains public; the work is measured against something outside the author."

23. Both Barton and Sternberg suggest that Wimsatt and Beardsley's *intention* about intention has been misunderstood. Barton, *Reading Old Testament*, 167–69; Sternberg, *Poetics of Biblical Narrative*, 8.

24. For an insightful evaluation and critique of the de-personalization and objectification of a literary work, see Ong, "Jinnee," 309–20.

25. The use of "historical" attaches significance to important and unavoidable extrinsic questions for biblical interpretation, such as the time and circumstances in which the author wrote. Text-theory, particularly as it relates to the Pentateuch, is a necessary component of a text-centered approach; as such, historical questions must be raised and then addressed. According to Barton (*Reading Old Testament*, 150), this appears to be Wimsatt and Beardsley's point as well. "Wimsatt and Beardsley were not structuralists! The meaning of a poem was for them still a *historical* meaning."

26. Patte's defense of authorial intent is all the more striking in light of an earlier article he wrote from a structural perspective. He wrote, "For indeed, the meaning of a story cannot be posited anymore than can the glitter of a jewel." And then, "The structuralist venture is based upon the awareness of the delusory fascination for making a fossil-like image out of a story's meaning." (Patte, "One Text," 4.) Patte's acceptance of

Similarly, as speech act theory points out, a linguistic statement does not make sense as long as one does not take into account the intentionality of the speaker . . . Yet the intentionality of the speaker, the subjectivity of the illocutionary force, are by nature largely elliptical. Therefore they need to be *inferred* on the basis of what is manifested in the statement, of its context, and this in terms of the rules which govern intentionality . . . Of course, this is what we do spontaneously when we listen to a speaker. Subconsciously making use of such rules, we infer what is the intentionality of the speaker; otherwise, the speech act would fail. In the case of "live speeches," this is a fairly reliable process which allows for communication to take place, even though it is somewhat haphazard, frequently involving trials and errors, guesses which are subsequently corrected, etc. In the case of texts, and especially texts from a removed historical period and from a foreign culture, the chance of error greatly multiplies. Yet, as long as we refuse to make the study of the subjectivity and the intentionality of the author a legitimate part of our critical investigation, we simply pretend that we can spontaneously apprehend them correctly! Actually, we occult this important dimension of meaning. A critical study of the intentionality of a text will allow us to recover it. For this purpose, unlike the spontaneous filling in of the ellipsis of live communication, we need to make a self-conscious use of the rules which govern intentionality.[27]

In short, texts have meaning because an author meant them to.

Roland Barthes, an opponent of authorial intent, illustrates the ramifications of severing a literary work from its author. In Barthes' words,

Once the Author is removed, the claim to decipher a text becomes futile. To give a text an Author is to impose a limit on that text, to furnish it with a final signified, to close the writing. Such a conception suits criticism very well, the latter then allotting itself the important task of discovering the Author (or its hypostases: society, history, psyche, liberty) beneath the work: when the Author has been found, the text is "explained"—victory to the critic . . . In precisely this way literature (it would be better from now on to say *writing*), by refusing to assign a "secret," an ultimate meaning, to the text (and to the world as a text), liberates

---

speech act theory resulted in his reevaluation of the role of authorial intent for biblical exegesis (Patte, "Speech Act Theory," 91, 95, 98).

27. Patte, "Speech Act Theory," 98; words in italics original.

what may be called an anti-theological activity, an activity that is
truly revolutionary since to refuse to fix meaning is, in the end, to
refuse God and his hypostases—reason, science, law.[28]

There are many indications, however, that biblical authors intel-
ligently and strategically composed their texts in order to convey a
particular meaning to their readers: the final form conveys the author's
intentions. Textually speaking, therefore, compositional strategy is synonymous with authorial intention.

Sternberg's study of the poetics of biblical narrative is one example
of a literary approach that affirms the importance of authorial intention. In his words, "As interpreters of the Bible, our only concern is with
'embodied' or 'objectified' intention; and that forms a different business
altogether, about which a wide measure of agreement has always existed.
In my own view, such intention fulfills a crucial role, for communication
presupposes a speaker who resorts to certain linguistic and structural
tools in order to produce certain effects on the addressee; the discourse
accordingly supplies a network of clues to the speaker's intention."[29]

Given the homogeneous literary patterns embracing the macro-
structure of the Pentateuch and larger complexes within the Pentateuch,[30]
the text-centered approach advocated here sees a direct correlation between a text's meaning and the authorial intention.[31] It is important to
note, however, that the author's intention can only be responsibly inferred by means of a careful literary analysis of the text itself, given the

---

28. Barthes, "Death of Author," 147. Elsewhere (ibid., 146) he writes, "We know now
that a text is not a line of words releasing a single 'theological' meaning (the 'message'
of the Author-God) but a multidimensional space in which a variety of writings, none
of them original, blend and clash." E. D. Hirsch (*Validity in Interpretation,* 5) concurs
with Barthes' understanding of the implications of the rejection of the author when
he writes, "To banish the original author as the determiner of meaning was to reject
the only compelling normative principle that could lend validity to an interpretation."
Another attempt to articulate the importance of the author is found in Vanhoozer, *Is
There a Meaning?*

29. Sternberg, Poetics of Biblical Narrative, 9.

30. For an explication of the literary patterns embracing the Pentateuch, see
Sailhamer, *Pentateuch as Narrative.*

31. This is clearly in contrast to structuralism, which is a method of interpretation
based on the hypothesis that a text's meaning is constrained by cultural norms and
rules inherent in language systems and literature; thus, there is little regard for authorial
intent. An entire journal volume is devoted to structuralist interpretations of Gen 2–3;
see Patte, "Genesis 2 and 3."

dearth of extrinsic information regarding the biblical authors available to modern OT exegetes.[32]

It Does Not Locate Meaning in the Reader

In Barthes' article on the death of the author, he posits that the entity of "author" is a dangerous myth imposed by a ruling elite. The "boundaries" of the meaning of a text are as limitless as the readers of one. The locus of meaning(s) is in the reader. Barthes states,

> Thus is revealed the total existence of writing: a text is made of multiple writings, drawn from many cultures and entering into mutual relations of dialogue, parody, contestation, but there is one place where this multiplicity is focused and that place is the reader, not, as was hitherto said, the author . . . We are now beginning to let ourselves be fooled no longer by the arrogant antiphrastical recriminations of good society in favour of the very thing it sets aside, ignores, smothers, or destroys; we know that to give writing its future, it is necessary to overthrow the myth: the birth of the reader must be at the cost of the death of the Author.[33]

Barthes' ideas influenced several schools whose theories were also applied to the study of Scripture, including semiotics, structuralism, and post-structuralism. Many of these newer methodologies agree with Barthes' proclamation of the death of the author and, as a result, are preeminently concerned with the role played by the reader in producing meaning.[34] Reader-response criticism, for example, argues that meaning is what the reader produces in the act of reading. Like structuralists, reader-response critics have also applied their theories to the interpretation of Genesis 1–3.[35] E. J. van Wolde, for example, argues for the coher-

---

32. Wimsatt and Beardsley, "Intentional Fallacy," 477–78. Wimsatt and Beardsley also argue for a difference between internal and external evidence for the meaning of a poem. Internal evidence is accessible to the public and "is discovered through the semantics and syntax of a poem, through our habitual knowledge of the language, through grammars, dictionaries, and all the literature which is the source of dictionaries, in general through all that makes a language and culture"; external evidence, however, "is private or idiosyncratic" and "not part of the work as a linguistic fact . . ." In other words, searching for meaning by means of external evidence is not constrained by the actual words of the text.

33. Barthes, "Death of Author," 148.

34. Barton, *Reading Old Testament*, 126–27. See especially his comments on Paul Beauchamp, "L'analyse Structurale et L'exégèse Biblique."

35. See Bernard, "Genèse 1 à 3," 109–28; Wolde, "Creation of Coherence."

ence of Genesis 1–3 on the basis of reader-response theory.[36] For van Wolde, the coherence of Genesis 1–3 derives primarily from the reader in the act of reading rather than the text. Van Wolde writes, "Coherence refers to the linguistic quality which is created by the reader's interpretation of a text as a meaningful whole: the reader can interpret the text coherently, that is to say, not a text itself *is* coherent, but a reader's interpretation *makes* it coherent."[37]

To be clear, van Wolde does not deny textual features produced by the author that contribute to the coherence of Genesis 1–3. However, its coherence is by and large the creation of the reader. This is clear when she writes, "The cohesive information is present in the text, but the mental representation of coherence is the result of an inferring process by the reader."[38] In other words, Genesis 1–3 *is* not a coherent text: rather, it *becomes* a coherent text in the act of reading.[39]

There is little doubt the reader plays a vital role in the communication continuum of author-text-reader. However, the concept of authorial intention and embodied intentionality (compositional strategy) discussed above provides the boundaries wherein the reader does the work of interpretation. Even van Wolde's article, though leaning toward a stronger emphasis on the role of the reader in creating coherence, represents a literary approach coming to terms with the recognition of the indispensible role of authorial strategy and embodied intentionality as the parameters for one's reading and interpretation: "Thirty years after the rise of structuralism in biblical exegesis, the division between the system and the individual, between the language system and the unique text written by an author or edited by a final redactor and read by an individual reader, should be removed. An approach should be defended

36. According to van Wolde, Gen 1:1–31 focuses on creation in general terms and 2:4—3:24 elaborates one specific day, namely the sixth day on which the man and woman are created and instructed to conquer the earth (Gen 1:26–28).

37. Wolde, "Creation of Coherence," 168–69. See also M. A. K. Halliday and Hasan, *Cohesion in English*. Van Wolde, however, does discuss various textual features out of which cohesion building is formed (such as the relationship of foreground and background clauses in the Hebrew text of Gen 1–3 and anaphoric and cataphoric elements).

38. Wolde, "Creation of Coherence," 171–72.

39. Barton, *Reading Old Testament*, 219: "It [reader-response theory] presents all reading as a matter of what we do with texts, and the texts themselves turn into merely the raw material for our adventures in reading, having no shape or meaning or coherence of their own."

in which the Hebrew language system, the authorial strategies, and the reader's mental representation are integrated."[40]

Elsewhere in the article, van Wolde is clear that meaning ultimately proceeds from the author to the reader via the text. She writes, "The author presupposes the reader's ability to integrate new knowledge into previously accumulated knowledge."[41] Readers, therefore, do not create meaning: rather, they discover it (intention) by means of a careful analysis of the text (embodied intention).

It Does Not Locate Meaning in the Canon

In his programmatic declaration of the demise of the Biblical Theology Movement and in his dissatisfaction with the inability of the critical methods to bridge between the world of the text and the world of the reader, Brevard Childs argued that the canon[42] is an essential context from within which to interpret the Bible.[43] Childs' canonical approach is a text-centered final-form focus whose primary goal is to read the Bible as sacred Scripture.[44]

There are, however, at least two facets of the canonical approach that differ from the methodology proposed in this book. The first facet has to do with the locus of meaning. In the canonical method, meaning is in some ways dislodged from the original meaning of pre-final form or pre-canonical texts (in our case, the intentionality of the essentially Mosaic Torah [Josh 1:8])) and is ultimately located within the community of faith. Meaning is somewhat fluid, an ongoing process of continual reinterpretation of the original meaning to meet the specific needs of the faith community.[45] The second facet is a corollary of the first, namely, the idea of *reinterpretation* of earlier texts as opposed to the accurate

40. Wolde, "Creation of Coherence," 161.

41. Ibid., 172.

42. Childs, *Biblical Theology in Crisis,* 99: "The status of canonicity is not an objectively demonstrable claim but a statement of Christian belief. In its original sense, canon does not simply perform the formal function of separating books that are authoritative from others that are not, but is the rule that delineates the area in which the church hears the word of God."

43. Ibid. See also Childs, *Introduction to Old Testament.* For more recent discussions on the relationship of canon and biblical interpretation, see Bartholomew et al., *Canon and Biblical Interpretation.*

44. Childs, *Introduction to Old Testament,* 82.

45. See Barton, *Reading Old Testament,* 87.

interpretation of earlier texts. Childs conceives of the development of the Hebrew Bible as a process by which earlier Scripture is continually reinterpreted (application) to meet new needs, regardless of the intentions of the earlier texts; earlier texts are reloaded with new meanings, rather than interpreted (historical intent), by subsequent biblical writers.[46] By placing the locus of meaning in the community and by proposing an ongoing reinterpretation (as opposed to interpretation) of earlier texts, meaning is loosed from the moorings of the intentionality of those responsible for the pre-final (pre-canonical) texts.[47]

For Childs, the meaning of an individual book is more than the sum total of its parts in its final form. The messages of the historical prophets (e.g., the eighth century prophets Hosea and Isaiah) are recast into entirely new molds in the finalized forms of their books regardless of their original intentions. In other words, the final form of Hosea or Isaiah does not represent a validation of the actual intentions of the historical prophets but an entirely new application (reinterpretation) of their original messages to suit entirely new situations, situations that were never envisioned by the prophets themselves, and so, bear meanings never intended by them as well. Deut 18:22, however, clearly states that accurate prophetic prediction was one way to distinguish between true and false prophets. This suggests that the authors of the Torah and the Prophets (i.e., the final form Torah, the book of Hosea, the book of Isaiah, etc.) took the intentions of the historical prophets (Moses, Isaiah, Hosea) seriously and literally. Thus, one does not have to posit a bifurcation between the meaning of pre-canonical texts and the authorial intent of their final forms. In my view, the Torah in its final form is the embodiment of authorial intent and its final form is an attempt

---

46. See, for instance, Childs' comments on the book of Hosea: *Introduction to Old Testament,* 377–84.

47. Barton, *Reading Old Testament,* 102: "On such a view of literature, authors, whether real or merely notional, do not ultimately matter. The meaning of a text inheres in the text, or in the setting within which it is read, not in the intentions of those who wrote it. The text an author writes has a life of its own, and what it means will depend on the context in which it appears. If the book of Ecclesiastes had been lost from all copies of the Bible, and were then discovered among the Dead Sea scrolls as a 'non-canonical' text, its meaning would be different from what it is now. This is one conclusion that plainly follows, once we abandon the author's intention as the criterion of meaning: that one and the same text can change its meaning, according to the context in which it is read."

to interpret accurately and faithfully the essentially Mosaic Torah (the pre-canonical Torah).[48]

What It Is

Briefly stated, the text-centered approach I am proposing is composed of the following characteristics. First, the text in its final form is the locus of meaning. Second, while the locus of meaning is in the text, the methodology does not minimize the importance of the events to which the text refers or the historical circumstances in which a text was produced. Rather, this method takes seriously the representational aims of the historical author(s). Therefore, while scholars living in the twenty-first century may desire to classify Genesis 1–3 as "myth," in my opinion, such a classification only distances the reader from ultimately understanding the intentionality and worldview of the historical author. The goal of this book, however, is not to defend the veracity of the events represented by the narrative (apologetics), but to explain the meaning of the narrative representation (interpretation). Third, a text is the embodiment of the historical author's intention. "A poem [text] does not come into existence by accident."[49] Biblical authors consciously and strategically assembled their sources, arranged them, and explained them for a purpose. To the extent that the strategy of a text is discerned, the intentions of its historical author are discovered.

The following section makes explicit the reasons behind my adoption of a text-centered approach by elaborating on the distinction between text and event as well as the components of textuality.

AN INTERPRETATION OF A TEXT RATHER THAN AN EVENT

Sailhamer has coined the phrase "text and event" to highlight and contrast two differing foci representing two distinct hermeneutical philosophies in the exegetical task.[50] A text-centered approach to exegesis focuses on

48. For a defense of this understanding of relationship between the historical intentions of the essentially Mosaic Torah and its final form, see Sailhamer, *Meaning*.

49. Wimsatt and Beardsley, "Intentional Fallacy," 469. (Words in brackets provided.)

50. Sailhamer, *Pentateuch as Narrative*, 16–22; Sailhamer, *Introduction,* 36–85. Bruce Waltke's use of these terms in his OT theology is more than likely taken from Sailhamer, although Waltke does not mention Sailhamer by name (Waltke and Yu, *Old Testament Theology*, 43–45).

the text as the locus of meaning, whereas an event-centered approach[51] attempts to interpret God's revelation in history through his actions, words, and deeds among God's people. While both approaches are concerned with "history," it is essential to note that in each case "history" has two quite distinct meanings. History can be understood as the narrative depiction of an event or the event itself. German uses two terms to distinguish between an event (*Historie*) and the recounting of an event (*Geschichte*). English, however, refers to both quite different things as "history." The phrase "text and event," therefore, provides a helpful way for English speakers to distinguish the two. This distinction is particularly necessary when dealing with biblical narratives purporting to portray historical events. A "text" centered focus, while not minimizing the importance of God's activity *in* history,[52] and while acknowledging that God has revealed himself *in* history, receives the text itself as the divine interpretation of God's activity in history. The text is not a photograph of the moments in time when God revealed himself; the text is divine revelation (see 2 Tim 3:16; 2 Pet 1:20–21). Meaning and interpretation are constrained and governed by the words of the text. According to Sailhamer,

> A text-oriented approach to the OT would insist that the locus of God's revelation is in the Scriptures themselves, in the text. There is no reason to discount the fact that God has made known his will in other ways at other times. But, given the theological priority of an inspired text (2 Tim 3:16), one must see in the text of Scripture itself the locus of God's revelation today. Thus, on the question of God's revelation in history, the sense of *history* in a text-oriented approach would be that of the record of past events. The history in which God makes known his will is the recorded history in the text of Scripture. When formulated this way, evangelical biblical theology is based on a revelation that consists of the meaning of a text, with its focus on Scripture as a written document. Even the formula "revelation in history" then concerns the meaning of a text.[53]

---

51. Event-oriented approaches are seldom exclusively event-centered. Rather, they are frequently a compendium of insights gleaned from both text and event.

52. By "history" here I mean the "event" itself and not the recounting of the event in the form of a narrative; that is, *Historie*, as opposed to *Geschichte*.

53. Sailhamer, *Pentateuch as Narrative*, 17.

Waltke also agrees[54] with Sailhamer when he writes, "The theologian has no access to the events except through the text itself. Archaeology can produce some artifacts that may shed light on the social customs of a particular historical time, but despite the best efforts of scholars in this field, the Bible remains the main and, for the most part, the only witness to these actions of God in history, and more important, the only authoritative interpreter of the events."[55]

Finally, Eep Talstra offers the following reason for opting for a linguistic (text) over a historical analysis for biblical exegesis:

> Newer developments—rightly, in my view—start from a different angle: to understand a text one must give up the idea of finding some external kernel hidden *behind* the raw data. There is no end to peeling away the historical. It may seem paradoxical, but if one accepts a text in full as it has been handed down by tradition, the effect is that it will have a much better chance of speaking for itself. This shift of interest to "text" and "reading" necessitates the implementation of linguistics as a more fundamental instrument. For that reason linguistic analysis has increasingly become an important topic in newer methodologies.[56]

A prevalent example of an "event" centered approach to Genesis 1–3, particularly among evangelicals, is the attempt to interpret the creation account of Genesis 1 in light of modern scientific theories.[57] For example, in Douglas Bozung's evaluation of Gorman Gray's theory regarding a gap of time between Genesis 1:1–2 and 1:3, he writes the following: "Gray is dissatisfied with the explanation of young-earth creationists for the origin and existence of starlight, which, according to modern astronomy, emanates from objects millions or even billions of light-years from the earth."[58]

---

54. Waltke's recent theology, however, at times mottles the distinction between text and event. For example, in Waltke's first of several reasons for adopting a text-centered approach to theology, Waltke suggests that biblical history is *Heilsgeschichte* and therefore events and texts are inseparable (Waltke and Yu, *Old Testament Theology*, 43). The concept of *Heilsgeschichte* in scholarly parlance, however, is indelibly linked with an event-centered approach to the study of the OT. See especially Sailhamer, *Introduction*, 58–72.

55. Waltke and Yu, *Old Testament Theology*, 43.

56. Talstra, "From 'Eclipse' to 'Art,'" 10.

57. See for example Gray, *Age of Universe*.

58. Bozung, "Evaluation," 406 n. 1.

Whether or not Bozung's evaluation of Gray is correct is beside the point. Important for my purposes is to note the fact that any need to account for an unspecified gap in time in Genesis 1 because of modern scientific theory is to confound the exegesis of the intent of the creation account within the Pentateuch for an explication of the event of creation itself by culling data both from the biblical text and the world of modern science. In Sailhamer's words, "Events [or extra textual data] stand open to multiple perspectives. The meaning or sense of an event lies in the ability of the onlooker to gather the appropriate data and evaluate it from a certain vantage point."[59]

Another subtler example of a behind-the-text-oriented approach to the creation account is John Walton's explanation of the intentionality of Genesis 1 by means of an analysis of ANE philosophical presuppositions of cosmology in contradistinction to modern philosophical presuppositions.[60] Walton argues that the debate between modern science and the biblical account of creation is not germane to the text itself. Rather the conflict is philosophical: namely, an attempt to force the modern understanding of material ontology into one's interpretation of a text whose ANE milieu is rooted in a functional ontology.[61] Walton writes, "We cannot understand outlooks on creation until we understand how someone thinks about ontology. Because the Bible is a document from the ancient world, we expect it to be framed in terms of its ancient cognitive landscape. We must see the world the way the text sees the world. Basically, we must see Genesis 1 as an ancient cosmological text."[62]

Based on a functional ontology, Walton argues that Genesis 1 does not account for the material origins of the universe in six days; rather, this text "is composed along the lines of a temple dedication ceremony in which, over a seven-day period, the functions of the cosmic temple are initiated and the functionaries are installed."[63] Walton continues, "The functions center on the royal and priestly roles of people, but the imagery is defined by the presence of God who has taken up his rest in the center of this cosmic temple. Through him, order is maintained, and nonfunctional disorder is held at bay—through him all things co-

59. Sailhamer, *Pentateuch as Narrative*, 22.

60. Walton, "Creation," 48–63; Walton, *Lost World of Genesis One*, 16–37.

61. Walton, "Creation," 55–57.

62. Ibid., 57.

63. Ibid., 61.

here. Genesis 1 is thus an account of the functional origins of the cosmic temple, and we need not force it to address material origins."[64]

The purpose in citing Walton is neither to corroborate his conclusions about ANE philosophical presuppositions nor to refute them,[65] but merely to note the fact that these conclusions regarding the meaning of the text are contingent on his assessment of "behind-the-text" data[66] that is open to numerous revisions which may result from re-evaluations of extant ANE cosmogonies or the finding of new data.[67] We recall Talstra's comments that "to understand a text one must give up the idea of finding some external kernel hidden *behind* the raw data."[68]

Thus it is important to underscore here what the difference between a text-centered approach and an event-centered approach looks like in the context of Genesis 1–3. A text-centered approach to Genesis 1–3 maintains that the meaning may be discerned by means of a careful literary analysis of this text in light of its larger literary context (ultimately the Pentateuch). A text-centered approach acknowledges the historical distance between the original readers and the modern reader. At the same time, a text-centered approach insists that the only access to the original author's[69] intentions and, ultimately, his philosophical presuppositions, is by means of a careful analysis of the text he produced. An event-centered (or behind-the-text centered) approach to Genesis 1–3, on the other hand, culls any and all data available on the biblical creation account, whether it is from modern science or from alleged sources from within the milieu of the ANE. Because this interpretation is achieved

64. Ibid.

65. Some of Walton's conclusions regarding the priestly and royal imagery in the creation account are substantiated by means of a thorough literary analysis. See for example Kearney, "Creation and Liturgy," 375–87.

66. I am not negating the importance of looking to ANE *texts* for elucidating the verbal meaning of Hebrew *texts*. Rather, the problem with Walton's thesis, as I see it, is the extent to which his own interpretation of Genesis 1 hangs upon his hypothetical identification of the ideal reader in his/her ANE context. In other words, Walton is primarily concerned with the meaning of Genesis 1 within the literary context of ANE texts and only secondarily concerned with the meaning of Genesis 1 within the literary context of the Pentateuch.

67. Walton's refutation of Gunkel's thesis regarding the presence of a *Chaoskampf* in Genesis 1 is in fact based on the discovery of additional Near Eastern creation accounts since the time of Gunkel.

68. Talstra, "From 'Eclipse' to 'Art,'" 10.

69. The individual(s) responsible for the final form of the Pentateuch.

by means of analysis of the data gathered outside the text and entirely
dependent on the critical reflections of the individual who has gathered
this data, meaning is wrested from the philological control of the text
and, ultimately, its historical author.

CONCEPT OF TEXTUALITY

Any discussion of a text-centered approach must account for textuality.
In other words, one must determine what a text is[70] before determining
how to interpret one. Gleaning from the insights of text theory and textlinguistics,[71] Yee-Cheung Wong describes the essential components of
every text.[72] First, a text is not the same as a sentence. Whereas a sentence
can be described by sentence grammar in a non-holistic manner, a text
must be described in terms of the whole, including such elements as
reference, pronominalization, tense, mood and voice, conjunctions and
back reference, nominalization and topicalization, optional locational
and temporal expressions, "mystery" particles, and coherence.[73] Second,
a text has its own properties. Wong cites Robert de Beaugrande and
Wolfgang Dressler's definition of a text. According to them, "A text will
be defined as a communicative occurrence which meets seven standards
of textuality. If any of these standards is not considered to have been sat-
isfied, the text will not be communicative. Hence, non-communicative
texts are treated as non-texts."[74]

---

70. Wong, *Text-Centered Approach*, 50.

71. Ibid., 52: "[A] text-theory attempts to describe what a text is by developing a theoretical framework in which texts can be defined and distinguished from non-texts . . .
[T]ext-linguistics attempts to describe and explain how a text is structured and formed,
concentrating particularly on the factors that give texts cohesion and coherence."

72. Ibid., 50–67. He begins his discussion by noting what a text is not: "To say that
the Old Testament is a *text* is equivalent to saying that it is not an *event*. Put simply, an
event is something that happens in time and space . . . On the other hand, a text, rather
than the event itself, is a depiction of these events . . . It is made up of words, phrases,
sentences, paragraphs and the like" (ibid., 50–51).

73. Longacre, "Texts and Text Linguistics," 259–66; Van Dijk, *Aspects of Text
Grammar*, 2.

74. Beaugrande and Dressler, *Introduction to Text Linguistics*, 2.

The seven standards of textuality noted by de Beaugrande and Dressler are cohesion,[75] coherence,[76] intentionality,[77] acceptability,[78] informativity,[79] situationality,[80] and intertextuality.[81] The third essential feature of a text, according to Wong, is the fact that a text has an author (see prior section on authorial intent). Fourth, and finally, a text has a communicative function.[82] Describing communicative function, Wong notes simply that a text can be viewed as

> a written linguistic communication between an *author* and a *reader*. It is the carrier of *information* from the *author* to the *reader*. It is also the means for accomplishing the communication between the *author* and the *reader*. Through the *text*, a "deficiency" of *information* between the two communication partners is overcome . . .The implication of understanding a text in its communication-situation is the concept of a text as a strategy of communication. Not only is a text a carrier of information from the author to the reader, it is, even more, a strategy of communication carefully designed by the author, the purpose of which is to guide the reader through the communication process, so that, the reader, on the one hand, can correctly receive the message conveyed by the author, and, the author, on the other hand, can be

75. Ibid., 3. Cohesion "concerns the ways in which the components of the surface text, i.e., the actual words we hear or see, *are mutually connected within a sequence*." (Words in italics original.)

76. Ibid., 4. Coherence "concerns the ways in which the components of the textual world, i.e., the configuration of concepts and relations which *underlie* the surface text, are *mutually accessible* and *relevant*." (Words in italics orginal.)

77. Ibid., 7. Intentionality concerns "the text producer's attitude that the set of occurrences should constitute a cohesive and coherent text instrumental in fulfilling the producer's intentions, e.g., to distribute knowledge or to attain a goal specified in a plan."

78. Ibid. Acceptability concerns "the text receiver's attitude that the set of occurrences should constitute a cohesive and coherent text having some use or relevance for the receiver, e.g., to acquire knowledge or provide co-operation in a plan."

79. Ibid., 8–9. Informativity "concerns the extent to which the occurrences of the presented text are expected vs. unexpected or known vs. unknown/certain."

80. Ibid., 9. Situationality "concerns the factors which make a text relevant to a situation of occurrence."

81. Ibid., 10. Intertextuality "concerns the factors which make the utilization of one text dependent upon knowledge of one or more previously encountered texts."

82. "Every text has a communicative function (e.g., legal texts to prevent crime, bereaved texts to console, etc.). For biblical texts, I maintain that the communicative function is theological." Lim, *Grace*, 71.

assured that his message is successfully passed through without any communication breakdown.[83]

An important corollary to the discussion of textuality is the acknowledgement that the OT is a text.[84] Thus, as I have tried to argue, the methodology employed for this study reflects a commitment to receiving and interpreting Genesis 1–3 as a textual unit within a larger text (the Pentateuch).[85] Treating Genesis 1–3 textually entails an expectation of the presence of the seven standards of textuality listed by de Beaugrande and Dressler. In an earlier chapter, I presented the work of a growing number of scholars who acknowledge the cohesion (a connectivity of the surface) and the coherence[86] (connectivity of the underlying content) of Genesis 1–3 in its final form regardless of the hypothetical sources in its compositional history.[87] Lim, for example, writes the following: "There is also a 'narrative coherence' (literary and theological) within the narrative text. The first eleven chapters (for that matter the Pentateuch as a whole) is to be read as a unified narrative which is derived from the arrangement of the text such as intertextual patterns of repetition, verbal and thematic linkages and others. Within that narrative coherence, there is a unified structure and a common purpose."[88]

Earlier in this chapter I argued for authorial intention, thus acknowledging the presence of the third element of textuality (intentionality). The acceptability (a text receiver's willingness to receive a text as

83. Wong, *Text-Centered Approach*, 67. (Words in italics original.)

84. Sailhamer, "Exegesis," 280. To be more specific, the OT is textual in nature (i.e., it is comprised of numerous texts). In the final chapter I also argue that the Tanakh is also a singular text with intentionality in its own right. My point here, however, is that one's methodology of biblical interpretation must be governed by the acknowledgement that the interpretation of a text is different than the interpretation of an event.

85. Ibid.: "A commitment to an understanding of the Old Testament as Scripture, then, implies an exegetical method and biblical theology that is a direct function of the meaning of a text. It means that exegesis must ask the question: How does a text have meaning? One must seek to discover the way in which authors of Scripture have construed words, phrases, clauses, and the like into whole texts."

86. On the distinction between cohesion and coherence, see Beaugrande and Dressler, *Introduction to Text Linguistics*, 13 n. 5; Wong, *Text-Centered Approach*, 60.

87. An important inroad into the recognition of cohesion on the surface structure and coherence in the deep structure of the biblical text came as a result of a growing appreciation of intertextuality, the seventh element of a text. See Hepner, "Verbal Resonance," 23.

88. Lim, *Grace*, 90.

cohesive, coherent, and to cooperate with its intentionality[89]) of Genesis 1–3 has been the presupposition of countless readers long before the rise of critical scholarship and continues to be the case in spite of it today. Lim has proposed that "reader responsible reading" will mean "reading a text in accordance with its genre[s] and exercising some kind of hermeneutical humility as we engage the text. It also means reading to *understand* rather than to *undermine* the text."[90]

In terms of "informativity," Sailhamer helpfully delineates between the known and the unknown in the communicative interplay between author and reader via the text in terms of "thema" and "rhema." Terms the author assumes are known to the reader he labels "thema" and the terms the author must explain to the reader in the text itself are called "rhema."[91] While there may be many opinions about the "situationality" of Genesis 1–3 within the Pentateuch, there is no doubt that Genesis 1–3 has one (the sixth standard of textuality).

The seventh element of textuality, "intertextuality," and its presence in Genesis 1–3 deserves a more thorough treatment, particularly because, as I argue later on, intertextuality plays a vital role in the interpretation of Genesis 1–3 on three levels: as it relates to the Pentateuch (inner-textuality), as it relates to other books in the OT (inter-textuality), and as it relates to the Tanakh as a whole (con-textuality).[92]

89. See footnote 75.

90. Lim, *Grace*, vii.

91. Sailhamer, *Pentateuch as Narrative*, 29–31. For the modern reader, thema terms pose a challenge, particularly because of the historical distance between the original reader and the modern one. Several such terms are used in Gen 1:1—2:4a ("the deep," "the expanse," "formless and void," "signs," "seasons," "the great sea monsters," etc.). According to Sailhamer, however, when interpreted within the larger structural context, the modern reader can ascertain the meaning of many thema terms.

92. These terms and definitions are taken from Sailhamer, *Introduction*, 156.

INTERTEXTUALITY AND INTERPRETATION

Intertextuality[93] has received a great deal of attention in Biblical Studies in recent years,[94] and, to date, definitions[95] and even terminology vary from scholar to scholar—some preferring the more general term "intertextuality,"[96] others preferring terms such as "inner-biblical allusion,"[97] "inner-biblical exegesis,"[98] "inner-biblical interpretation,"[99] "echo,"[100] or "resonance."[101] There are even scholars who assign different meanings to some of these terms.[102] For the purposes of clarity I use the

93. To recall, Beaugrande and Dressler define "intertextuality" as "the ways in which the production and reception of a given text depends upon the participants' knowledge of other texts" (Beaugrande and Dressler, *Introduction to Text Linguistics*, 182). According to Ben-Porat ("Poetics," 107), "The literary allusion is a device for the simultaneous activation of two texts."

94. Boda, "Reading," 277–91; Broyles, "Traditions," 157–75; DeClaissé-Walford, "Intertextual Reading," 139–52; Fishbane, *Biblical Interpretation*; Hays, *Echoes*; Hays, "'Who Has Believed?'" 25–49; Hepner, "Verbal Resonance," 3–27; Kim, "Jonah," 487–528; Leonard, "Identifying Inner-Biblical Allusions," 241–65; Lyons, "Marking Innerbiblical Allusion," 245–50; Markl, "Hab 3," 99–108; Noble, "Esau, Tamar, and Joseph," 219–52; Ortlund, "Intertextual Reading," 273–85; Plank, "By Water," 180–94; Schneider, "Texte–Intertexte," 361–76; Sommer, *Prophet*; Sommer, "New Light," 646–66; Steymans, "Blessings," 71–89; Weyde, "Inner-Biblical Interpretation," 287–300; Williamson, "Isaiah 62:4," 734–39.

95. See Biddle, "Ancestral Motifs," 619–20, 620 n. 4; Beaugrande and Dressler, *Introduction*, 182; Sommer, *Prophet*, 61; Trimpe, *Von der Schöpfung*, 17; Zakovitch, *Introduction*, 9.

96. Sailhamer, *Introduction*.

97. Leonard, "Identifying Inner-Biblical Allusions."

98. Fishbane, *Biblical Interpretation*.

99. Zakovitch, *Introduction*.

100. Hays, *Echoes*.

101. Hepner, "Verbal Resonance."

102. Sommer, *Prophet*, 6–18. Sommer (ibid., 7) argues that "intertextuality" is focused on the text itself or the reader (not intentional on the part of the author), whereas "allusion" and "influence" are focused on the author and the text (intentional). He writes, "This distinction between intertextuality, on the one hand, and allusion and influence, on the other, is basic to contemporary theoretical discussions of the relations between texts, though many readers continue to confuse them. In brief, intertextuality is concerned with the reader or with the text as a thing independent of its author, while influence and allusion are concerned with the author as well as the text and reader. Intertextuality is synchronic in its approach, influence or allusion diachronic or even historicist. Intertextuality is interested in a very wide range of correspondences among texts, influence and allusion with a more narrow set. Intertextuality examines the relations among many texts, while influence and allusion look for specific connections between a limited number of texts" (ibid., 8).

more general term "intertextuality." However, I understand intertextuality in terms of a relationship between one text and some other text(s) whereby its historical author *intended* it to be *recognized* by the reader. In Mark Biddle's words,

> The term "intertextuality" finds a number of usages in the literature. In the contexts of the act of reading, it often refers to the implication of the observation that any reader approaches any "text" (including non-written texts such as films or works of art) as a component in a nexus of other "texts." The act of reading establishes relationships between texts regardless of genetic dependence. The focus of this study, in contrast, will be on intertextualities which the author (a) intended as such and (b) expected his or her readers to recognize as such so that their reading of one or both of the related intertexts would be shaped.[103]

These two elements of intertextuality (intentionality on the part of the author and recognizability on the part of the reader) bring to the fore one of the more difficult issues in the scholarly discussion of intertextuality, namely, the problem of discerning the difference between intentional intertextuality and an unintentional congruence of language.[104] Richard Hays, for example, argues that the "identification of intertextu-

103. Biddle, "Ancestral Motifs," 619–20. Biddle (ibid., 620, n. 4) cites Ulrich Broich, "Formen der Markierung, " 31, who writes, "Intertextualität [liegt] dann vor, wenn ein Autor bei der Abfassung seines Textes sich nicht nur der Verwendung anderer Texte bewußt ist, sondern auch vom Rezipienten erwartet, daß er diese Beziehung zwischen seinem Text und anderen Texten als vom Autor intendiert und als wichting [sic] für das Verständnis seines Textes erkannt." Translation: "Intertextuality [exists] then if an author is himself aware not only of the use of another text in the composition of his text, but also expects of the recipient that he recognizes this relationship between his text and other texts as intended by the author and as important for the understanding of his text." (Translation my own.)

104. Sommer (*Prophet*, 32) writes, "All students of allusion must distinguish between two types of textual similarity: cases in which one writer relies on another and cases in which two writers use similar language coincidentally. Several texts may use the same vocabulary not because a later author depends on an earlier one but because they utilize a common tradition, or because they are discussing a topic that naturally suggests certain vocabulary. This problem becomes acute in a highly traditional literature such as the Bible." Hays ("'Who Has Believed?'" 29) concurs: "Identifying allusions and echoes of an earlier text in a later one, however, poses a daunting challenge, especially when we encounter texts that come to us from the ancient world . . . Thus, this sort of interpretative task calls for close attention and discernment by the reader, or more precisely, by the reading community. The danger of rampant subjectivity and misinterpretation is very great." See also Noble, "Esau, Tamar, and Joseph," 227.

ality is not a science but an art[105] practiced by skilled interpreters within a reading community that has agreed on the value of situating individual texts within a historical continuum of other texts (i.e., a canon) . . . The ability to recognize—or to exclude—possible allusions is a skill, a reader competence, inculcated by reading communities."[106]

While there certainly is some degree of subjectivity in identifying intertextuality, there is an overall consistency among scholars regarding the presence of certain core linguistic (lexical) criteria, and further, there is agreement that the likelihood for intertextuality grows on a scale of cumulative evidence. According to Sommer, "The argument that the author alludes, then, is a cumulative one; assertions that allusions occur in certain passages become stronger as patterns emerge from those allusions. The critic must weigh evidence including the number of markers and their distinctiveness, the presence of stylistic or thematic patterns that typify the author's allusions, and the likelihood that the author would allude to the alleged source. The weighing of such evidence (and hence the identification of allusions) is an art, not a science."[107]

Ronald Bergey agrees with Sommer: "That some, or any of the linguistic affinities presented above indicate intertextuality should not be assumed. One wonders whether a given parallel resulted from other causes, such as, a common language tradition used in thematically and genre related passages or even coincidence. Linguistic parallels, are, however, the most sure guide in terms of determining whether textual correlations have been consciously or deliberately made if they are corroborated by other lines of evidence."[108]

Fishbane likewise notes that "the identification of aggadic exegesis where external objective criteria are lacking is proportionally increased to the extent that multiple and sustained lexical linkages between two texts can be recognized and, where the second text (the putative *traditio*) uses a segment of the first (the putative *traditum*) in a lexically reorganized and topically rethematized way."[109]

105. So also Sommer, *Prophet*, 34–35.

106. Hays, "'Who Has Believed?'" 30.

107. Sommer, *Prophet*, 35.

108. Bergey, "Song of Moses," 47.

109. Fishbane, *Biblical Interpretation*, 285.

In a recent publication, Jeffery Leonard offers eight guidelines for identifying intertextuality,[110] guidelines which will form the underlying methodological foundation for my identification of intertextuality in Genesis 1–3 in subsequent chapters of this book:

> (1) Shared language is the single most important factor in establishing a textual connection.[111] (2) Shared language is more important than non-shared language.[112] (3) Shared language that is rare or distinctive suggests a stronger connection than does language that is widely used. (4) Shared phrases suggest a stronger connection than do individual shared terms.[113] (5) The accumulation of shared language suggests a stronger connection than does a single shared term or phrase.[114] (6) Shared language in similar contexts suggests a stronger connection than does shared language alone. (7) Shared language need not be accompanied by shared ideology to establish a connection.[115] (8) Shared language need not be accompanied by shared form to establish a connection.[116]

Leonard's eight guidelines are, in my opinion, the most helpful list of criteria currently available.

In addition to these eight guidelines, Leonard also attempts to delineate criteria wherewith one can discern the directionality of the allusion. Once again it is worth quoting Leonard at length:

---

110. See also seven helpful criteria provided by Hays, *Echoes*, 29–32; Hays, "'Who Has Believed?" 34–45.

111. According to Leonard ("Identifying Inner-Biblical Allusions," 246–47.), "verbal parallels provide the most objective and verifiable criteria for identifying these allusions."

112. Ibid., 249: "The use of nonshared language has no bearing, though, on the existence of the allusion itself."

113. Ibid., 252: "While individual terms may well point toward a connection between texts, the sharing of longer phrases tends to strengthen such a connection."

114. Ibid., 253: "An implication flowing from the principle outlined here is the notion that strong evidence for allusions in some cases can lend support to less certain allusions elsewhere. Each additional connection found in a text provides supporting evidence for affirming less obvious allusions."

115. Ibid., 255: "A writer who depends on a particular text or tradition will often draw on the language of that underlying tradition. There is no reason to expect, though, that a later writer would understand or feel compelled to duplicate the ideological concerns of the earlier treatment."

116. Ibid., 246.

If we accept the premise that some biblical texts do rely on others, it remains to consider what sorts of evidence offer insight into the direction of the textual relationship. Here I suggest a series of fundamental questions can guide our search: (1) Does one text claim to draw on another? (2) Are there elements in the texts that help to fix their dates? (3) Is one text capable of producing the other? (4) Does one text assume the other? (5) Does one text show a general pattern of dependence on other texts? (6) Are there rhetorical patterns in the texts that suggest that one text has used the other in an exegetically significant way?[117]

Leonard's third principle ("Is one text capable of producing the other?") has great potential for evaluating the nature of the literary relationship between Genesis 1–3 and the remainder of the Pentateuch. To illustrate, Leonard discusses the intertextual relationship between Genesis 12:10–20 and the exodus narrative.[118] According to Leonard, "the similarities are so striking that the two must be directly connected."[119] The question is, however, which story is borrowing from the other? In response Leonard writes, "The answer seems obvious. It is easy to imagine that a skillful tradent might have modeled a tradition from the Abraham narratives on the pattern of the exodus. It is nearly impossible, though, to understand how an isolated pericope in Abram's story could have given birth to the great complex of traditions that make up the exodus story."[120]

To reinforce his point, Leonard demonstrates that the description of the plagues in Psalm 78 is far sketchier than the plague narrative in Exodus. According to Leonard, one could hardly conceive how the plague narrative could have developed from Psalm 78, whereas, Psalm 78 clearly assumes familiarity with the larger story found in Exodus.[121] Leonard's findings are particularly relevant to one's assessment of the intertextual relationship of Genesis 1–3 with the rest of the Pentateuch. As I argue later, the nature of the textual relationship of Genesis 1–3 with

---

117. Ibid., 258.

118. For an insightful discussion on the innertextual connections between Gen 12:10–20 and the exodus, see Sailhamer, *Pentateuch as Narrative*, 37–39.

119. Leonard, "Identifying Inner-Biblical Allusions," 260.

120. Ibid.

121. Ibid., 260–61. The fourth principle ("Does one text assume the other?") is fairly similar to the previous principle as well. He argues that the oblique references in Ps 106:14–15 suggest that the reader must know the larger story found in the Pentateuch in order to make sense of these verses.

the remainder of the Pentateuch as well as the Tanakh as a whole suggests that it was composed with Israel's story or biblical history already
in mind (perhaps prophetically), and that the author expected his readers to recognize this in his or her attempt to discern its meaning in the
final form of the Pentateuch.[122]

In discussing Genesis 1–3, however, one is challenged by the fact
that "intertextuality" generally deals with a "later" text's allusion to an
"earlier" text. The terms "later" and "earlier" as I use them here have
nothing to do with dating. Rather, I use these terms to identify a reading strategy. That is, when the Pentateuch is treated as one book with
a compositional strategy, it is clear that Genesis 1–3 is the earlier (the
earliest) text in the Pentateuch. How would the reader, therefore, identify
"intertextuality" in Genesis 1–3?

Sailhamer's concept of "narrative typology" provides a useful
framework for understanding the role of intertextuality in Genesis 1–3.
To understand what is meant by narrative typology, it is necessary to
return to Sailhamer's discussion (see my chapter 3) of the role of "the
last days" in the compositional strategy of the Pentateuch. According to
Sailhamer, the poetic seams introducing larger poems in the Pentateuch
(particularly Gen 49, Num 24, and Deut 32–33) provide the interpretative framework for evaluating the meaning of the Pentateuch as a
whole.[123] In each of these poems a central figure calls together (imperative) a group of people to proclaim (cohortative) what will happen "in
the last days" (Gen 49:1; Num 24:14; Deut 31:28–29). Moreover, each
of these poems reflects upon the relationship of Israel's history (as recorded in the Pentateuch) to Israel's future (eschatology).[124] Thus, the
temporal framework provided by the Pentateuch intentionally embraces
the "beginning" (Gen 1:1) and the "end." In fact, Sailhamer highlights the
unusual nature of the very first word in the Hebrew Bible by noting that
ראשית ("beginning") is never used elsewhere in the Pentateuch for the
adverbial notion of a punctiliar "beginning."[125] Rather, ראשית ("begin-

---

122. Gen 1–3, for example, as will be argued later, clearly presupposes the existence
of the narrative description of the tabernacle in Exod 25–40 (the fact of which totally
undermines Wellhausen's theory of JEDP).

123. Sailhamer, Pentateuch as Narrative, 34–44.

124. Sailhamer, "Creation," 89–106.

125. Ibid., 94–96. Elsewhere in the Pentateuch ראשונה and תחלה are used.

ning") is deliberately chosen for its semantic resonance with the "last" (אחרית) days in the final form Pentateuch.[126] In Sailhamer's own words,

> By the use of the terms רֵאשִׁית and אַחֲרִית, God's activities are divided into a "beginning" (רֵאשִׁית) and an end, a "last days" (אַחֲרִית הַיָּמִים). This also implied a "time between" in which fell Israel's own history. By opening the Torah with the statement that "in the beginning (בְּרֵאשִׁית) God created the heavens and the earth," the author assigns the earlier chapters of Genesis to a larger eschatological schema in which its events are cast as those of the *Urzeit*.
>
> Within that broad schema, there are remarkable parallels between the *Urzeit* of Genesis 1–11 and the *Endzeit* described in the poetic texts of the Pentateuch.[127]

Returning to the concept of "narrative typology," Sailhamer argues that earlier narratives intentionally anticipate later narratives: later narratives are written to remind the reader of earlier narratives.[128] Sailhamer offers the following examples: (1) Genesis 12:10–20 (Abraham's exodus from Egypt) anticipates Israel's exodus from Egypt; (2) the spread of sin in Genesis 1–11 anticipates the defilement of the camp in Leviticus 11–16; and (3) Pharaoh's attempt to thwart Israel in the early chapters of Exodus anticipates Balak's attempt to thwart Israel in the Balaam narratives.[129] If Sailhamer has correctly identified the importance of the relationship between the beginning and the end in the Pentateuch, then one would expect to find literary allusions (intertextuality) to other narratives in the earlier chapters of Genesis.

TYPES OF INTERTEXTUALITY

Before leaving the topic of intertextuality, brief mention should be made of the types of intertextuality and the names for these types employed in this book.

---

126. This thesis is bolstered by the unusual fact that the word ראשית appears in all the major poems about "the last days" (Gen 49:3; Num 24:20; Deut 33:21). For a more thorough study of the role ראשית plays in the final composition of the Pentateuch see Postell, "Eschatological Reading."

127. Sailhamer, "Creation," 96.

128. Schmutzer, "Creation Mandate," 109: "We contend that stories within Genesis 1–11 regularly anticipate later narratives, and these advance and even parody earlier content."

129. Sailhamer, *Pentateuch as Narrative*, 37–44.

In-Textuality—According to Sailhamer, there are various levels wherewith a textual strategy can be traced (in-, inner-, inter-, and con-textuality).[130] At the smallest level, in-textuality is the lexical means by which inner cohesion is provided to the smallest units of a text. This cohesion may be expressed by means of key terms (*Leitworten*), structural patterns, inclusions, and others. Although the conclusion to the creation narrative in Genesis 1 is highly contested, the repetition of "create" (ברא), "the heavens" (השמים), and "the earth" (הארץ) in 2:4a either functions as an in-textual inclusion to mark the conclusion of the first discrete unit in the opening to the Pentateuch, namely Gen 1:1—2:4a, or it may be used to link the first textual unit with the one that follows.[131] Another possible in-textual clue to the isolation of the smallest textual unit in Genesis 1 is the preponderance of "sevens" and multiples of seven throughout the narrative. I use the term "in-textuality," therefore, to identify the literary strategies used to bring coherence to the smallest textually complete unit.

Inner-textuality—Inner-textuality is the literary tool employed to bring coherence to all of the individual textual units in the composition of a complete book ("inner-linkage").[132] Such links are used, according to Sailhamer, to thematize whole books. One example of inner-textuality would be the ways the author of the Pentateuch linked Gen 1:1—2:3 with Gen 2:4—3:24. Regardless of the putative sources behind Genesis 1–3, the final form evidences uniform compositional features.[133] Vocabulary

130. Sailhamer, *Introduction*, 206–15.

131. This hotly contested issue is discussed in a subsequent chapter.

132. Shepherd, *Daniel,* 10: "The first step to discovery of the author's compositional strategy is to develop an appropriate text theory. It is evident that the author did not compose his work of whole cloth in one sitting. The text has been put together somewhat like musical tracks on a well-shaped compact disc recording. Musical artists lay down tracks at various times and places, but they work to make those tracks appear on disc as parts of a larger whole so that the placement of the first track, the last track, and those in-between gives the recording an overall contour. In the same way, the author of the Pentateuch has composed various narratives, poems, genealogies, and laws into a well-crafted whole."

133. Noble, "Esau, Tamar, and Joseph," 247: "It is difficult to conceive how a theory which rests so much upon the supposed independence of origin and the development of a book's various parts can account for the multitudinous allusions of one part to another that we find in its final form. Allusion entails authorship; and wide-ranging allusion entails wide-ranging authorship. What I am arguing, then, is that the time may be ripe for studies in the formation of Genesis to undergo an author-oriented revolution, similar to that which has recently occurred in the study of Isaiah."

plays an important role. One example would be the use of "not good" in 2:18 (see also 3:6; 6:2), a likely inner-textual allusion to the proclamation of "good" and "very good" in Genesis 1. Another inner-textual link is the phrase "living soul" (נפש חיה; 1:20, 24, 30; 2:7, 19). An additional inner-textual link comes by way of the first person proclamation of divine intent to create humanity. In Genesis 1:26, the first person plural cohortative (נעשה) is used for the creation of collective humanity (אדם) as a plurality, namely, as male and female (זכר ונקבה). In Genesis 2:18, however, the first person singular cohortative[134] is used in the creation account of a singular individual (woman). Whatever one makes of the meaning of this inner-textual allusion, the overall effect of binding the first creation account to the second is achieved. What is more, not only do inner-textual relationships provide lexical and thematic unity to a biblical book, but they also frequently fall within the parameters of Sommer's narrower definition of inner-biblical exegesis, namely, the attempt "to explain the meaning of a specific older text."[135] If, for instance, Numbers 24:17—the reference to a king (שבט) who will come in the last days (24:14) and crush the heads of Israel's enemies—is an inner-textual allusion to Genesis 3:15 (and Gen 49:10),[136] it is, therefore, an exegetical attempt to explain the meaning of an earlier text.

Intertextuality—Intertextuality, as Sailhamer defines it, and as it is used in this book, is "the study of links between and among texts."[137] This

---

134. See Wenham, *Genesis 1-15*, 47. Many Hebrew manuscripts (e.g., *Miqroth Gedoloth, Sefer Berashit*, based on the Hebrew Text of Jacob Ben Chaim's Second Rabbinic Bible) do not include the *mappiq* in the *he* (ה). The LXX and the Targums have taken אעשה as a cohortative (Tg. Onq., Tg. Ps-J., and Tg. Neof.). The Kittel edition of the *Biblia Hebraica* does not include the *mappiq* (so also GKC §75 l). It is clear that the translator of the LXX perceived an inner-textual link between 1:26 and 2:18 and, consequently, altered the first person singular subjunctive to the first person plural subjunctive to conform to 1:26 (ποιησωμεν).

135. Sommer, *Prophet*, 23: "I intend the term 'exegesis' in the narrow sense outlined above: an exegetical text purports to explain the meaning of a specific older text. (My definition differs from the much broader use of the term in the phrase 'inner-biblical exegesis' in the work of Sarna, Fishbane, and Zakovitch. For them this phrase refers to any case in which one biblical passage borrows from or is based on another. Most examples of what they call inner-biblical exegesis are not, strictly speaking, exegetical; they are allusions. It is for this reason that I prefer to call the phenomenon 'inner-biblical allusion and exegesis.')"

136. See Hamilton, "Seed of Woman," 253–73; Sailhamer, "Creation," 98.

137. Sailhamer, *Introduction*, 212.

term specifically denotes one biblical book's literary allusions, whether implicit (echoes and allusions) or explicit (citations), to another biblical book or books. Frequently, intertextuality involves Sommer's concept of inner-biblical exegesis. One example of an intertextual (inner-biblical) exegesis of Genesis 1–3 that is discussed in greater depth in a subsequent chapter is found in 1 Kings 1–11. Numerous textual allusions to Genesis 1–3 suggest that the author of Kings not only interpreted Genesis 1–3[138] as the depiction of a wise royal-priestly figure whose fall is folly, but also as a prophetic "prefiguration" of Solomon.

Con-textuality—Con-textuality, a name apparently coined by Sailhamer, relates to the semantic effect of the arrangement of books.[139] Sailhamer is clear that con-textuality does not entail an intentional linkage. Elsewhere, however, Sailhamer argues for a deliberate canonical redaction of the Tanakh, whereby an individual (or individuals) links the Pentateuch to the Prophets and the Prophets to the Writings, by means of canonical seams.[140] In a subsequent chapter the theory of "canonical seams" is investigated and an attempt is made to view Genesis 1–3 in light of these seams in order to determine if there is a guiding theological intention behind the formation of the Tanakh as a unified composition; in the form of a question, "Is there a discernibly exegetical theme of the final form of the Tanakh?"

Compositional Analysis

Having discussed key components of a text-centered approach—"text" centered interpretation, textuality, and intertextuality—it is necessary to discuss one other distinctive component of the text-centered methodology employed in this book, namely, "compositional analysis" or "composition criticism." Compositional analysis is "the attempt to describe the semantics of the arrangement of source material in the biblical text."[141]

138. These intertextual allusions strongly suggest that the author of 1 Kings regarded Gen 1–3 as a cohesive and coherent text.

139. Sailhamer, *Introduction*, 213: "*Con-textuality* is the notion of the effect on meaning of the relative position of a biblical book within a prescribed order of reading. What is the semantic effect of a book's relative position within the OT Canon?" (Italics original.)

140. Ibid., 239–41.

141. Sailhamer, *Pentateuch as Narrative*, 34.

Georg Fohrer states the task of composition criticism in the following
manner:

> Composition criticism explains the character and manner of
> the joining of units and, if necessary, the character and manner
> of the alterations carried out by a composer, and particularly
> inserted sections. It examines the question, for example, how
> the Abraham and Jacob cycles, the narrative threads of the
> Pentateuch/Hexateuch, the earliest composed collection of com-
> plexes of proverbs and songs, and the book of Kings have been
> assembled. What ways have the composers in the process broken
> new ground? What function does the unit to be exegeted have
> within the composition?[142]

A compositional analysis pays close attention to the relationship of
the part and the whole for discerning the compositional strategy of
a given book. In the case of the Pentateuch, a compositional analysis
attempts to uncover the strategy governing the assembly of the various
narratives (e.g., Gen 1 and Gen 2–3), laws (e.g., the covenant code, the
holiness code, the priestly code, etc.), poems (e.g., Gen 2:23; 3:14–19;
Gen 49, Exod 15, etc.), and genealogies (e.g., Gen 5) into a cohesive and
coherent text.[143]

142. Fohrer et al., *Exegese des Alten Testaments*, 142. (Translation my own.) "Die
Kompositionskritik soll die Art und Weise der Zusammenfügung von Einheiten
und gegebenenfalls die Art und Weise der von einem Kompositor vorgenommenen.
Änderungen und eingefügten eigenen Abschnitte erklären. Sie untersucht die Frage,
wie z.B. der Abraham- und der Jakobzyklus, die Erzählungsfäden des Pentateuchs/
Hexateuchs, die ersten komponierten Sammlungskomplexe von Sprüchen und Liedern
oder die Königsbücher zusammengestellt worden sind. Welche Wege haben die
Kompositoren dabei beschritten? Welche Funktion hat die zu exegesierende Einheit
innerhalb der Komposition?"

143. In at least two ways, compositional analysis and rhetorical criticism as it is
practiced in the OT share a similar concern to explain the texture of a literary unit and
the structure or overall design of the final composition (the part and whole). See Trible,
Rhetorical Criticism, 27.

5

A Text-Centered Analysis of Genesis 1–3, Part 1

$\mathbf{N}$OW THAT I HAVE reviewed the works of numerous scholars who notice parallels between the earlier chapters of Genesis 1–3 and Israel's history, and having made my working methodological assumptions explicit, in this chapter I attempt to substantiate my thesis: namely, that Genesis 1–3 prophetically foreshadows Israel's exile (as a result of their failure to keep the Mosaic Covenant) in order to wed the final form Pentateuch[1] with a prophetic eschatology.

Due to certain space restrictions, I cannot treat Genesis 1–3 exhaustively. There are many exegetical issues left untouched since my purpose is to trace intentional inner- and intertextual links between Genesis 1–3 and Israel's later biblical history (inner- and intertextuality). Thus, the analysis is limited to issues directly related to the thesis.

---

1. In his recent theology of the OT, Bruce Waltke acknowledges both the existence of a Mosaic core and a much later final form Pentateuch. Regarding the creation narrative he writes, "The creation narrative, though part of the original Mosaic core of material, likely reached its final form during Israel's exile in Babylon" (Waltke and Yu, *Old Testament Theology*, 177). Conservative biblical scholars have been aware of the presence of "Post-Mosaica" for a long time, but have frequently treated these "anachronisms" apologetically in order to defend the Mosaic authorship of the Pentateuch. See for example, Hengstenberg, *Dissertations*, 122–282. My purpose here is not to explain away the "Post-Mosaica" apologetically but to understand their significance exegetically. The "Post-Mosaica" are a vital and indispensable testimony for discerning the intentionality of the Pentateuch itself (see for example the inner-biblical interpretation of Deut 18:15 in Deut 34:10). Like Waltke, I affirm a Mosaic core. However, I am interested in understanding the final form. Henceforth, I will refer to the individual(s) responsible for the final form Pentateuch as the author. The presence of Deut 34, a canonical seam linking the Torah with the Prophets, suggests that the final form is quite late. As stated in my methodology section, however, I do not regard the final form as a manipulation of the intended meaning of an earlier form(s), but as an attempt to interpret and represent it faithfully. For this reason, I do not believe it is problematic when quoting the Pentateuch to state, as do the NT authors, "Moses says."

There are four sections in this discussion. Section one looks at Genesis 1–3 in light of the Pentateuchal "land theme." Section two views Genesis 1–3 from the perspective of a prototypical Sinai Covenant between God and Adam. In section three (beginning in the next chapter), I investigate the relationship between Genesis 1–3 and Israel's failure to keep the Sinai Covenant and the consequences of that broken covenant. The final section investigates two macro-structural inclusions in the final form Pentateuch: (1) the inclusion of pessimistic realism in the beginning and end of the Torah indicating the certainty of Israel's failure to keep the Sinai Covenant; and (2) the inclusion of hope at the conclusions of Genesis and Deuteronomy portraying Jacob and Moses as paradigmatic examples for the ideal reader who must wait hopefully in exile until God fulfills his promises concerning "the last days."

In this fourth section I attempt to show that the final form Pentateuch is not tethered to a Second Temple priestly agenda (contra Wellhausen) or to the Sinai Covenant per se. Instead I argue that, in light of the certainties of covenant violation and exile, the Pentateuch's compositional strategy is eschatological in nature. The Pentateuch represents the candid confession (Lev 26:40; see also Dan 9) of covenant failure and the deserved consequences of the broken covenant (Lev 26; Deut 4:46—28:68; 31:28–29). Nonetheless, the Pentateuch also represents a deep-rooted hope in God's faithfulness to deal with Israel's uncircumcised hearts (Lev 26:41; Deut 30:6), to atone both for their transgression and for the land (Lev 26:41–45; Deut 32:43), and to fulfill his promises of redemption in the last days (Gen 49:1; Num 24:14; Deut 4:30; 31:29; see also Gen 49:18) through the provision of a coming, conquering king (Gen 49:8–12; Num 24:7–9, 17–19; Deut 33:5, 7).

RELATIONSHIP OF THE "TWO" CREATION ACCOUNTS

Much ink has been spilled over the relationship between the supposed "P" and "J" creation accounts. A much discussed issue in biblical scholarship concerns the purpose of Gen 2:4. Does this verse form the conclusion to the "first" creation account or the introduction to the "second?"[2] The majority of historical-critical scholars, past and present, regard Gen

---

2. For a thorough history of interpretation of this verse since the eightenth century, see Stordalen, "Genesis 2,4," 163–77.

2:4a as the conclusion to the "P" creation account.[3] The reasons for this view generally fall along three lines: (1) the terminological similarities between 1:1 and 2:4a[4] suggesting that 2:4a is the conclusion to the "first" creation account; (2) differing literary and linguistic styles in 2:4a and 2:4b;[5] and (3) a change in the divine names in verse 4b.[6]

There are good reasons, however, for taking all of 2:4 as the introduction to the following section. First, if 2:3 is regarded as the conclusion to the first account, then "land," a key word in the creation account, is used twenty-one times. If, however, Gen 2:4a is included the tally rises to twenty-two uses of the word "land." When trying to make a case for or against either position on the basis of numbers, however, the sword cuts both ways. The conflicting data (see footnote 5 on the word ברא) means that the case must not be decided on the basis of numerical evidence alone.

Second, a linguistic argument for a division between 2:4a and 2:4b on the basis of differing words for "create" is flawed. It is a foregone conclusion among critical scholars that Gen 5:1–28 belongs to the priestly source. Gen 5:1, a verse attributed to the same source (and also syntactically parallel to 2:4), uses the two different words for create as well. Throughout Genesis 1, also a text universally attributed to one source, ברא and עשׂה are used. In 1:26 God expresses his intentions to "make" man and in 1:27 we are told that God "creates" man. Therefore, attempts to divide 2:4a from 2:4b on the basis of two different words for create is not grounded in the textual data.

---

3. Otto, "Die Paradieserzählung Genesis 2–3," 184–87. Among those who have argued for this position are J. Wellhausen, J. Skinner, B. S. Childs, and R. Rendtorff. So also Robert Alter, *Five Books of Moses*, 20. According to Stordalen, ("Genesis 2,4," 163): "The opinion that Genesis 2,4 should be divided in two half verses assigned to two different sources is truly a classic in modern biblical scholarship."

4. Both verses refer to "the heavens and the earth" and use the term "create" (ברא).

5. Alter, *Five Books of Moses*, 20. One supposed linguistic difference is the verbs for create (ברא in 2:4a and עשׂה in 2:4b). An example of the supposed literary shift concerns the use of "seven" (a key denominator in the Sinaitic legislation) in the "first" creation account and its total absence in the second. When Gen 2:4a is reckoned as part of the opening creation account, the word "create" (ברא, a word that is less than marginal for the biblical account of creation) is used a total of seven times (1:1, 21, 27 [3 x]; 2:3, 4a). On the prominence and importance of the number seven for the feast days and their sacrifices, see for example Ashley, *Book of Numbers*, 562. On the pervasive use of sevens in the "first" creation account see Wenham, *Genesis 1–15*, 6.

6. Stordalen, "Genesis 2,4," 174.

Third, according to Otto,[7] the use of the phrase "these are the generations" with "in the day" immediately following is not limited to Gen 2:4 (see Gen 5:1; Num 3:1). In these cases, "these are the generations" always introduces the following section and never stands as a conclusion to the previous section. This strongly suggests that Gen 2:3 serves as the conclusion to the initial creation account.[8]

In his comprehensive analysis of Gen 2:4, Stordalen comes to the following conclusions:

> 1) אלא תולתות in Gen 2,4 shall introduce the story of the progeny, the "product" of heaven and earth, *not* the story of the genesis of these two themselves. 2) This story of the "product" is undoubtedly the "J" story in Gen 2–3. No other story presents itself as a possible substitute. 3) The ביום clause in Gen 2,4b is a conventional extension of the תולדות formula, so both halves of Gen 2,4b are to be read as a literary unit. 4) Gen 2,4 presupposes Gen 1. Thus the narrator in this way introducing Gen 2–3 was familiar even with Gen 1 in its present place. Therefore we locate him relatively late in the literary process of Genesis, presumably subsequent to the first fashion of the story now given in Gen 2.[9]

Regardless of the existence of hypothetical sources, Stordalen's comments strongly suggest that Gen 2:4 is the work of the author of Genesis (the Pentateuch), who strategically employed verse 4 to link the preceding narrative with the one that follows. To recall, a text-centered compositional analysis attempts to discern the semantics of the arrangement of the final form (compositional analysis) rather than pitting the theology of one source against another.

According to Stordalen's findings regarding the use of the "תולדות formula" in Genesis 1–11, Gen 2:4—3:24 is not intended to repeat the "first" creation account, but serves as an introduction to "material which parallels and yet not quite conforms to the preceding text."[10] More specifically, Stordalen maintains that Genesis 2–3 is not a creation story at all, but rather a narrative of what becomes of the "heavens and the

---

7. Otto, "Die Paradieserzählung Genesis 2-3," 184–88.

8. So also Keil and Delitzsch, *The Pentateuch*, 70; Sailhamer, *Genesis*, 40; Stordalen, *Echoes of Eden*, 213, 219; Wenham, *Genesis 1–15*, 49.

9. Stordalen, "Genesis 2,4," 173.

10. Ibid., 174.

earth" later on (the "aftermath"[11] of creation). Otto contends that Genesis 2–3 not only presumes the previous narrative, but must be understood as a commentary and further explication of Gen 1:1—2:4.[12] Sailhamer argues, based on a literary analysis of Gen 2:5–7, that Genesis 2–3 focuses on aspects of the land (already mentioned in the previous narrative) affected by the curse.[13] This is evident in at least five ways. First, the narrator notifies the reader he is narrating events that had taken place "before" (טרם) any "herbage of the field" (עשׂב השׂדה) "sprouted" (יצמח), terms specifically used later on to refer to the curse upon the ground (3:18). Second, Gen 2:5 refers to a time before the Lord had "caused rain (המטיר) to fall upon the ground (על הארץ)." With the exception of Job 38:26, this phrase is found only in the Flood Narrative (Gen 7:4).[14] Third, this is a time before there was a man "to work the ground" (לעבד את האדמה), again a phrase used to describe the penalty of exile as a consequence of Adam's disobedience (3:23). Fourth, in verse 6, the text focuses on a mist that watered the "face of the land." Throughout Genesis 1–11 the "face of the land" is a key concern (see 4:14; 6:1, 7; 7:4, 23; 8:8, 13). Even the use of the term אד (v. 6), like אדם, is a likely play on the word אדמה, revealing the author's concern with the "land" and what became of it after Adam's transgression. Finally, verse 7 notes that man is taken from the "dust of the ground." According to Sailhamer, "One can also see in this picture of man's origin an anticipation of his destiny. After the Fall, mankind would again return to the "dust of the ground" (3:19).[15] Thus, Genesis 2–3 serves as a commentary on how God's "very good" creation (1:31) has become a place where the reader experiences the curse, exile, and death (see 3:6; 6:2).

11. Ibid., 175.

12. Otto, "Die Paradieserzählung Genesis 2–3," 184–85.

13. Sailhamer, *Genesis*, 40. Syntactically, Gen 2:5–6 should be regarded as necessary background material communicated by the author to the reader (x + *yiqtol* [3 x]; nominal clause [3 x], *qatal* [1 x], x + *qatal* [2 x]). This information provides the necessary context for interpreting the narrative. For an explication of the role of the *yiqtol* and the *qatal* in Hebrew narrative, see Schneider, *Grammatik*, §48; also see Blokland, *In Search*; Niccacci, *Syntax*; Sailhamer, "Notes on Syntax"; Talstra, "Text Grammar Theory," 169–74; Talstra, "Text Grammar Syntax, 26–38; Talstra, "Syntax and Composition," 225–36.

14. A central motif of the Flood Narrative is the alleviation of the curse upon the ground (see Gen 5:29).

15. Sailhamer, *Genesis Unbound*, 154.

Ewald's pre-Wellhausen understanding of the compositional intentionality of the Pentateuch sheds helpful light on the semantic effect
of the final arrangement of Genesis 1 followed by 2–3.[16] According to
Ewald, the final Pentateuch is the cooperative product of five narrators
whose work reflects various vantage points within the development of
Israel's history.[17] The earliest sources of the Pentateuch, according to
Ewald (e.g., the Book of Origins[18]) were preeminently focused on Israel's
law, or Sinai.[19] Yet, Israel's ongoing chafing against the divine law and
its restrictions on human freedom[20] led subsequent prophetic narrators
(particularly the fourth[21]) to develop an ever-expanding eschatological
universalism. In Ewald's words:

> If we then regard closer the truths which are here forced upon
> us, we shall have to confess that they flow from a height of pro-
> phetic activity and advanced national culture totally foreign to

16. I already noted that Ewald's understanding of the Pentateuch's compositional
history from a priestly to a prophetic form is defended by H.-C. Schmitt.

17. I am not endorsing Ewald's views of the history of the Pentateuch's composition,
but concur with his understanding of a prophetic final form.

18. Most critical scholars would attribute this material to "P," but contrary to Ewald,
they date it as the latest source in the Pentateuch.

19. Commenting on the narrator responsible for the Book of Origins, Ewald (*History
of Israel*, 82) writes, "For we then discover the remarkable fact, that the author's most
heartfelt sympathy and greatest fullness of narration are called forth only when he is
treating a question of legislation, and can fill the frame of his narrative with elucidations
of such judicial or moral sanctions as have their origin in antiquity." Later (ibid., 85) he
writes, "This ground-thought, in conformity with the supreme aim of the work, deals
solely with the two-fold question: What is Law and Right to man in general? and, What
is Law and Right for Israel in particular?"

20. Ibid., 85–86.

21. Ibid., 101–2. Ewald ascribes to this narrator many of the key poetic texts in the
Pentateuch (e.g., Gen 9:25–27; 25:23; 27:27–29, 39–40; Num 23:7—24:24), arguing that
they are Messianic insertions. Moreover, Ewald (ibid., 104), argues that this narrator's
central dogma was faith, and that, specifically in contrast to the earlier religion of Israel:
"Prophetic activity attained at that time its culminating point in Judah, and had already
produced a multitude of lofty and eternally true thoughts. Now as these forced their
way even into the contemplation of history, and sought admission into the yielding
domain of primitive history, the old conceptions of it were evidently no longer universally sufficient, and new ones arose imperceptibly. The Divine blessing awarded to
the Patriarchs was now no longer confined as in the Book of Origins . . . to the single
nation of Israel, but extended, according to the true Messianic view, over all nations of
the earth: and that everything ultimately depends upon faith and the proof of faith, was
now the great prophetic dogma, which was soon to transform the primitive history into
accordance with itself."

the Book of Origins. The developed Messianic expectations, the truth of the infinite all-surpassing grace of Jahve beside the deep sinfulness and corruption of the earthly (or natural) man,[22] the similar truths of the non-casual origin of the wicked principle in man—these are such illustrious thoughts, which the sun of these ages was the first to elicit from the sacred soil.[23]

Ewald's take on the developmental history of the Pentateuch from a book of law to a book of eschatology provides the necessary context for understanding his understanding of the intentionality of the juxtaposition of Genesis 1 with 2–3. It is worth quoting Ewald at length:

Such is the oldest narrative [Genesis 1] in the form it took at the time of the highest glory of the ancient nation in all the calmness of its pride; and well does it show the marks of the happily-contented elevation of that time. But however strikingly the peculiar lofty nature of man as a creature was indicated in those few traits of imperishable truth and beauty, there came upon the ancient community soon enough times when the growing corruption of all mankind was profoundly felt. With new force the question then arose, What is man in his essential original being, as also his degenerate present and whole future, and how may the glaring contradiction be explained, that a creature raised so high above all others could nevertheless sink down even deeper than all others? A real enigma was thus presented in the earnest contemplation of things; and the enigma was capable of a thorough solution only as the eager eye perceived more vividly the original divine destiny of man, and kept this firmly and purely before it in its eternal significance. Man, as he steps into view before us now in the midst of the current of unfinished human history, under the burden of error and sin, is not man as he ought to be, not man in his real intention and according to the divine will, and therefore not as he originally was when he went forth from the hand of the Creator wholly pure and good, nor as he at last must become if his divine destiny is not to prove futile. Thus the first step for our narrator in the solving of the problem was to distinguish strictly between man conceivable as originally created in his pure determination according to the will of God and the historical man, between the typical, archetypal man and the man of today, between the spiritual and the carnal man, the man of God and the man of sin. What high doctrine and what fascina-

22. For textual support Ewald cites Gen 3:1–23; 8:21; 18:1—19:28; Exod 32–34.
23. Ewald, *History of Israel*, 101–2.

tion may lie in this distinction as it is vividly realized in thought! And our narrator presents it with all sharpness of outline, not merely placing side by side man as conceived in his divinely-given original glory, and man as fallen from it, but as a genuine historical thinker he explains and sets forth the possibility of the transition from the former to the latter, and also makes apparent the other possibility, viz. the restoration of the erring and strayed. Only with this does the narrative attain the charming complete-ness which distinguishes it.[24]

Though Ewald's theories on composition are largely "behind-the-text," his understanding of the compositional strategy of the Pentateuch is insightful. It is a book whose final form is existentially bound up with the present realities of Israel's sin and punishment. However, the current problems are presented in view of the glories of the distant past, in order to point the reader toward a hopeful future. In my opinion, Ewald elo-quently describes the compositional intentionality behind the juxtaposi-tion of Genesis 1–3. To repeat the thesis of this book: When understood as the introduction to the Pentateuch, Genesis 1–3 foreshadows Israel's failure to keep the stipulations of the Sinai Covenant and their exile from the Promised Land in order to point the reader to a future work of God in the "last days."

THE LAND IN GENESIS 1–3

In this section I argue that the intention of Genesis 1–3 is to draw a par-allel between the "good land" of creation and the "good land" promised to Abraham and his descendants. The initial phases of the creation week allude to important redemptive themes elsewhere in the Pentateuch, including Israel's redemption from the land of Egypt. The depiction of the garden as a gift for Adam intimates of God's intentions for Israel in the future as well. In essence, God graciously prepares and gives a special "land" to Adam (Israel). Occupation of this special land is contingent on his fulfillment of the creation mandate to subdue and conquer[25] the inhabitants of the "land" (1:26, 28) as well as on his obedience to the divine commandments in the form of dietary restrictions (2:16–17). These parallels provide the necessary backdrop for understanding the significance of the creation mandate in the Pentateuch.

---

24. Ibid., 126–27. (Words in brackets provided.)

25. I address the meaning of this term at length later in this chapter.

"Earth" or "Promised Land" in Genesis 1?

Even a cursory reading of Gen 1:1—2:3 reveals the author's predominant focus upon the ארץ ("land"). The word ארץ appears twenty-one times,[26] while שמים ("sky") appears only eleven times.[27] Although an exhaustive treatment of the relationship of Gen 1:1 to the following verses (vv. 2–3) is beyond the scope of this book, the issue must be addressed if we hope to understand Genesis 1–3 as the introduction to the Torah.

The first verse of Genesis could not offer a more eloquent[28] and compositionally strategic[29] opening to the first book of the Hebrew Bible.[30] "In the beginning God created the heavens and the earth."[31] What

26. 1:1, 2, 10, 11 (2 x), 12, 15, 17, 20, 22, 24 (2 x), 25, 26 (2 x), 28 (2 x), 29, 30 (2 x); 2:1.

27. 1:1, 8, 9, 14, 15, 17, 20, 26, 28, 30; 2:1.

28. This is evidenced in at least three ways. First, the verse contains seven words and twenty-eight letters. According to Wenham (*Genesis 1–15*, 6), "1:1 consists of 7 words, 1:2 of 14 (7 x 2) words, 2:1–3 of 35 (7 x 5) words. The number seven dominates this opening chapter in a strange way, not only in the number of words in a particular section but in the number of times a specific word or phrase recurs. For example, 'God' is mentioned 35 times, 'earth' 21 times, 'heaven/firmament' 21 times, while the phrases 'and it was so' and 'God saw that it was good' occur 7 times."

Second, the first two words are alliterated, both of which begin with the letters ב, ר, א. See Bar-Efrat, *Narrative Art*, 203. And finally, according to Sailhamer, ("Genesis," 35.) there is likely alliteration between the verbs ברא and ברך in order to develop the theme of blessing (see 1:21–22, 27–28; 2:3a, b; 5:2a, b).

29. Earlier I discussed the likelihood that ראשית was chosen because of its semantic relationship with the word אחרית. It cannot be fortuitous that in each of the three macro-structural poems about the "last days," (Gen 49:1; Num 24:14; Deut 31:28–29), the word ראשית also appears (see Gen 49:3; Num 24:20; Deut 33:21). Kenneth A. Mathews (*Genesis 1—11:26*, 126) writes, "The occurrence of 'beginning' . . . in 1:1 suggests that it has been selected because of its association with 'end.' . . . If so, the author has at the outset shown that creation's 'beginnings' were initiated with a future goal intended, an eschatological purpose."

30. By "first book," I am not referring to Genesis, but to the Pentateuch as a single composition.

31. I am aware of the syntactical issue regarding whether or not בְּרֵאשִׁית should be interpreted as an absolute ("In the beginning God created") or as a relative ("In the beginning when God created the heavens and the earth"), and if a relative, whether the main clause begins in verse 2 or verse 3. For a succinct and fair treatment of the various positions, see Lim, *Grace*, 103–8. Lim's conclusion, however, is far from conclusive. In his words, "All three translations are possible. However, which one is the most probable? In my judgment, it is difficult to adjudicate based on grammatical, syntactical, linguistical or lexical investigations alone. Ultimately, in spite of all the arguments given by all the different sides, it boils down to the reader's personal preference and presuppositional pool concerning his or her understanding of God. In other words, a person's view of God determines his or her translation" (ibid., 108).

purpose does the first verse of this passage serve?[32] According to Lim, there are four ways this verse has been understood:

1. V. 1 is to be taken as a summary statement[33] and v. 2 describes the original condition of the world.

2. V. 1 is to be taken as a superscription and v. 2 describes the situation prior to creation, the pre-existing chaos. However chaos may simply be a state of condition and not an antagonistic monster like other Near Eastern literature.

3. V. 1 is to be taken as a first act of creation. This takes v. 1 as an independent main clause, which is the most ancient and traditional reading of Gen 1:1–3. This approach interprets the first three verses chronologically. V. 1 is the first creative act, v. 2 is the consequence of v. 1, and v. 3 is the first creative word.

4. V. 1 is to be taken as a perfect creation but between vv. 1 and 2 something happened that is commonly attributed to the fall of Satan resulting in the convulsion and contamination of creation (hence this is commonly called the "gap theory"). Some even put the destruction of dinosaurs at this time. Hence vv. 3–31 are understood as recreation/reconstruction. The conjunction in v. 2 "and" is translated disjunctively "but." The verb "was" is translated "became." [34]

Of these four options, the fourth option will not be considered by virtue of its "behind the text" theological speculations. In other words, there are no indications from within the text itself (authorial intention) that the author is pointing to a fall of Satan. By understanding verse 1 as a superscription and or summary statement, options one and two allow for the presence of pre-created material, whereby creation does

---

Scholars whose religious presuppositional pools are quite diverse have defended the traditional view. See Barr, "Hebrew Lexicography," 147; Eichrodt, "Beginning," 1–10; Sailhamer, "Genesis," 21; Wenham, *Genesis 1–15*, 3; Westermann, *Genesis 1—11*, 97. Therefore I find it difficult to accept Lim's conclusions regarding the overriding influence of one's religious presuppositions in this particular instance.

32. For a thorough treatment of the grammatical, syntactical, and theological issues related to Gen 1:1, see Hasel, "Recent Translations," 154–67.

33. One proponent of this view is Waltke. See Waltke and Yu, *Old Testament Theology*, 179.

34. Lim, *Grace*, 108–9.

not begin until the third verse.[35] A significant theological implication of options 1 and 2, therefore, is a non-traditional understanding of creation *ex nihilo* such that "darkness and the watery chaos" may in some way be considered "co-terminus, co-eternal and autonomous from God";[36] or that Scripture is simply silent about when or if God actually created the ארץ ("land") and the מים ("water") of the תהום ("deep") in verse 2.[37]

Sailhamer, however, puts forth three objections to the "title" or "summary view."[38] First, Gen 1:1 is a complete sentence, whereas titles in the Hebrew Bible are never formed as complete sentences.[39] Second, the presence of the conjunction in the second verse strongly militates against regarding verse 1 as a title.[40] Finally, the first chapter contains a summary statement in 2:1, rendering the need for a second summary statement unnecessary and, therefore, unlikely.

Option three, the traditional option, appears to be the best.[41] Taking Gen 1:1 as God's first work of creation (with verses 2ff. as a description of subsequent and different creative acts[42]) eliminates the problem of explaining any pre-created material. But, the traditional understanding is also not without its problems. If Gen 1:1 and vv. 2ff. refer to different and subsequent creative acts, in what sense are verses 1 and 2–3 different?[43]

35. Lim, *Grace*, 109–10.

36. Ibid., 11. See also Sailhamer, *Genesis Unbound*, 23.

37. According to Waltke (*Old Testament Theology*, 180), "Like other ancient Near Eastern cosmogonies and Homer's *Iliad*, the Genesis account assumes the existence of primordial water—there is no word of God that commands its existence. Although the origin of primordial water is unknown, the summary in verse 1, along with other biblical texts, represents it as a temporal reality; only God is eternal." See also Wenham, *Genesis 1–15*, 11.

38. Sailhamer, *Genesis Unbound*, 102–3.

39. Ibid., 253, ch 9 n. 1. According to Sailhamer, when a summary statement appears at the beginning of a narrative, it is typically a nominal clause (see Gen 2:4a; 5:1; 6:9; 11:10). At the end of a narrative it appears as a verbal clause (see Gen 2:1; 25:34b; 49:28b).

40. Ibid., 253, ch 9 n. 2. If verse 2 was in apposition to verse 1, it would not begin with a conjunction (see 2:4a; 5:1). In Sailhamer's words, "This is perhaps the most telling argument against understanding Genesis 1:1 as a title or a summary of the first chapter. Though it might seem like a minor point, Hebrew grammar uses this conjunction carefully. If verse 1 were a title, the section immediately following it would surely not begin with the conjunction 'and'" (ibid., 103).

41. Lim, *Grace*.

42. Ibid; Sailhamer, *Genesis Unbound*, 103.

43. Sailhamer, *Genesis Unbound*, 57.

Evidence strongly suggests that the phrase "heavens and earth" in 1:1 should be understood as a merism, namely, the use of opposite words to refer to the totality of the created universe (everything).[44] But if verse 1 is not a title or summary of what follows, a tension arises between verse 1, the description of the creation of the "heavens and the earth" (the finished universe)[45] and verse 2, which describes an unfinished place not fit for human habitation. Mathews lucidly describes this tension when he writes,

> The most formidable argument for interpreting v. 1 as a summary is the phrase "the heavens and the earth," which uniformly means in Scripture the universe as a completed organization—the cosmos as we know it. Verse 2 describes the earth in a negative state, a chaos of elements, which is opposed to creation (cf. Isa 34:11; Jer 4:23); therefore the well-ordered universe of v. 1 and the negative elements of the earth cannot have existed contemporaneously. If the "heavens and earth" declares existence of the well-ordered cosmos, how can it also be that the "earth" is disorganized and incomplete as portrayed in v. 2?[46]

Mathews, who in fact argues for the traditional understanding of verse 1, obviously feels this tension. He is only able to maintain the traditional view by arguing that the phrase "the heavens and the earth" is used uniquely in Genesis 1, "since it concerns the exceptional event of creation itself."[47]

Although Sailhamer understands "the heavens and the earth" in 1:1 as a merism, he does not share Mathews' exceptional understanding of it. Sailhamer attempts to resolve the tension between the description of the completed universe in verse 1 and the uninhabitable ארץ ("land")

---

44. Mathews, *Genesis 1—11:26*, 142; Sailhamer, *Genesis Unbound*, 56; Waltke and Yu, *Old Testament Theology*, 179; Westermann, *Genesis 1–11*, 101.

45. A phrase always used elsewhere to refer to a finished universe. The phrase את השמים ואת הארץ appears thirteen times (Gen 1:1; Exod 20:11; 31:17; Deut 4:26; 30:19; 31:28; 2 Kgs 19:15; Isa 37:16; Jer 23:24; 32:17; Hag 2:6, 21; 2 Chr 2:11); as השמים והארץ two times (Gen 2:1, 4); as ארץ ושמים two times (Gen 2:4; Ps 148:13); and as שמים וארץ eleven times (Gen 14:19, 22; Jer 33:25; 51:48; Joel 4:16; Pss 69:35; 115:15; 121:2; 124:8; 134:3; 146:6).

46. Mathews, *Genesis 1—11:26*, 140. Waltke and Yu, *Old Testament Theology*, 179, write, "Verse 1 and 2 cannot mean respectively that God created the organized universe (v. 1) and at that time the earth was disorganized (v. 2), without arousing rational 'nonsense' (i.e., 'nonsense')."

47. Mathews, *Genesis 1—11:26*, 142.

in verse 2 by arguing that ארץ in verse 2 does not refer to the entire universe (world), but to a specific place in the world,[48] namely the land that is later promised to Abraham and his descendants.[49] In his words, "I contend that two distinct time periods are mentioned in Genesis 1. In the first period (the 'beginning,' Genesis 1:1), God created the universe; no time limitations[50] are placed on that period. In the second period (Genesis 1:2—2:4a), God prepared the garden of Eden for man's dwelling; that activity occurred in one week."[51] In this view, God creates the entirety of the universe (including the heavenly luminaries,[52] the seas, the dry land, the plants and the animals[53]) *ex nihilo* in an undefined period of time called "the beginning" (v. 1); in 1:2—2:4a, God then prepares a specific land in the course of seven days to give as a gift to the first human beings.[54]

48. Sailhamer argues for a localized meaning of the term ארץ in verse 2 since it is no longer part of the merism, "heavens and earth," and also because of its primary usage throughout the first chapter (1:11, 20, 24, 28). This also suggests that a more fitting translation of שמים in 1:2—2:4a is "sky" (see Exod 20:4). See Sailhamer, *Genesis Unbound*, 48–50.

49. Ibid., 14.

50. Ibid., 38–42. Sailhamer's understanding of 1:1 as an undefined period of time rather than a specific moment in time is also based on an unexceptional interpretation of the Hebrew word ראשית ("beginning"), a word used elsewhere to refer to an initial indeterminate period or duration of time (see for example Gen 10:10; Deut 11:12; Jer 28:1; Job 8:7). Sailhamer (ibid., 40), writes, "When understood in this way, the text does not say that God created the universe in the first moment of time; rather it says that God created the universe during an indeterminate period of time before the actual reckoning of a sequence of time began. In Genesis 1, the period which follows 'the beginning' is a single, seven-day week, which itself is followed by a vast history of humanity, leading ultimately to Abraham and the people of Israel." Rashi long ago argued that ראשית is not the proper Hebrew word for the initiation of a sequence of time. He writes, "And the Scripture is not here to teach the order of creation, that is to say that these things came first, because if it was there to teach this, it would have been written, 'בראשונה' ('In the beginning, God created the heavens,' etc." Miqraoth-Gedoloth, *Berayshit*, 4. (Translation from Hebrew my own.)

51. Sailhamer, *Genesis Unbound*, 29.

52. According to Sailhamer, *Genesis*, 34, God does not create the luminaries in 1:14 but merely determines their purpose: "Let the lights in the expanse of the sky divide between the day and the night. And they will be for signs and seasons and for days and years" (translation of Hebrew my own).

53. Sailhamer, *Genesis Unbound*, 56.

54. The merit of Sailhamer's position is its seemingly nice fit within the Pentateuch and its theology as a whole. Sailhamer writes (ibid., 82), "In reading Genesis 1 and 2, therefore, we need to ask several questions: What is the overall purpose of the

Sailhamer offers four reasons for identifying ארץ ("land") in 1:2–
2:4a as the Promised Land.[55] First, the close textual connection between
chapters 1 and 2 suggests that chapter 2 is an intentional elaboration of
the first chapter. In other words, the preparation of the "land" in chapter
1 parallels the preparation of the Garden of Eden (or Eden as a whole)
in chapter 2.[56] It is clear, moreover, that there is an immediate shift in
2:4 from the universal ("the heavens and the earth") to the specific in
2:5–7 ("and before any plant of the field was in the land"). The context
makes it clear that the land referred to in 2:5 is "Eden" (vv. 8–15). Second,
throughout Genesis 1–11 there is an ongoing comparison between the
"land" and "Babylon" to the east. This movement away from the "land"
(Gen 3) toward Babylon in the east (Gen 11) seems to identify the "land"
in Genesis 1 and 2 as the Promised Land. Sailhamer finds support, among
other places, in Gen 11:1–2 where all the inhabitants of the "land" travel
eastward until they find a plain in the land of Babylon.[57] In other words,
Genesis 1–11 portrays an eastward movement farther and farther away
from the "good land" to Babylon (a recapitulation of Israel's story).[58] A
reversal in the eastern exilic progression takes place when God calls
Abram out of Babylon back to the good "land," namely, the land already
referenced in Genesis 1–2.

Third, two central themes in the Pentateuch are the Sinai Covenant
and God's gift of the "land" to his people. The author's interest in the Sinai

---

Pentateuch? What is its central theme? In what way do Genesis 1 and 2 help us understand that theme? How do these early chapters prepare us for understanding and
appreciating all that follows in the Pentateuch?"

55. Ibid., 50–53.

56. If, as I have already argued, verse 4 belongs to what follows, the identification of
the "land" in chapter 1 with the land in chapter 2 is quite clear:

A. In the beginning God created the heavens and the earth (1:1)	A'. This is the account of what became of the heavens and the earth when the Lord God made the land and the sky (2:4)
B. And the land was uninhabitable and darkness was upon the deep and the Spirit of God hovered upon the surface of the water.	B'. And before any shrub of the field was in the land and before any herb of the field sprouted (for the Lord God had not yet brought rain upon the land) and there was no person to work the ground.

57. Sailhamer, *Genesis Unbound*, 51–52.

58. See Gen 3:24; 10:30; 11:2 (see also 4:10–14, where Cain's murder is depicted as
a defiling of the Promised Land [Num 35:33]. While his parents were only exiled from
the garden [Jerusalem?], he is exiled from Promised Land altogether).

Covenant is already transparent throughout Genesis 1, for instance, the reference to the "appointed times" (1:14) and the Sabbath (2:1–3). One would also expect, therefore, other central themes, such as the gift of the land, to emerge in the very first chapter of the Torah as well.[59] One corroborating piece of evidence that strengthens Sailhamer's identification of the "land" in Genesis 1–2 is the wording of the Creation Mandate in 1:28. This call to "conquer the land," within the context of the Pentateuch, is highly suggestive of Israel's mandate to do the same (see Num 32:22, 29; Josh 18:1). Fourth, and finally, later inner-biblical interpretation seems to identify the "land" of Genesis 1–2 as the Promised Land (see Jer 27:5–6; Isa 51:3; Ezek. 36:35; Joel 2:3; see also Jer 4:23–26[60]).[61]

A particularly strong piece of evidence in support of Sailhamer's thesis is the correspondence between the boundaries of Eden (2:10–14) and the land promised to Abraham (Gen 15:18). The author goes to great lengths to provide the reader with a detailed explanation[62] of the boundaries of the Garden of Eden. According to Sailhamer, the Garden of Eden is located by means of the geographical information about the four rivers.[63] The wording suggests that the text moves from the rivers least known (the Pishon) to those the most known (the Euphrates) to the readers. Although we are not able to identify the locations of the first two rivers with certainty, it cannot be fortuitous that later in Genesis (especially ch. 10) the author provides important clues as to their whereabouts. The Gihon flows around the land of "Cush," a place later linked to Egypt in Gen 10:6. Thus with good reason, Sailhamer identifies the Gihon as the "river of Egypt."

59. Sailhamer, *Genesis Unbound*, 52.

60. Ibid., 54, 65. These verses from Jeremiah, in my opinion, lend the strongest support to Sailhamer's thesis. As God had lovingly prepared the Promised Land for his people in the distant past, so here he is pictured as reducing it to its primeval uninhabitable state. See Sailhamer's comments on Jer 27:5–6 as well.

61. It may also be the case that these verses merely compare the land of Canaan with Eden. *At the very least*, one can say there is a strong typological link between the Promised Land and the Garden of Eden.

62. Gen 2:10–14 contains ten nominal clauses, one x + *yiqtol* clause, and one *weqatal* clause. The narrative progression ceases in Gen 2:9a and is not resumed until v. 15 (note the *wayyiqtol* clauses in these verses). The use of these background and discourse clauses in the narrative suggests that the author is communicating directly to the readers in order to provide them essential textual information necessary for the interpretation of the intentionality of the Garden of Eden in the Pentateuch.

63. Sailhamer, *Genesis Unbound*, 70–73.

Sailhamer does not elaborate on the Pishon River, but the text also provides helpful clues for discerning its whereabouts: it flows around the land of "Havilah." The author identifies Havilah as a land with good gold and precious stones. As a personal name, "Havilah" is identified as one of the sons of Cush (Gen 10:7; see 1 Chr 1:9). But "Havilah" is also used as the name of a descendant of Shem (Gen 10:29; see 1 Chr 1:23). The mention of the name "Ophir" later in the same verse—the name of a place also associated with gold, wood, and gems (1 Kgs 10:11)—however, suggests that there is a likely link between the location of the Pishon and the geographical location of the descendants of Shem. In a rather rare second person address to the reader by the author, we are told elsewhere in Genesis that the descendants of Ishmael (Shemites) "settled from Havilah to Shur which is close to Egypt[64] as you go toward Assyria" (Gen 25:18; see also 1 Sam 15:7). Moreover, Gen 10:30 notes that their (Ophir, Havilah, and Yobab, the sons of Yoktan) dwelling place is associated with "Mesha in the direction of Sephar, the hill country of the east." Thus, though the identification of this river is uncertain, one can say with a fair degree of certainty that this river was located on the southeastern border of the land of Canaan.

The other rivers mentioned in Genesis 2, however, can be identified with certainty: the Euphrates and the Tigris Rivers, both of which are located north and east of the Promised Land. It would appear, therefore, that the four rivers mentioned in Genesis 2 correspond nicely with the boundaries around the land promised to Abraham and his descendants (see Deut 1:7; 11:24; Josh 1:4).[65]

I find Sailhamer's thesis regarding the identity of the "land" in Genesis 1–2 convincing. Here, however, I believe it is necessary to offer additional support to Sailhamer's position. In my discussion of the history of interpretation and more recent studies, I mentioned that scholars have noticed inner-textual parallels between Adam and Abraham. Not only does the text thematically link Abram to Adam (a "new Adam")[66]

64. Although the NASB and NKJV translate על פני as "east," the NET, NRSV, and NJPS all render this Hebrew phrase as "alongside" or "close to." This could be next to Egypt on at least three sides. However, the mention of "Asshur" ("Assyria") suggests that Havilah was in fact a land that was located next to Egypt on the east.

65. See Sailhamer, *Genesis Unbound*, 72.

66. Thematic links include the following: Abram clearly inherits Adam's creation mandate to be fruitful and multiply and to be a channel of blessing. Both individuals are taken from one place and brought to a "good land" (2:15; 15:7).

but Genesis 15–16 appears to be an intentional recapitulation of Adam's story in Genesis 2–3, namely, the provision of a good land and a "Fall." Genesis 15 is a pivotal text in the Pentateuch, with tentacles reaching back to the earlier chapters of Genesis and forward, anticipating subsequent stories. Genesis 15 is one of the pillar passages in the macro-structural "faith theme" in the Pentateuch.[67]

When Genesis 15–16 is read in light of Genesis 2–3, certain striking parallels emerge. First, in both passages the central figure undergoes a deep and divinely induced slumber (Gen 2:21; 15:12).[68] Second, both passages provide homogenous geographical information regarding the boundaries of a divinely provided land (Gen 2:10–14; 15:18). Third, while Genesis 2 does not mention a covenant as does Genesis 15, it is clearly covenantal in nature.[69] Fourth, the recounting of divine slumber and the provision of a beautiful land in both cases are followed by "Fall Narratives" in terminology that is strikingly similar. Sailhamer writes, "The account of Sarah's plan to have a son has not only been connected with the list of nations in chapter 15, but also appears to have been intentionally shaped with reference to the account of the Fall in Genesis 3."[70]

Parallels noted by Sailhamer include the following:[71]

---

67. See Schmitt, "Redaktion des Pentateuch." There are homogenous literary patterns and lexical repetitions in Gen 14–15, Exod 2–4, 18–24, and Num 10–21. In each passage there is an appearance of a Gentile priest who blesses an individual and serves "bread" (Gen 14:18, 20; Exod 2:16; Exod 18:1, 12; and Num 10:29). Following the appearance of a Gentile priest there is a theophany in fire (Gen 15:1, 17; Exod 3:2; Exod 19:16–18; 20:18; Num 10:34). In each of these passages, "to believe" plays a primary role (Gen 15:6; Exod 4:1, 5, 8, 31 [see 14:31]; Exod 19:9; Num 14:11; 20:12). For an explanation of the significance of these patterns for the theology of the Pentateuch, see Postell, "Where's the Faith?!"; Sailhamer, "Parallel Structures"; Sailhamer, *Meaning of Pentateuch*, 346–47.

68. The Hebrew expression נפל + תרדמה is only used these two places in the Pentateuch (elsewhere in 1 Sam 26:12; Job 4:13; 33:15; Prov 19:15).

69. Brueggemann, "Same Flesh and Bone," 540. The covenantal nature of Gen 2 will be discussed at length in the last section of this chapter.

70. Sailhamer, *Pentateuch as Narrative*, 153.

71. Ibid.

Table 3. Comparison of Adam and Abram (Sailhamer)

Gen 16:2a	Gen 3:2
"so she [Sarai] said to"	"The woman said to"
Gen 16:2b	Gen 3:17
"Abram listened to Sarai"	"you listened to your"
Gen 16:3a	Gen 3:6a
"Sarai . . . took"	"she took some"
Gen 16:3a	Gen 3:6b
"and [she] gave to her husband [Abram]"	"she also gave some to her husband"

These parallels not only suggest a correlation between Adam and Abram, but more importantly for my purposes here, an identification (if not *actuality*, then at the very least *typologically*) of the "land" given to Adam in Genesis 2 with the land promised to Abram in Genesis 15.

Before moving on to my analysis of Gen 1–3 in light of the Pentateuchal theme of the land, it is necessary to deal with one substantial objection to the identification of the "land" in Gen 1:2—2.4a as the Promised Land. Two verses seemingly include Gen 1:1 as part of the narrative of the six-day creation:

> For [in] six days the LORD *made* the heavens and the earth, the sea, and everything in them and he rested on the seventh day. (Exod 20:11a)

> For [in] six days the LORD made the heavens and the earth and on the seventh day he rested and he was refreshed. (Exod 31:17b)

Sailhamer's response to these verses is twofold.[72] First, he argues that the phrase את השמים ואת הארץ ("the heavens and the earth") in Exod 20:11a is not used as a merism since the text provides a longer list of things God made—the sky, the land, and the seas (and everything in them). These are the same three things God makes during the first three days in Genesis 1. The remainder of the days God makes "everything in them." Therefore, a better translation of את השמים ואת הארץ would be "the sky and the land." Second, the text does not say that God "created"

---

72. Sailhamer, *Genesis Unbound*, 106–8.

these things. The word used is עשׂה ("made"), and not ברא ("create"). In other words, Exod 20:11 (and 31:17b) is not referring to Gen 1:1, where it states that God "created" the universe. Rather, this passage points to God's work of "making" the land, sky, and seas suitable for human habitation in a six day period, a key word throughout God's preparation of the land in 1:2—2:4.[73] Elsewhere in the Hebrew Bible the term "make" is used for the preparation of already existing entities, such as the "cutting" of one's fingernails (Deut 21:12), "washing" one's feet (2 Sam 19:25), and the "trimming" of one's beard (2 Sam 19:24). Sailhamer also notes that this word can mean "to appoint" or "to acquire." God is not creating something that does not exist in Gen 1:2—2:4a; instead he is setting it in good order.

The soundness of Sailhamer's response to these verses may be challenged on a couple of levels. First, while the phrase את השמים ואת הארץ in Exod 20:11 is part of a longer list, the same is not the case for Exod 31:17b. Sailhamer is aware of this problem and thus argues that this verse and others like it "are most likely understood as abbreviated forms of this same expression."[74] But the fact that this phrase does not appear as part of a longer list is problematic for Sailhamer's position, and one could easily understand this verse as a reference to the creation of the entire world. A second objection has to do with Sailhamer's explanation of ברא ("to create") and עשׂה ("to make"). Is there in fact such a great semantic distinction between these terms? Are there times (including this one) when these terms are simply used synonymously?[75] A semantic distinction between ברא and עשׂה is essential for Sailhamer's interpretation of Exod 20:11 and 31:17 to stand. On several occasions in the Bible ברא and עשׂה are used in the same verse,[76] and in some cases they do appear to be used synonymously (see especially Gen 5:1; 6:7; Isa 41:20; 43:7; see also Gen 1:26, 27). This is most evident in Gen 1:26–27, verses in the creation narrative itself. According to verse 26, God declares his intention to "make" man in his image. The verb used to carry out this activity, however, is "create" (v. 27). And in Gen 5:1, an obvious allusion

---

73. Gen 1:7, 11, 12, 16, 25, 26, 31; 2:2, 3, 4.

74. Sailhamer, *Genesis Unbound*, 107.

75. The translators of the LXX, our closest link to living informants, obviously understood these terms synonymously (compare Gen1:1 and Exod 20:11). On the LXX's use of "make" instead of "create" see Schmidt, "ברא *br*," 256.

76. Gen 2:3, 4; 5:1; 6:7; Exod 34:10; Isa 41:20; 43:7; 45:7, 12, 18; and Amos 4:13.

to the creation of man in 1:26–27, both terms are used again: "in the day when God *created* (ברא) man in the likeness of God he *made* (עשׂה) him." J. Vollmar and Westermann argue, contra Sailhamer, that only in Gen 3:21 is עשׂה ever used to refer to God's making something out of existing materials in the OT.[77]

While the force of these arguments against Sailhamer's position must not be minimized, in my opinion, the evidence against Sailhamer's thesis is not entirely airtight. First, it is evident that the phrase את השׁמים ואת הארץ does appear in a longer list in Exodus 20:11, and therefore, this phrase is likely not intended to be a merism. And though this phrase is typically used as a merism, the fact that Exodus 31:17 uses the verb עשׂה (rather than ברא), as well as the reference to God's rest suggests that this verse is a reflection on the preparation of the land in Gen 1:2—2:3. Second, although עשׂה ("to make") and ברא ("to create") in 1:26–27 may be taken as synonymous terms when isolated from the larger context, the juxtaposition of chapters 1 and 2 does in fact indicate that the creation of mankind involved both a "creating" (1:27) and a "fashioning" out of preexisting materials (יצר; 2:7). Moreover, although Vollmar and Westermann claim that the use of עשׂה for preparation from existing materials in 3:21 is unique to the entire OT, this is simply not the case. In Gen 2:18, God expresses his intention to create the woman with a singular cohortative[78] from the verb עשׂה: "I will make." Verse 21 then elaborates on what "making" entails: namely, the preparation of the woman from existing materials. Therefore, while Sailhamer's position admittedly has its problems, I believe that this position is best suited to the immediate context (Gen 1–2), the compositional strategy of the Pentateuch, and the inner-biblical testimony of the OT. Moreover, of all the other scholarly explanations regarding the relationship between verses 1 and 2, Sailhamer's position has the merit of being the least problematic.[79] I concur with Sailhamer that the "land" God prepares in Gen

77. Vollmer, "עשׂה *'śh*," 950: "Gen 3:21 occupies a special position because it is the only passage in the OT in which *'śh* refers to God manufacturing, preparing from materials at hand." See also Westermann, *Genesis 1–11*, 269.

78. This is an obvious allusion to Gen 1:26. The singular cohortative in 2:18 may be explained by virtue of the fact that here God is only creating an absolutely singular entity, the woman, whereas in 1:26 God creates a composite entity, male and female.

79. Although there will certainly be those who contest the identification of the "land" in Gen 1:2 as the Promised Land, it is difficult to deny the strong typological connections between the two. So whilst a literal identification of Eden with the land—

1:2—2:4a. is the same "land" he prepares in 2:5–14, namely, the land he later promises to give to Abraham and his descendants.

Prototypical Parting of the "Exilic" Waters

The creation narrative is initiated with a term that anticipates the temporal scope and goal of the entire Pentateuch: ראשית ("beginning"). A "beginning" implies an "end." This term is not only strategically employed at the beginning of the Torah, but appears in each of the major poems about the "end" days (see Gen 49:3; Num 24:20; Deut 33:21). God's "end" time purposes for the land are intentionally foreshadowed in the "beginning." Deuteronomy 11:11–12 aptly captures the semantic connotations of "beginning" (as the antithesis of the "end") already anticipated in Gen 1:1 and also highlights God's gracious concern for this land throughout the entire Pentateuch: "And the land which you are crossing over[80] to possess, a land of mountains and valleys, it drinks water from the rains, a land which the LORD your God seeks with care, the eyes of the LORD your God are always on it from the beginning (ראשית) of the year and until the end (אחרית) of the year." The author of the Pentateuch intentionally depicts the creation account with an eye to later events, particularly God's purposes for the land and his people. Thus, the use of ראשית provides the reader an important semantic clue for understanding the intentionality of what follows.

Key terms are used to describe the initial condition of the land in Gen 1:2. First, the land is described as being in a state of תהו ובהו. Although the English versions typically translate this phrase "formless and void,"[81] Jeremiah uses this phrase to describe the condition of the Promised Land after the conquest of the invading force from the north (Jer 4:23; so also Isa 34:11). When תהו is used of land elsewhere, it refers to desert conditions or a place not fit for human habitation, frequently

---

the case for which I have made in the main text—reinforces the thesis of this book, it is ultimately not essential to my more fundamental point. Even if readers are not fully persuaded by the case for the *identification* of Eden with the Promised Land, the case for the typological linking of the two is very strong indeed.

80. Just as water must be parted for Israel to enjoy the Promised Land (see for example, Deut 2:29), so here, water must be divided for the first man to enjoy God's "good land."

81. See for example ESV, NASB, KJV, NKJV, NCV, NIV, NLT, RSV, NRSV, NJPS; see also HSCB, *The Message*. The LXX translates this phrase as ἀόρατος καὶ ἀκατασκεύαστος, and similarly the Vulg., *inanis et vacua*.

the result of the ravages of a conquering army (see Deut 32:10; Isa 34:11; 45:18; see Gen 2:5–6).[82] Thus, תהו ובהו as a description of the land in Genesis 1 anticipates the condition of the Promised Land at the time of the Babylonian exile. This concern for the Babylonian exile and a return to the land is confirmed in the narrative progression of Genesis 1–11 as a whole: from the Promised Land (Gen 1–2) to Babylon (Gen 11). Abram's departure from Ur of the Chaldeans to Canaan, in its narrative context, anticipates Israel's eventual journey from Babylon back to Canaan (Gen 12:1–5). In other words, the Primeval History has been intentionally framed by allusions to the Babylonian exile (Gen 1:2 and 11:1–9).

A second term used to describe the condition of the land in verse 2 is תהום ("deep"), likely an alliteration of the word תהו. Elsewhere in the Pentateuch תהום refers to the waters of the flood (Gen 7:11; 8:2) and to the waters that covered the Egyptian army (Exod 15:5, 8; see also Isa 51:10; 63:13; Ps 106:9). The waters covering the darkened land present a barrier to man's enjoyment of the good land, and must therefore be divided (vv. 6–10).[83] The רוח ("Spirit") over the waters becomes a central theme later on in the story of Israel's redemption from bondage and exile.[84]

> And the land was uninhabitable and darkness was upon the *deep water* (תהום), and the *Spirit* (רוח) of *God* (אלהים) brooded upon the face of the *water* (מים). (Gen 1:2)

82. The translation of this phrase in the Targums appears to be more textually derived. The Frg. Tg. Recension P reads, "desolate [תהיא], chaotic [בהיא], and desolate [צדיא] of people, and empty [ריקנא] of all worship [פולחן]." Similarly, the Frg. Tg. VNL (although "worship" is replaced with "beast" [בעיר]). Tg. Neof., a conflation of the aforementioned fragmentary Targums says, "And the land was desolate, and chaotic, and desolate of people and from animals and empty of all worship." Tg. Onq. says, "desolate [צדיא] and empty [רוקניא]," and Tg. Psa-J., "desolate [תהייא], chaotic [בהיא], desolate [צדיא] of human beings and empty [ריקנייא] of all animals." The reference to worship in Tg. Neof. and the Fragmentary Targums suggests that the translators perceived the purpose of creation as the establishment of worship in the land.

83. Sailhamer, *Genesis Unbound*, 125. The word used for divide (בדל; v. 6) is a key term elsewhere in the Pentateuch in the legislation of the Mosaic Covenant (see for example Exod 26:33; Lev 10:10; 11:47; 20:25; Num 8:14). Its appearance here is one clue of many that the author is interested in the relationship between creation and the Sinai Covenant.

84. The centrality of the work of the Spirit throughout the Pentateuch strongly suggests that "Spirit" here is a better translation than "wind" (see Gen 41:38; Exod 31:3; 35:31; 11:29; Num 24:2; 27:18; Deut 34:9). For Coccejus' excellent treatment of this passage, see chapter 2, footnote 19.

And God remembered Noah and all the living creatures and all the cattle which were with him in the ark and *God* (אלהים) made a *wind* (רוח) to pass over the earth and the *water* (מים) receded and the springs of the *deep water* (תהום) were shut up. (Gen 8:1–2a).

And with the *breath* (רוח) of your nostrils the *water* (מים) was heaped up, it stood up like a heap of water, the *deep waters* (תהום, pl.) condensed in the heart of the sea (ים). (Exod 15:8).[85]

It is little wonder that Israel's initial entry into the Promised Land in the book of Joshua is described in terms that resonate with the Pentateuchal theme of the removal of water so that God's people could enjoy the good land.[86]

A confirmation that Gen 1:2 anticipates redemptive themes, such as the crossing of the Red Sea, is found in Deuteronomy 32, a song about the "last days" (Deut 31:29). There, a cluster of terms from the creation account—a cluster appearing nowhere else in the entire Hebrew Bible—describes Israel's redemption using these same terms: "He found him in a desert land and in an *uninhabitable* (תהו) howling wasteland, he surrounded him, he attentively considered him, he protected him as the apple of his eye. As an eagle stirs up its nest, *brooding* (ירחף) over its chicks, he carries him upon his pinions" (Deut 32:10–11).

Thus, the opening of the Pentateuch describes the land in the same condition in which we find it during the exilic period.[87] The allusions to redemption from an exilic situation, however, are intended to offer hope

---

85. See Exod 15:10; also Exod 14:21.

86. See Josh. 3:13, 16 (cf., Exod 15:8).

87. "I saw the land (הארץ) and behold it was uninhabitable (ובהו תהו), and the skies (השמים), and their light (אור) was not there . . . I saw and behold the man (האדם) was not there, and every flying creature (כל עוף) in the skies fled. I saw and behold the garden-land (כרמל), a desert" (Jer 4:23, 24–26a). The allusions to the creation account in Gen 1 are unmistakable. Moreover, Stordalen (*Echoes of Eden*, 36–40), in his exhaustive study of the word גן ("garden") includes כרמל ("garden-land") within its semantic range or sense relation. This suggests that the "garden-land" in v. 26 is a reference to the Garden of Eden. Jeremiah's interpretation of the creation account together with the Paradise Narrative as a coherent unit has at least two important implications for one's understanding of Gen 1–2. First, Jeremiah identifies the land in Gen 1 as the garden in Gen 2. Second, the absence of light in v. 23 is not the absence of the sun, but the darkness of a hopeless condition, suggesting that Gen 1:3 is also not describing the absence of the sun, but the state of a gloomy proto-exilic land. To recall, the syntax of Gen 1:14–16 does not depict God's creation of the luminaries but the establishment of their purpose.

to the reader:[88] God has not forgotten the land, nor has he forgotten his people. Just as God brooded over the land and his people in the primeval, pre-exilic past, so God continues to brood over the land and his people in the present. Just as God parted the waters in the "beginning" (and throughout Israel's history), so God will do the same for Israel in the future (see for example Isa 11:15–16; 43:2).

Prototypical Preparation of the Promised Land

Genesis 1 and 2 portray God as a loving father preparing the very best gift for his children (see Deut 32:6–7). Verse 2 describes the land in such a way that the land is foreshadowed in its eventual exilic state. The remainder of chapter 1 and also chapter 2 describe the preparation of the Promised Land much the same way that the later prophets describe God's future preparation of the Promised Land for the exiled people of God.[89] Oddly, the land is initially described with terms elsewhere used to describe the "desert" (a place without water) and at the same time as a place covered with water (surely not a desert). The point of using "mixed metaphors," however, is not to muddy the waters of linguistic clarity (excuse the pun). Rather, the author's selective use of descriptions of the land anticipates God's redemptive acts of bringing his people both through the "water" (Exod 14–15) and also the "desert" (Exod 15:22ff.) to bring them to the Promised Land.

In Gen 1:11–12, we are told that God covers the land with green grass and fruit trees. Later on in the Exodus Narrative, the same terms are also used of the destruction of the land of Egypt. The brooding of the רוח ("Spirit") in Genesis 1 intimates of "very good" things to come. For Egypt, however, the רוח ("wind") over the land (and also over the water, Exod 14:21) brings devastation in its wake (see Exod 10:13). Locusts cover the land and devour all the herbage (עשׂב) of the land, and all the fruit of the trees (פרי העץ) and nothing green (ירק) remains on the trees and of the herbage of the field (עשׂב השׂדה) in all the land of Egypt (com-

---

88. Although commenting on the limited theological concerns of the priestly writers, Brueggemann ("Kerygma," 413) lucidly describes the Pentateuchal hope of a return to the land from exile when he writes, "The kerygmatic key to priestly theology is that the promise of the land of blessing still endures and will be realized soon ... What I have argued is that the historical point of contact, the way in which exiled Israel experienced chaos and creation, was an exile and restoration."

89. See for example Isa 40–55.

pare Exod 10:15 with Gen 1:11–12, 29–30).[90] Later in the Pentateuch, however, the land of Canaan is described as a fruitful land (see Num 13:20, 27; Lev 26:4; Deut 1:25; 7:13). In a rehearsal of Israel's history, Jeremiah recalls God's having brought Israel out of Egypt, through the desert, and into a garden-land (כרמל) in order to eat its good fruit (see Jer 2:6–7). Moreover, Israel is also warned that one of the consequences for their disobedience would be the devouring of the fruit of the Promised Land (see Lev 26:20; Deut 28:33, 42, 51; see also Jer 7:20). The bounty of the Promised Land would be ravaged even as it had been in the land of Egypt due to God's judgment. In spite of Israel's transgression, God in his faithfulness will once again restore the fruitful bounty of the Promised Land in the future (Isa 4:2; 65:21; Ezek. 34:27; 47:12).

Prototypical Mandate to Conquer the Land

The language of the creation mandate provides an important thematic link between the land in Genesis 1–2 and the land of Canaan. Integral to God's purposes for the first humans is to take dominion (רדה) over all the created beings[91] (1:26b, 28b) and to conquer (כבש) the land (1:28a). The language of the creation mandate is both royal[92] and overtly militaristic.[93] Iain Provan, discussing the terminology of the creation mandate, writes, "The second verb (in English "subdue") is a translation of the Hebrew

90. Enns, *Exodus*, 204–5. Enns describes the plagues in terms of a "reversal of creation."

91. Lohfink, "Subdue the Earth?" 3, n. 6. Lohfink perceptively notes the text-critical problem in 1:26. He writes, "We do not expect to find the earth in the midst of the various groups of animals." Instead of "land," the Syriac has "animals" (חיה). He also suggests that the Syriac may be the preferred reading because elsewhere רדה always refers to the dominion over living things (see 1 Kgs 5:4; Ps 72:8). While I believe the MT preserves the better reading, Lohfink's observations suggest that the reference to the dominion over the *land* serves as an attention grabber.

92. Many scholars affirm the royal overtones of the creation mandate. See for example Hart, "Genesis 1:1—2:3," 324, 331; Provan, "Creation and Holistic Ministry," 297–98; Rowe, *God's Kingdom*, 55 n. 194; Schmutzer, "Creation Mandate," 156; Van Seters, "Creation of Man," 341; Westermann, *Genesis 1–11*, 158. Adam and Eve are portrayed as the first king and queen divinely appointed to rule over the Promised Land.

93. Keiser, "Genesis 1–11," 87–88; Lohfink, "Subdue the Earth?" 9; See Provan, "Creation and Holistic Ministry," 297–98; Schmutzer, "Creation Mandate," 143, 150–51. Concerning the Hebrew word כבש, Schmutzer (ibid., 150–51) writes, "As שבכ is used in the balance of the Old Testament, it shows harsh and even militaristic connotations. From the king's perspective, in Esther, for example, he believes Haman is 'assaulting' (כבש) the queen (7:8; cf. Neh 5:5)."

verb *kabash*. It is the language of conquest, usually military conquest. It reappears in passages like Numbers 32:22, 29 and Joshua 18:1, where we read of the land being 'subdued' before God and his people; or 2 Samuel 8:11, where we read of David 'subduing' all the nations. Warfare therefore lurks in the background of this verb."[94]

Its use here, however, gives rise to a legitimate question: Why would a "very good land" require such a militaristic (violent) take over?[95] Keiser points to this tension when he writes, "The utilization of כָּבַשׁ implies that the earth needs to be subdued, thus logically creating the impression that something within creation requires such action. But this notion goes against the nearly universal presupposition that God's creation was perfect in the sense of being unimprovable or finished."[96] Not only does this militaristic description motivate one to ask why the land needs to be conquered, but also who would need to be conquered in such an ideal place.

Both questions are resolved when Gen 1:26–28 is read within its immediate literary context (Gen 1–3) and within the Pentateuch as a whole: God's mandate to Adam and Eve to conquer the land and its inhabitant (the serpent) foreshadows God's mandate to Israel to conquer the land and its inhabitants (the Canaanites),[97] thus establishing a link between the land God gives to Adam and Eve and the land God gives to Abraham and his descendants. To put it in other terms, the whole earth belongs to God, but within the Pentateuch (and within the Hebrew Bible) there is only one land among many other lands that must be conquered for God's purposes to be fulfilled.

94. Provan, "Creation and Holistic Ministry," 297.

95. Lohfink's essay, "Subdue the Earth?" appears to be motivated by his discomfort with the thought of the human exploitation of the earth and its resources—a notion that is distasteful to modern sensibilities. He minimizes the force of this term by limiting his interpretation of Gen 1:28 to "P" theology. Some scholars, ancient and modern, attempt to downplay the militaristic overtones by understanding "subdue" as a reference to cultivation and caregiving or as an equivalent to "filling the earth." See for example, Cassuto, *Commentary*, 36 [Hebrew]; Fretheim, *Pentateuch*, 75; Miqraoth-Gedoloth, *Berayshit*, 44; Ramban.

96. Keiser, "Genesis 1–11," 88.

97. The term "Canaanite" is used generically for all inhabitants of Canaan, here and throughout the remainder of the book. The mandate to conquer the land and its inhabitants only finds ultimate fulfillment with the coming eschatological king who will conquer Israel's foes and reign over the land (see Num 24:19; Ps 72:8 [Zech. 9:10]; Ps 110:2).

Rashi appears to have understood Genesis 1 within the Pentateuchal theme of the conquest of Canaan as well. He writes,

> Rabbi Isaac said, "The Torah should have begun with 'This month is for you' (Exod 12:2) because it is the first commandment that was commanded to Israel." And what is the reason he began with Genesis? Because according to Ps 111:6, "He declared to his people the power of his works to give them the inheritance of the nations." That if the nations of the world should say to Israel, "You are robbers, because you conquered [כבשתם] the lands of seven nations," they [Israel] can say to them, "The whole land belongs to the Holy One blessed be He. He created it [ברא‎ה] and gave it to whomever he thought right in his eyes. It was his desire to give it to them and it was his desire to take it away from them and to give it to us."[98]

Here we see that Rashi regards Genesis 1 as a strategic introduction to the remainder of the Pentateuch and its central themes. Why does the Pentateuch begin the way it does? It does so in order to justify Israel's conquest of the Promised Land. His comments suggest that Rashi may have understood the "land" in Genesis 1 as the Promised Land ("lands of the seven nations") and not the entire earth. In this light, Rashi perceives a thematic link between the "creation mandate" and the divine mandate given to Israel to conquer the land from the Canaanites. Moreover, the accusation leveled against Israel (they are "robbers" who have forcibly taken the land from others) implies a militaristic understanding of the "conquest" in Gen 1:28 as well.

Like Rashi, Lohfink also perceives a connection between the wording of the creation mandate and later references to the conquering of the Promised Land. Lohfink writes, "Precisely in a text in which the verb *kbš* appears in a context that has a priestly echo and that has the *land* of Canaan as its object, namely Num 32:22, 29, the parallel passages in Deut 3:20, 31:3; Josh 1:15 show, with the word *yrš* used in the corresponding place, that what is at issue is that the land has become the possession of YHWH or of the Israelites."[99]

---

98. Miqraoth-Gedoloth, *Berayshit*, 2, 4 (Rashi on Gen 1:1; translation my own).

99. Lohfink, "Subdue the Earth?" 10. As noted earlier, however, Lohfink minimizes the militaristic connotations of the term "subdue" by regarding this term as a synonym of ירש. He writes, "It is therefore best to translate the text of Gen 1:28 also as undramatically as possible, somewhat as I have done above: 'Take possession of it [i.e., the earth].'"

The militaristic overtones of the creation mandate, therefore, make
sense only when understood as the prototypical mandate to conquer the
Promised Land.[100] The purpose of the militaristic terminology is not to
give license for the exploitation of the natural resources in the world.
Rather, it prepares the reader for understanding what should have been
Adam and Eve's response to the serpent in Genesis 3, and also supplies
Israel with their marching orders in the remainder of the Pentateuch
(and in the Tanakh).[101] The author employs this terminology in order
to establish a link between God's purposes in the "beginning" and his
ultimate purposes in the "end." The royal terminology used in the creation mandate suggests that Adam is the prototypical king who is called
to conquer the Promised Land.[102] The depiction of Adam, a conquering king in the time of the ראשית ("beginning"), provides the proto-
logical template for the coming of another conquering king in the time
of the אחרית ("end") who, unlike Adam, will successfully conquer the
Promised Land (see Num 24:14, 19; Ps 2:8). When interpreted within the
compositional strategy of the Pentateuch, therefore, God's purposes for
humanity do not come to fruition until the land promised to Abraham
is ultimately under the regal authority of Abraham's Seed (Gen 3:15; Pss
72:8; 110:2).

Once the creation mandate is interpreted in the light of the compositional strategy of the Pentateuch, another exegetical issue is resolved

---

100. Bovell, "Genesis 3:21?" 365: "The phrase 'subdue the land' appears again in
Numbers 32:22, 29 and Joshua 18:1 to refer to the driving out of the enemies with clear
intentions of occupation. There is no reason to apologize for the strong language here.
The ability to subdue the land is part of God's *blessing*, and the welfare of Israel in later
narratives tends to be evaluated in terms of their success in dispossessing the land of its
ungodly inhabitants. Genesis 1 had opened the door for an antagonist even in contrast
to domesticated animals; they are the hallmark of a dangerous, uninhabitable land."

101. The fact that the creation mandate already anticipates the temptation narrative
strongly supports the unity of Genesis 1–3. The creation mandate to militaristically
conquer the land makes no sense when it is isolated from the identification of the antagonist who must be conquered.

102. Westermann, *Genesis 1–11*, 158, 161: "The verb רדה means 'to tread the wine
press' in Joel 4:13; it means 'to subdue' in Num 24:19 and Lev 26:17, and is used of the
dominion of the king in 1 Kgs 5:4; Pss 110:2; 72:8; Isa 14:6; Ezek 34:4 . . . The second verb
[כבש], like רדה, belongs to the context of subordination or domination. In the Qal it is
used of slaves: Jer 34:11, 16; Neh 5:5; 2 Chr 28:10; in the Niphal it is used of a land which
has been brought into subjection: Num 32:22, 29; Josh 18:1; 1 Chr 22:18. It is possible
that this verb too derives from the rule of the king . . . even though it is not used in this
context in the Old Testament." (Words in brackets provided.)

as well. From whom do Adam and Eve need to conquer the land? The unexplained presence of a seditious entity in the paradisiacal garden has long perplexed interpreters and readers of the Bible alike. Why is it there? How did it come to be the way it is? Was there a fall of Satan during a supposed time gap between verses 1 and 2 in Genesis 1? Sousan succinctly summarizes this exegetical bewilderment created by the appearance of the serpent when he writes,

> What can be the reason for the intervention of the serpent? This question is perplexing. Generally, the arrival of the serpent has been seen as "absolutely inexplicable"; for W. Zimmerli, followed by Westermann and by H-J. Fabry, "It appears suddenly [and] will remain there as a riddle"; for Trible, the serpent's motives are "obscure" and could be a literary artifice used to raise the issue of life and death; likewise, B. Vawter considers the serpent as "the symbol of an unexplained source of mischief and wrong for which no accounting is given." Jacob holds that the serpent is a metaphor for the evil inclination . . . and for ἡδονή, Philo's term for the sensual desire that incites to transgress the divine prohibition; he writes that the "envious, cunning, and animalistic thoughts of man are put in the mouth of an animal for they arise from the animal in man;" however, he does not explain why such thoughts would arise. Cassuto follows suit, although he recognizes that in popular belief the serpent is a symbol of Leviathan, over which God will triumph (Isa 27:1); he sees the serpent as a "principle of evil" which manifests itself through the woman when she looks at the forbidden fruit, and which, as God told Cain (Gen 4:7), needs to be dominated, for it always "lies in wait for man."[103]

Traditional Jewish and Christian exegetes have identified the "serpent" as Satan. Attempts have also been made to identify the role of the serpent by means of comparative studies and extra-biblical sources from the ANE.[104] Others have argued that the serpent is a symbol of the Canaanite fertility cults.[105] Westermann has challenged the latter view, however, because Gen 3:1 specifically states that God made the serpent. How could God be the originator of Canaanite fertility cults?[106]

103. Sousan, "Woman in Eden," 154–55.

104. Wenham, *Genesis 1–15*, 72–73; see the brief history of interpretation in Wolde, "Reader-Oriented Exegesis," 15–17.

105. Among those holding this position, according to Westermann (*Genesis 1–11*, 237), are J. A. Soggin; J. L. McKenzie, J. Daniélou, J. Coppens, and O. Loretz.

106. Ibid., 238.

The solution to this exegetical mystery, in my opinion, is found in a text-centered approach. While the serpent is "absolutely inexplicable" in isolation from the compositional strategy of the Pentateuch, its role is quite clear when Genesis 1–3 is interpreted as the introduction to the Pentateuch. The most likely explanation for the serpent is its role as a prototypical Canaanite.[107] It is the "original" evil inhabitant of the land.[108] The author's purpose is not to offer the reader exhaustive details about the identity of the serpent; rather, the intention is to give the reader insight about the present inhabitants of the land by looking at their "forefather" (Gen 3:15). Thus, Adam's entrance into the garden to conquer the serpent anticipates Israel's entrance into the Promised Land to conquer the Canaanites. Adam is "brought"[109] (Gen 2:15) into a good land wherein dwells an evil inhabitant. This inhabitant must be subdued. Later, Israel is "brought" into a good land wherein evil inhabitants dwell. Israel, like Adam, must subdue them (Lev 18:1–5).[110] As we shall see, Adam and Eve's failure to subdue this inhabitant and their fall into temptation foreshadows Israel's eventual failure to totally subdue the Canaanites and their fall into temptation.

Several clues in the text itself suggest that the author intended the reader to identify the serpent as the "forefather" of the later Canaanites. First, the temptation narrative (Gen 3) is set upon the stage of human sexuality (Gen 2:25). The Sinaitic legislation regarding the exposure and covering of nakedness is frequently motivated by a warning about the practices of the inhabitants of the land of Canaan (see Gen 9:22; Lev 18:6–7, 24–25). An explicit connection between sexual immorality and the Canaanites appears as early as Genesis 9. Second, the literary parallels between Noah's fall and Adam's fall link the "cursed" serpent in Genesis 3

---

107. This identification also answers Westermann's query. While God is not the originator of the Canaanite fertility cults, he certainly is the originator of the Canaanites, a fact that is confirmed by the genealogies of Genesis.

108. Although this link does not explain why God made Eden with a snake or Canaan with Canaanites, it is important to keep in mind that the author's purpose for looking at the past is primarily to explain the present and the future, not to answer all our philosophical, historical, and theological struggles about the past.

109. Many scholars have argued that the verb employed for "bring" (נוח) in Gen 2:15 is the standard term for Israel's possession of the land (see Deut 12:9; 25:19; 1 Kgs 8:56). See for example Blenkinsopp, *Pentateuch*, 66.

110. Ibid. Blenkinsopp, who also interprets Gen 2–3 as replication of the course of the Primary History, regards the serpent as a symbol of the cults practiced by the native inhabitants of the land. See also Bovell, "Genesis 3:21?" 362–64.

with the "cursed" Canaan in Genesis 9. Sailhamer points to the following literary parallels between the transgression of Adam and the drunkenness of Noah:[111] Both narratives record the "planting" (ויטע) of a garden/orchard (Gen 2:8; 9:20). In both narratives, an individual(s) partakes of the "fruit" and finds himself "naked" and "uncovered" (3:6–7; 9:21). In both narratives, the "nakedness" of the "fallen" character(s) is "covered" (3:21; 9:23). The author depicts Noah's sin as a replication of Adam's sin. In this light a necessary detail emerges for determining the identity of the serpent's "seed" in Gen 3:15. Canaan and the serpent are parallel figures, thereby establishing a textual link between the Canaanites and the serpent:

And the Lord God said to the serpent ... "Cursed are you." (Gen 3:14)	And he said, "Cursed is Canaan." (Gen 9:25)

The parallels between Adam's Fall and Noah's Fall suggest that the curse pronounced on Canaan is intended to link the original inhabitant of the land to the subsequent inhabitants of the Land. The exploitation of human sexuality in the garden by the original inhabitant of the land[112] becomes indicative of the behavior of the subsequent inhabitants of the land.

Third, the early introduction of Canaan in the Pentateuch (Gen 9:18) and the abundance of details regarding the peoples descended from Canaan as well as the description of their territory according to specific borders in the Table of Nations (Gen 10:15–19)[113] reinforces the likelihood that the Canaanites and their land are already in focus in Genesis 1–3 as well. A primary concern of the creation mandate, therefore, is the reality of Adam and Eve's unfinished business and the need for the eventual subduing of the godless inhabitants of the land (Gen 3:15). It may simply be an example of a lexical coincidence, but it is worth mentioning that even the name "Canaan" (כנען) comes from a root that also means "to subdue." This root is used elsewhere in the context of God's promise to Israel that he would "subdue" the inhabitants of Canaan for his people: "And you shall know today that the LORD your God is the one who is

111. Sailhamer, *Pentateuch as Narrative*, 129–30.

112. I am not arguing that the serpent engaged in sexually illicit relations with Eve, but merely pointing to the fact that the temptation takes place in the context of human sexuality.

113. Alexander, *From Paradise*, 135.

passing before you, a consuming fire, he will destroy them and he will
subdue them (יכניעם) before you, and you will dispossess them and you
will destroy them quickly, just as the Lord spoke to you." (Deut 9:3) Thus,
the Canaanites' name memorializes their ultimate fate: submission.

Jewish commentators apparently perceived a textual link between
the serpent and the Canaanites as well. Commenting on the curse of the
serpent in Gen 3:14, the ancient rabbis quote Rabbi Levi as follows: "In
the eschatological future everything will be healed except the serpent
and the Gibeonites. The serpent of whom it is written (Isa 65:25), 'And
the serpent's food is the dust. They will do no harm and they will not act
corruptly, etc.' The Gibeonites (Ezek 48:19), 'And the workers of the city
will serve it from all the tribes of Israel.'"[114]

At first sight, the rationale for associating the serpent and the
Gibeonites on the basis of an obscure verse in Ezekiel is not apparent.[115]
Yet, the textual data in Joshua 9 suggests that the author of Joshua intentionally draws a parallel between the Gibeonites' deception of Israel and
the serpent's deception of Adam and Eve. In the larger context of the
book of Joshua, Joshua, like Adam, is a royal figure[116] who is also called to
"conquer" (Josh 1:3; 18:1) the Promised Land[117] by subduing its evil inhabitants. The author of Joshua is well aware of Israel's eventual failure to
fulfill the "creation mandate" (Josh 24:20; see Deut 31:28–29), namely, to
totally subdue the evil inhabitants of the land. Joshua 9 should be understood as a sneak preview of the initial compromises with the inhabitants
of the land that eventually lead to Israel's following after the Canaanite
practices. The Gibeonites, after having heard of Israel's military success
(v. 24), trick Joshua into entering into a covenantal relationship (v. 6).
Such a relationship is explicitly forbidden by the Lord in the law (Exod
23:32–33).

According to verse 4, the Gibeonites distinguish themselves from
among all the other inhabitants of the land (vv. 1–3) by acting "craft-
ily" (בערמה), a word used only this once in the Former Prophets (Josh–

114. Kantrowitz, *Judaic Classics Library*, Gen. Rab. 20.5. (Translation from Hebrew
my own.)

115. According to Josh 9:23 (see v. 27), the punishment for the Gibeonite deception
is that they would never cease to be servants (slaves) of the temple. In Ezekiel, however,
those who serve in the eschatological temple and city will be from all the tribes of the
house of Israel. The Midrash attempts to resolve this apparent contradiction.

116. Compare Josh 1:7–8 with Deut 17:19–20.

117. Compare Josh. 1:4 with Gen 2:10–14.

2 Kgs).[118] The use of this term to describe their behavior clearly echoes the behavior of the serpent who is also described as being more "prudent/shrewd" (ערום) than all the other animals (inhabitants) of the land (Gen 3:1).[119] Once Joshua discovers he has been tricked, he says, "Why have you *deceived* (רמה) us?" an accusation that resonates with Eve's accusation of the serpent in the garden (Gen 3:13).[120] Immediately after Joshua accuses the Gibeonites he pronounces a curse upon them, "Cursed are you" (ארורים אתם; v. 23), much like God, upon accusing the serpent, pronounced a curse upon it: "Cursed are you" (ארור אתה; Gen 3:14). The Gibeonites' perpetual state of servitude serves as a link to the perpetual humiliation of the serpent (i.e., crawling on the belly and eating dust, Gen 3:14) and also to the curse on Canaan as a "servant of servants to his brothers" (Gen 9:25).[121] The midrashic association of the Gibeonites and the serpent appears, therefore, to be warranted by details from the text itself.[122]

In light of all that has been said, therefore, the creation mandate sets the stage for the drama about to take place in the garden. God prepares a "very good land" (see Num 14:7) to give to Adam and Eve as a gift. The possession of this "good land" is contingent on Adam's obedience to the Lord's commandments. These commandments include the conquering of the "prudent/shrewd" inhabitant and dietary restrictions. This depiction of Adam and Eve is not coincidentally related to Israel's story, but integrally and strategically linked to it. In the following section I discuss the foreshadowing of the Sinai Covenant in Genesis 1–3. There I argue that Adam and Eve's relationship with God is essentially a proto-Sinaitic relationship with the Creator, the purpose of which is to demonstrate the certainty of Israel's failure under the Sinai Covenant and the need for a future work of grace.

118. Elsewhere, this word appears three times in Proverbs (1:4; 8:5, 12) and once in Exodus (21:14).

119. This meaning of this term is discussed in a subsequent section.

120. The word for "deceive" is different in Gen 3:13 (נשא, hi.).

121. "The lowest servant."

122. For a biblical defense of the exegetical practices of midrashic interpretation, see Seeligmann, "Voraussetzungen."

THE SINAI COVENANT IN GENESIS 1–3

Critical scholars have uniformly identified Gen 1:1—2:4a as "P."[123] This identification is made on the basis of distinctive vocabulary and phrases,[124] literary style,[125] festive concerns,[126] the provision of dietary restrictions and the classification of various creatures according to their kinds,[127] statements of inspection and benediction unique to the creation account and the construction of the tabernacle (and later temple),[128] and the use of the divine name Elohim.[129] Regardless of the existence of a hypothetical priestly source, one can say with great confidence that the Sinai Covenant plays a central role in the compositional strategy of Genesis 1.[130] Unfortunately, the division of Genesis 1–3 into two different sources ("P" and "J") blurs the fact that Genesis 2–3 is equally concerned with the Sinai Covenant and its legislation. While Genesis 1 foreshadows the construction of the tabernacle, Genesis 2–3 (Eden) anticipates the physical appearance of it.

---

123. See for example, Bernhard Anderson, *From Creation to New Creation*, 45, 48; Bauks, "Genesis 1 als Programmschrift"; Firmage, "Genesis 1"; König, *Genesis*, 132; Levenson, 100; Wenham, *Genesis 1-15*, xxxi, 1–40; Westermann, *Genesis 1-11*, 18.

124. Such as בדל (Gen 1:4, 7; Exod 26:33; Lev 20:25, 26; Num 8:14); מין + ל + pronominal suffix (Gen 1:11, 12, 21, 24-25; 6:20; 7:14; Lev 11:14, 16, 19, 22, 29); זרע *hiphal* (Gen 1:11, 12; Lev 12:2); מאור, used both in the plural and the singular as a reference to the light of the sun and moon in Gen 1:14, 15, 16; elsewhere in the Pentateuch, however, it is used as a reference to the lampstand in the tabernacle or its light (Exod 25:6; 27:20; 35:8, 14, 28; 39:37; Lev 24:2; Num 4:9, 16); שרץ (Gen 1:20–21; 7:21; 8:17; 9:7; Exod 1:7; 7:28; Lev 11:29, 41–43, 46); רמש (Gen 1:21, 26, 28; 7:14, 21; 8:17; Lev 11:44, 46); פרו ורבו ומלאו (Gen 1:22, 28; 9:1); נפש חיה (Gen 1:24, 30; 9:12, 15, 16; but also Gen 2:7, 19).

125. The use of "seven" and its denominators are pervasive in Gen 1:1—2:3 and throughout the Sinaitic legislation as well.

126. The purpose of the luminaries to mark the "appointed times" (מועדים; Gen 1:14; Lev 23:2) clearly anticipates the Sinai Covenant. The land has been divinely designed with the Sinai Covenant in mind. The Sabbath is depicted as the pinnacle of the preparation of the land (Gen 2:1-3) as well; see Dumbrell, "Genesis 2:1-17," 55; Levenson, *Creation*, 109–110.

127. Gen 1:29-30; 9:3; Leviticus 11.

128. Gen 1:31; 2:1-3; Exod 39:43; 40:33; see also 1 Kgs 7:40; 8:14.

129. Wenham, *Genesis 1-15*, 38-39: "Gen 1 has been called a festive overture to P, for it introduces themes that are characteristic of and developed in much greater detail in other priestly material later in the Pentateuch. By tracing back to creation the classificatory system among plants and animals, the Sabbath, and the origins of divine blessing, the writer is giving these institutions the authority of primeval antiquity. Though there is little in the chapter that relates directly to worship, the prime interest of the P material, the references to the fixed times (v. 14), and to the seventh day (2:1-3) may be construed as hints of the editor's preoccupation with the cult."

130. Sailhamer, *Pentateuch as Narrative*, 28-29.

While Adam is a "king" in Genesis 1, he is a prototypical "Sinaitic priest" in chapters 2–3. The ongoing possession of Eden on the basis of obedience to commandments, the theme of curse and blessing, and even the structure of the divine curses in Gen 3:14–19,[131] all presume essential components of the Sinai Covenant as well.

Many scholars recognize the above-mentioned links between the Sinai Covenant and Genesis 1–3. But it is generally assumed that these links serve to provide a pre-Sinaitic rationale, basis, and apologetic for the ongoing maintenance of the Sinai Covenant. In other words, Genesis 1–3 is intended to encourage the reader to keep the Sinai Covenant. Is this the case? Do these chapters in fact function as a prologue to the Sinai Covenant and its legislation, or is it more fitting to regard the introduction to the Torah as a prophetic commentary on Israel's historical experiences under the Sinai Covenant and their need for divine intervention? These questions are vital for evaluating the theological intentions of the Pentateuch in its final form. To address these questions I will begin by looking at the depiction of Adam as a "prototypical Israel" (as well as Israel's prototypical king) serving God under a "prototypical Sinai Covenant."

131. The curse in Gen 3 not only provides the *raison d'être* for the purity laws (Lev 11–15) but also the outline for their structure as well. Scholars have recognized the obviously literary affinities of the animals listed in the dietary laws (Lev 11) with those described in the creation account in Gen 1. But if one considers Gen 2–3 in light of Lev 11, the details provided about the serpent in Gen 3 presume knowledge of the dietary laws as well. Significantly, after the serpent seduces Eve, he is doomed to "crawl on his belly" (תלך על גחנך; Gen 3:14), a phrase elsewhere only appearing in Lev 11:42. And in Gen 1–3 as well as Lev 11, the serpent is the last of the animals to be mentioned. Moreover, while it has often been pointed out that Eve adds to the Lord's commands in Gen 3:3, "do not eat … do not touch" (לא תגעו … לא תאכלו), many have failed to notice the fact that the juxtaposition of these two verbal phrases ("do not eat … do not touch") is only found elsewhere in the legislation of the dietary laws (Lev 11:8; Deut 14:8). Eve's conversation with a serpent, the most detestable of all unclean foods, about dietary laws appears almost comical. Turning again to the structure of the purity laws, it is important to note that following the dietary laws (Lev 11) come instructions related to the uncleanness of a woman in childbirth (Lev 12:2ff.; אשה + ילד), described with language strikingly similar to the curse in Gen 3:16. The final section of purity laws relate to a man (אדם) and his skin (see Lev 13:2ff.; Gen 3:17–19, 21), again reminiscent of the immediate effects of the curse upon Adam's skin. Thus, the resemblance of the structure of the purity laws (serpent crawling on belly + a woman in child birth + a man and his skin) to the poetic structure of the curse in Gen 3 is likely not fortuitous. For a recent attempt to argue that the purity laws are structurally related to the curse in Gen 3, see Kiuchi, *Leviticus*, 29, 38–40. For a similar position on the relationship of the curses and the purity laws, see Sailhamer, *Pentateuch as Narrative*, 39–41. For support regarding an intentional link between Gen 3:14 and Lev 11:42, see Alter, *Five Books of Moses*, 588.

Prototypical Tabernacle and Priesthood

Above I noted how critical scholars identify Genesis 1 as "P" because of its numerous affinities with other purportedly priestly sources, most notably the Tabernacle Narrative (Exod 25–31, 35–40). P. J. Kearny persuasively argues that the giving of the design for the tabernacle in seven divine speeches (Exod 25:1; 30:11, 17, 22, 34; 31:1, 12) is patterned after the seven-day creation week.[132] The Sabbath's appearance in the seventh divine speech coupled with the use of כלה ("complete") at the conclusion of the tabernacle's blueprints strongly suggests that the association of the giving of the tabernacle and the seven-day preparation of the Promised Land is intentional (see Exod 31:12–17, 18; Gen 2:1–2).

Table 4. Comparison: Seven Days of Preparation and Seven Divine Speeches

Seven Days of Preparation	Seven Divine Speeches
Day 1: Gen 1:5	Speech 1: Exod 25:1
Day 2: Gen 1:8	Speech 2: Exod 30:11
Day 3: Gen 1:13	Speech 3: Exod 30:17
Day 4: Gen 1:19	Speech 4: Exod 30:22
Day 5: Gen 1:23	Speech 5: Exod 30:34
Day 6: Gen 1:31	Speech 6: Exod 31:1
Day 7: Gen 2:1–3: SABBATH	Speech 7: Exod 31:12: SABBATH

Other conspicuous parallels between Genesis 1 and the tabernacle also exist. Michael Fishbane (and also Peter Enns) notes that "the closing chapters of the Book of Exodus disclose unmistakable echoes of the language of Genesis 1:1—2:4*a*."[133] In both accounts, there is (1) a statement that the "work" (מלאכה) of construction is "complete" (כלה; Exod 40:33; see 39:32; Gen 2:1); (2) an "inspection" (וירא את כל ... והנה, "and he saw everything ... and behold") of the completed work (Exod 39:43; Gen 1:31); and (3) a "benediction" (ויברך) of the completed work (Exod 39:43; Gen 1:22, 28; 2:3). In both accounts, the "Spirit of God" (רוח אלהים) appears as the empowering agent of creation (Gen 1:2; Exod 31:3).[134] Finally, following both accounts there is a Fall Narrative (Gen 3;

132. Kearney, "Creation and Liturgy," 375.

133. Fishbane, *Biblical Text*, 12. Enns, *Exodus*, 550–52.

134. Enns, *Exodus*, 543; Sailhamer, *Pentateuch as Narrative*, 309.

Exod 32), which is introduced by the word בוש ("to shame one another," "delayed;" יתבששו, בשש) in the *hithpolel/polel* stem (Gen 2:25; Exod 32:1).[135]

Table 5. Comparison of Preparation of the Land and Tabernacle

	Consummation of Preparation of the Land	Consummation of Preparation of the Tabernacle[136]
Statement of Completion	"By the seventh day God completed (כלה) his work (מלאכה) which he had done." (Gen 2:2)	"And Moses completed (כלה) the work (מלאכה)." (Exod 40:33b; see 39:32)
Inspection	"And God saw (וירא) everything (את כל) which he made, and behold (והנה), it was very good." (Gen 1:31a)	"And Moses saw (וירא) all (את כל) the work, and behold (והנה) they did it just as the Lord commanded, thus they did." (Exod 39:43a)
Benediction	"And God blessed them (ויברך אתם)." (Gen 1:22, 28; see 2:3)	"And Moses blessed them (ויברך אתם)." (Exod 39:43b)
Role of God's Spirit	"And the Spirit of God (רוח אלהים) was brooding over the surface of the waters." (Gen 1:2)	"And I have filled him with the Spirit of God (רוח אלהים), with wisdom, with understanding, and with the knowledge of all work."
Fall Narrative Introduced with ב-ש-ש[137]	"And they did not shame one another (יתבששו)." (Gen 2:25b)	"And the people saw that Moses delayed (בשש) to descend from the mountain."

135. Erlich ("Story of Garden," 25) argues that the use of the root בוש in the *polel* and *hithpolel*, only in Gen 2:25 and Exod 32:1, is intentional.

136. A case can be made that the actual completion of the tabernacle is reported in Num 7:1, where the sanctuary is sanctified and the tools are anointed. Even there, the language clearly resonates with Gen 2:1ff., namely, the completion of creation and the sanctification of the seventh day. The tabernacle in essence becomes a perpetual "seventh-day" space for the people of Israel.

137. I am aware that ב-ש-ש is not the root of either of these verbs. The similarity of these verbs and their location at the introduction of two compositionally strategic Fall Narratives in the Pentateuch, however, amongst the many other innertextual parallels, leads me to believe that the resemblance here is intentional.

The parallels linking God's preparation of the Promised Land (Gen 1) and Israel's preparation of the tabernacle (Exod 25–31, 35–40) set the narrative stage for the author's depiction of the Garden of Eden in Genesis 2–3. The implicit link between Genesis 1 and the tabernacle becomes more explicit in Genesis 2–3. The Garden of Eden, much like Mount Sinai later in Exodus, serves as the divine template for the tabernacle's (and temple's) design. According to Wenham, the Garden of Eden is portrayed as an archetypal sanctuary, "a place where God dwells and where man should worship him. Many of the features of the garden may also be found in later sanctuaries, particularly the tabernacle or Jerusalem temple. These parallels suggest that the garden itself is understood as a sort of sanctuary."[138]

Jewish and Christian scholars alike have noticed numerous links between the Garden of Eden and the tabernacle.[139] Wenham enumerates eight parallels:

1. The verb "walk" (התהלך) in Gen 3:8 is also used to described God's presence in the tabernacle (Lev 26:12; Deut 23:14).

2. The cherubim who guard access to the tree of life on the east (Gen 3:24) are also embroidered on the tabernacle's curtains and stand guard over the ark. The tabernacle, like Eden, is entered from the east (Gen 3:24; Exod 25:18–22; 26:31).

3. The design of the menorah in the form of a seven-branched tree with fruit is highly suggestive of the fruit trees in Eden and the Tree of Life (Exod 25:32–36).

4. The terms "cultivate" (עבד) and "keep" (שמר), used to describe Adam's occupation in the garden, are terms most frequently used elsewhere in the Pentateuch (Gen 2:15; Num 3:7–8; 8:26; 18:5–6) to describe the Levites' occupation in the tabernacle. This phrase is also used to describe obedience to the precepts of Sinai (see Deut 13:5).[140]

---

138. Wenham, "Sanctuary Symbolism," 399.

139. See, for example, Rashi's comments on Lev 26:12.

140. The juxtaposition of עבד and שמר in Gen 2:15 as terms specifically tied to the service of God in the Mosaic legislation was clearly noticed by the translators of the early Targums. Frg. Tg. P renders עבד as למיהוי פלח באוריתיה ("to serve the Torah") and שמר as למיטר פיקודוי ("to observe the commandments"); see also Frg. Tg. VNL, Tg. Neof., and Tg. Ps-J.

5. The phrase "to clothe with tunics" (לבשׁ hiphal + כתנת) in Gen 3:21 is only used elsewhere in the Pentateuch to describe garments for the priests (Exod 29:5, 8; 40:14; 8:13 [see also Lev 16:4; 8:7]). These garments were intended to cover their nakedness (see Exod 20:26).

6. The precious materials in the garden or in its vicinity—gold, onyx, and bdellium (Gen 2:12)—are found in abundance in the tabernacle. Gold is the primary metal for much of the tabernacle's furnishings as well as the vestures of the high priest. Onyx is used for decorating the tabernacle, temple, and high priestly vestments and breastplate (Exod 25:7; 28:9–14, 20). Bdellium is the term used to describe the appearance of the manna which was stored in the ark in the Holy of Holies (Num 11:7).

7. The Tree of the Knowledge of Good and Evil is suggestive of the Book of the Law stored in the Holy of Holies (Exod 25:16; Deut 31:26; see Ps 19:8–9).[141]

8. The description of the garden as the source of abundantly flowing water (2:10–14), though not present in the tabernacle's design, is a typical description for later sanctuaries in the Scripture (Ps 46:5; Ezek 47). One of the names of the rivers surrounding the garden, Gihon (Gen 2:13), is also the name given to the water source surrounding Jerusalem (1 Kgs 1:33, 38, 45; 2 Chr 32:30; 33:14).[142]

What purpose do these parallels serve in the final form Pentateuch? In one real sense, the garden serves as the prototypical reality of which the tabernacle serves only as a copy or a type (see Exod 25:9, 40; 26:30; Num 8:4). The tabernacle and its operation are permeated with an aroma of Eden. A link is forged between God's creation purposes and the construction of the tabernacle, whereby the Mosaic tabernacle and its priesthood perpetuate, albeit imperfectly, the "sanctuary" in Eden and its "priesthood." When interpreted through the wider lens of the creation mandate to conquer the land, moreover, the preservation of the prototypical sanctuary from all uncleanness is integral to Adam's priestly role

---

141. This is the weakest of all possible parallels noted by Wenham.
142. Wenham, "Sanctuary Symbolism," 399–404.

(see Num 3; Lev 10:11).[143] What better animal could have been chosen
for the antagonist to Adam's vocation than a serpent, for the serpent embodies more than the sexual perversity of the future inhabitants of the
land; it also represents the epitome of all uncleanness in the dietary laws
(see Lev 11:42–43; Gen 3:14). Thus, these innertextual links anticipate
Israel's service to God in the wilderness and eventually in the Promised
Land. So far Adam is not only the forerunner of Israel's "future," but
its embodiment. Adam is "brought in" to the Promised Land/Garden
Sanctuary to fulfill royal and priestly duties (see Exod 19:4–6).

Prototypical Sinai Covenant

The goal of this section is to argue that Adam and Eve's relationship with
God—the contingency of their enjoyment of the land, their duties in
the garden, and the consequences of their disobedience—foreshadows
Israel's life under the Sinai Covenant.

In the introduction to this study I discussed the work of Sousan
at length. Sousan interprets Genesis 2–3 as a metaphor of the prophets'
interpretation of the Sinai Covenant, namely, as the marriage between
God and his people. Thus, the narrative plot of Genesis 2–3, according
to Sousan, outlines God's program for Israel. God brings Adam from the
desert (Gen 2:5) to a paradisiacal garden. Adam's ongoing possession of
the garden is contingent upon the keeping of the commandment not
to eat of the tree. According to Sousan, the plot "has a covenantal character that recalls the transport of Israel from a desert to the Promised
Land under the terms of the Covenant at Sinai."[144] Many scholars, like
Sousan, argue that this plot flows from the covenant theology found in
Deuteronomy and, later on, in the Deuteronomistic History.[145] Schökel,
for instance, noticed connections between Genesis 2–3 and key passages
in the Pentateuch as well as later events in the biblical history (Joshua 1
to 2 Kings 25). The parallels noted by Schökel include (1) the narrative
depiction of covenant-sin-punishment-reconciliation in Adam/Israel's

---

143. Schmutzer, "Creation Mandate," 348: "Just as Eden is God's garden-sanctuary,
the prototypical temple, so the terms 'keeping and guarding' ... are used for priests who
'serve' God in the temple and 'guard' it from all unclean things."

144. Sousan, "Woman in Garden," 176.

145. Blenkinsopp, *The Pentateuch*, 66; Gardner, "Gen 2:4b—3," 15; Otto, "Paradieserzählung Genesis 2–3," 172; Schmitt, "Spätdeuteronomistische Geschichtswerk,"
261–79; Schökel, "Motivos Sapienciales," 305–6.

covenantal relationship with God in Genesis 2–3 and in Exodus 19–34;[146] (2) the depiction of Adam's being taking from outside the garden and placed ("rested"[147]) inside it and Israel's being brought from outside the land of Canaan and being placed inside it;[148] (3) Adam's downfall following his "cleaving" to a woman and the downfall of Israel at Baal Peor as well as the downfall of Israel's subsequent kings due to their having cleaved to seductive women; (4) the apodictic laws of the garden and the apodictic laws of Sinai; and (5) the covenantal style of the consequences of disobedience in the garden, such as curses and exile, and the consequences of disobedience to the Sinai Covenant.

Without trying to repeat what has already been said, I believe it would be helpful to put forward several reasons in support of viewing Genesis 1–3 as the establishment of a prototypical Sinai Covenant between God and Adam (and Eve). First, the literary design of Genesis 1–3 suggests that it has been composed with the Sinai Covenant in view. This is evidenced in the following ways. First, the pattern of creation/fall/restoration in Genesis 1–3 anticipates the preparation of the tabernacle (Exod 25–31), and the fall and restoration of Israel in the Golden Calf Narrative (Exod 32–34). Second, the structure of the curses and their effects on the serpent (animal; Gen 3:14–15), the woman (Gen 3:16), and the man (Gen 3:17–19) anticipate the structure of and rationale for the

---

146. Otto ("Paradieserzählung Genesis 2–3," 178, 191–92) argues that the fixed sequence of creation/fall/restoration in the Primeval History is patterned after the Sinai pericope as a whole. In other words, Gen 2–3 has been composed with the Sinai Narrative in mind.

147. This is a stock term for Israel's future possession of the Promised Land, the root of which bears the notion of "rest" (see Deut 3:20; 12:10; Josh 1:13, 15; 22:4). The theme of "rest" is pervasive in the Flood Narrative, forging a link between the loss of rest in Gen 3 (the curse) and the temporary restoration of rest from the curse (see Gen 5:29) through Noah (נוח), whose name means "rest." The root "נוח" as well as words sharing two of its consonants (ח-נ) provide cohesion and coherence to the narrative block as a whole. "Noah" (נוח) "brings comfort" (נחם) from the curse (Gen 5:29). God is "sorry" (נחם) that he made mankind (Gen 6:6a, 7b), but "Noah" finds "favor" (חן) in God's eyes. The ark "rests" (נוח) on the mountain in the seventh month (Gen 8:4a), but the dove sent out from the ark finds no "rest" (מנוח) for its feet (Gen 8:9a). The Flood Narrative reaches its conclusion when "Noah" offers an offering with a soothing aroma (ניחוח, from the root "נוח"). The association of the "land" and "rest" in the remainder of the Pentateuch suggests that "rest" is a key theme in the book. On the importance of "rest" in the Pentateuch and also in the Prophets, see Sailhamer, *Genesis Unbound*, 149.

148. See Gen 2:15; Deut 3:20; 30:3–4; Josh. 1:13, 15; Jer 27:11; Ezek. 36:34; 37:14, 21; Isa 14:1.

Purity Code in Leviticus 11–15.[149] Third, the language used to describe the appearance (theophany) of God in the garden for Adam and Eve's "trial" and their fearful retreat suggest that this passage was composed in light of God's appearance to Israel on Mount Sinai and Israel's fearful retreat.[150] Finally, the description of Eve's temptation, Adam and Eve's fearful retreat, and the provision of covering for their nakedness also anticipate the structure of the Sinai pericope. Adam and Eve's violation of the commandment is depicted as an infraction against the tenth commandment (compare Gen 3:6 and Exod 20:17). In Wenham's words: "The woman's covetousness is described in terminology that foreshadows the tenth commandment. 'Delight,' תאוה, and 'desirable,' נחמד, are from roots meaning 'to covet' (Deut 5:21; see also Exod 20:17)."[151]

Having violated the tenth commandment, Adam and Eve distance themselves from God because of fear (Gen 3:8). Although they feebly attempt to cover their nakedness, God provides a covering (Gen 3:21). In similar fashion, God appears to the people in Exodus 19:19. The people hear the Decalogue (Exod 20:1–17), in which the tenth commandment forbids coveting (v. 17). The narrative picks up with the people's fearful retreat (Exod 20:18–21), and concludes with a command to cover one's nakedness in worship (Exod 20:26). Thus, on several levels, the compositional structure of Genesis 1–3 anticipates and presumes the contents of the Sinai Narrative.

Second, the phraseology used to describe Adam's life and duties in the garden portrays an individual who is fulfilling the conditions of the Sinai Covenant (Gen 2:15). Although I have already discussed the significance of עבד and שמר, it is important to recall the fact that these words, when used together, describe the responsibilities of the Levites as well as the obligations of obedience to the commandments of Sinai later in the Torah.

Third, God's commandment to Adam in Gen 2:16–17 in the form of a prohibition is characteristic of the laws of the Sinai Covenant.[152]

149. Lev 11 deals with impurities related to animals; chapter 12, with the impurities related to a woman; and 13:1, impurities related to a man.

150. Only in Gen 3:8 and Exod 19:19 is there ever a description of a "voice" or "sound" (קול) "walking" (הלך). The use of this phrase in conjunction with Adam and Eve's fearful retreat (vv. 8–9) strongly suggests that Adam and Eve's trial anticipates Exod 19–20. See Sailhamer›s comments in *Pentateuch as Narrative*, 105.

151. Wenham, *Genesis 1–15*, 75.

152. Ibid., 67: "The restriction is blunt and firm. 'Never eat,' literally, 'you shall not

Fourth, a *leitmotif* throughout Genesis 1–3 is "food" (אכלה; 1:29, 30; see also 6:21; 9:3) and "eating" (2:16, 17; 3:1, 2, 3, 5, 6, 11, 12, 13, 14, 17, 18, 19, 22; see also 6:21; 9:4), an important concern in the Sinai Covenant as well. Man's dynamic relationship to God is reflected throughout the Pentateuch by means of the addition of dietary regulations.[153] The likelihood that the dietary restriction in 2:16–17 is intended to foreshadow the laws of Leviticus 11 is bolstered by the content of the dialogue between the serpent and the woman. Following the detailed description of all the other creatures according to their kinds in Genesis 1,[154] the serpent is the final creature of the creation account to be mentioned, thus anticipating the structure of Leviticus 11, where the serpent also appears at the end of the list of animals (compare Gen 3:14 with Lev 11:42). Eve's recapitulation of the commandment to the serpent "not to eat" includes an addendum: "not to touch" (3:3).[155] The only two other places in the Hebrew Scriptures where the commandment "Do not eat" and "Do not touch" appear, and in a manner grammatically identical to

---

eat; resembles the Ten Commandments: לא 'not' followed by the imperfect is used for long-standing prohibitions; cf. 'Do not steal, murder,' etc. (Exod 20:3–17). To it is appended a motive clause: 'for on the day you do (eat), you will certainly die' (cf. Exod 20:5, 7, 11), a characteristic feature of Hebrew law (cf., B. Gemser, 'Motive Clause in Old Testament Law,' . . 50–66)." See also the comments on Gen 2:16–17 in Alter, *Five Books of Moses*, 21.

153. A case can be made that the addition of the food laws in the Pentateuch (Gen 9:3–4 and Lev 11) is directly related to sin. This is quite clear in Gen 9, but clues in the compositional arrangement of Lev 9–11 suggest the same there as well. אכל is also a *Leitwort* in Lev 9–11 and provides both cohesion and coherence to the text as a whole. In Lev 9:24, we are told that fire "eats" (אכל) the offering, but in 10:2 fire "eats" (אכל) the offerer. Nadab and Abihu's transgression, depicted in a manner similar to Noah's transgression (compare the action of the two sons of Noah with the two sons of Uzziel in Gen 9:23 and Lev 10:4–5 and the behavior of Noah in Gen 9:21 and the new legislation in Lev 10:9), results in a dispute between Moses and Aaron regarding ambiguities in what should or should not have been eaten (10:12, 13, 14, 17, 18, 19). The dispute provides the context for the giving of more legislation elucidating the issue of what should and should not be eaten (Lev 11). In their literary context, therefore, the dietary laws of Lev 11 are directly related to the transgression of Nadab and Abihu.

154. The classification of the creatures and the vocabulary used to describe them in Gen 1 are quite similar to the classification of the creatures and the vocabulary of Lev 11.

155. Scholars debate whether Eve has done something wrong by adding to the commandments about the tree. For a helpful survey of various proposals, see Townsend, "Eve's Answer," 399–402. A better solution is to treat this addition as part of the overall compositional strategy of the Pentateuch. Eve's words ought to be understood in the context of the Sinai Covenant and its legislation.

Gen 3:3,[156] are Lev 11:8 and Deuteronomy 14:8, the dietary regulations for the people of Israel.[157] Eve discusses the food laws of Sinai with the most unclean of all the animals while her husband stands passively by (3:6b; see Num 30:6–15). Thus, the temptation narrative is painted with Sinaitic colors.

A fifth reason for understanding Adam's relationship to God as proto-Sinaitic has to do with the element of contingency. To recall, God "takes" (לקח) Adam out of an "uninhabitable" or "desert" land (Gen 1:2; 2:5–7), and "causes him to rest" (הניח) in a paradisiacal "land" prepared by God. As noted by Schökel, לקח is used elsewhere in the Hebrew Bible for bringing Israel out of exile (Deut 30:4–5; Ezek 37:21) and also as a term for election (Gen 24:7); הניח, inversely, is the word associated with God's bringing Israel into the Promised Land (Deut 3:20).[158] Thus, God takes Adam out to bring him in, as is the case in God's dealings with Israel. Adam's ongoing enjoyment of the "land" is clearly contingent on his obedience to the divine commandments, a concept that is central to the Sinai Covenant (see Exod 20:12; Deut 30:15–20).[159] Adam is offered two choices: (1) obedience resulting in life in the garden (see Gen 3:24), and (2) disobedience resulting in exile and death. Leviticus 18:5 is an apt description for the nature and conditions of God's covenant-like relationship with Adam: "And you shall keep my statutes and my judgments of which the individual who does them will live by them."[160]

Finally, the consequences for Adam and Eve's disobedience anticipate the consequences for disobedience to the commandments of Sinai. Adam's disobedience results in curses (Gen 3:14–19), exile (Gen 3:23–24), and death (Gen 3:19), all of which are part and parcel of the penalties enumerated in the Sinai Covenant. This is most clearly seen in the final chapters of the Torah, where the curses for the violation of the covenant are listed (Deut 28:15–68). A prominent theme in this list, as in Genesis 3, is "exile" (vv. 36, 41, 64, 68), "death" (vv. 45, 48, 53–57, 63),

156. לא + *yiqtol*, 2nd, masc. plural.

157. Townsend, "Eve's Answer," 406–7. On the basis of the parallels in Lev 11 and Deut 14 to Eve's words, Townsend concludes that the original readers would have identified the Tree of the Knowledge of Good and Evil as an unclean food.

158. Schökel, "Motivos Sapienciales," 305.

159. Sailhamer, *Genesis Unbound*, 94.

160. Lev 18:5 is used as a theological summary of God's expectations for his people under the Sinai Covenant elsewhere in the Tanakh (Ezek 20:11, 13, 21; Neh 9:29) and also in the NT (Rom 10:5; Gal 3:12).

and the desolation of the land itself (vv. 24, 38–40, 42, 51; Gen 3:17–19). There is even a play on the Hebrew word עבד in Deut 28: 47–48, possibly an allusion to the same word play found in Gen 2:15 and 3:24. In verse 47 עבד means "worship" and in verse 48 it refers to "servitude."[161] Israel's punishment here is also described in terms possibly alluding to Genesis 3 as well (Adam's Fall and "exile" from the garden):"And you will serve (ועבדת; see Gen 3:24) your enemies (איביך; see Gen 3:15) whom the Lord will send (ישלחנו; see Gen 3:23), in hunger and thirst and in nakedness (עירם; see Gen 3:7) and with the lack of everything, and he will put an iron yoke upon your neck until he destroys you." (Deut 28:48)

Even the spelling of "nakedness" here is the same one found in Gen 3:7. Sailhamer argues that the spelling of "nakedness" (עירם) in Gen 3:7—a play on the word "prudent/shrewd" (ערום) in 3:1 and "naked" in 2:25 (ערומים)—anticipates Israel's future condition under divine judgment as a result of their disobedience. He writes,

> [T]here is a difference in meaning between עָרוֹם ("naked") in 2:25 and עֵירֹם ("naked") in 3:7. Although both terms are infrequent in the Pentateuch, the latter is distinguished by its use in Deut 28:48, where it depicts the state of Israel's exiles who have been punished for their failure to trust and obey God's word ... In distinguishing the first state of human nakedness from the second, the author has introduced a subtle yet perceptible clue to the story's meaning. The effect of the Fall was not simply that the man and the woman came to know they were עָרוֹם ("naked"). Specifically, they came to know that they were עֵירֹם ("naked") in the sense of being "under God's judgment," as in Deuteronomy 28:48 (cf. Ezek 16:39; 23:29).[162]

All the reasons mentioned above strongly support the thesis that Genesis 1–3 typifies and anticipates Israel's life (and history) under the Mosaic Covenant.

---

161. See Sailhamer's comments on the connotations of "work" before and after the Fall in *Pentateuch as Narrative*, 100–101.

162. Ibid., 103.

6

A Text-Centered Analysis of Genesis 1–3, Part 2

SEDUCTION AND EXILE IN GENESIS 1–3

The purpose of this section is to argue that Adam and Eve's seduction by the "inhabitant" of the land foreshadows Israel's future seduction by the inhabitants of the land and subsequent exile. Although Genesis 3, in the earliest version of the Pentateuch (Mosaic core), might have once warned Israel before their impending conquest to beware of the seductive Canaanites, this cannot be the case in the final form Pentateuch.[1] If the Pentateuch attained its final form, as Waltke states, in the exile or at some time after, then Genesis 1–3 must be regarded as a commentary on Israel's historical experiences of failure under the Sinai Covenant, and, at the same time, a confirmation of Moses' prophetic warning (see Deut 31:28–29). Thus, Genesis 3 offers theological reasons for Israel's exile while, at the same time, reinforcing their eschatological hopes by ensuring an eventual victory over the serpent in spite of their failures (Gen 3:15). Thus, a dynamic exists in the Pentateuch between prediction and verification, between the past and the future, between the "Mosaic core" and the final form. The final form is, in essence, a prophetic validation of Moses' predictions regarding the certainties of seduction, failure, and exile (see Deut 4:25–30; 30:1–2; 31:28–29). The confirmation of the accuracies of Moses' predictions of failure in the final form Pentateuch engenders faith and hope with respect to the certainties of his promises regarding "the last days."

---

1. I am not arguing for or against the existence of a Mosaic core, but merely suggesting that this narrative could have provided a fitting warning to the Israelites about the Canaanites before the conquest, but makes no sense as a warning after the exile had already occurred.

Prototypical Canaanite

The serpent's role in the garden has long occupied Jewish and Christian biblical scholars.[2] Wenham's comments illustrate the exegetical perplexities surrounding the figure of the serpent: "Why, it is often asked, did the snake appear and tempt the woman? *Very diverse answers have been offered, though none appear entirely satisfactory.*"[3] Earlier I argued that a text-centered approach offers the best solution. Attempts to establish its identity and purpose via appeals to the ANE run the risk of hypothetical interpretations moving beyond the confines and control of the text itself. Attempts to identify the serpent as a symbol of "the cults practiced by the native inhabitants of the land"[4] run up against a *crux interpretum*: why would the text say that God made the serpent (Gen 3:1) if it is a symbol of the Canaanite cults? The solution, one that makes excellent "textual sense," is to understand the serpent as a prototypical Canaanite.[5] This solution alleviates any possible suggestion that God is responsible for the origin of the Canaanite cults or evil in any way. While not the originator of the Canaanite cults, God is clearly portrayed in Genesis as the originator of all humanity, including the Canaanites. The primary purpose of Genesis 3 is not to elaborate on *how* the serpent became a tempter nor on *why* it inhabits the land, any more than the author intends to elaborate on *how* the Canaanites became tempters[6] and on *why* they inhabit the land. The point of the narrative, rather, is to identify *who* the serpent is vis-à-vis the Canaanites. The serpent is simply present when Adam is brought into the garden, just as the Canaanites are present when the Israelites are brought into the Promised Land. The "Garden-Land" is a beautiful place, but also a dangerous place. Throughout the remainder of the Pentateuch the author continually warns the Israelites about the seditious Canaanites whom they were going to encounter and

2. Fretheim, "Genesis 3," 149.

3. Wenham, *Genesis 1–15*, 72. (Italics provided.)

4. The view espoused by Blenkinsopp, *Pentateuch*, 66.

5. The poetic promise of mankind's ultimate victory over the serpent in Gen 3:15 suggests that the serpent is also more than simply a garden variety of snakes. The poem in Gen 3 (see also Num 24:17) opens wide the door for the NT's later identification of the serpent as Satan (Rev 12:9).

6. The parallels between Gen 3 and 9:18–27 suggest that "uncovered" sexuality after the Fall (sexual perversity) typifies the moral depravity of the Canaanites (see Lev 18).

emphasizes their need to conquer them completely.[7] If the Canaanites remain in the land, the Israelites will fare no better than Adam and Eve did in the garden. The certainty of Israel's failure in the conclusion of the Pentateuch (see Deut 31:28–29), moreover, and the presence of exilic/post-exilic "post-Mosaica" (see Deut 34:10) in the Pentateuch,[8] strongly suggest that the author of the final form Pentateuch observes Israel's history from the vantage point of one who is intimately acquainted with Israel's bitter failures to keep Sinai throughout their history. From the perspective of the final form Pentateuch, therefore, it is precisely *because* the Canaanites were permitted to remain in the Promised Land that Israel fared no better than Adam and Eve. "They did not destroy the peoples as the Lord said to them. And they had fellowship with the nations and they learned their deeds. And they worshipped their idols and they were a snare to them. And they sacrificed their sons and their daughters to the demons . . . And he gave them into the hand of the nations and those who hated them ruled over them."[9] Because the serpent and his descendants still remain, the unfinished business of the creation mandate remains as well. The serpent and his descendants must be, and will be, conquered in the future through the Seed of the woman (Gen 3:15; Num 24:8, 17).

The author describes the serpent as "more ערום (*'rwm*) than" all the creatures of the field that the Lord God made." It is noteworthy that ערום is most often used positively in Scripture[10] ("sensible" or "prudent"), and with the exception of Genesis 3:1, appears exclusively in Wisdom Literature.[11] Among other things, it is specifically employed here for its literary value. Not only are the words "crafty" (or, as I argue later, "prudent") and "naked" (2:25; see also 3:7) homonyms, but it is likely a play on the word "skin" (עור; 3:21), both sharing two of the same consonants in Hebrew. Moreover, ערום ("crafty/prudent") is assonant with the word "curse" (ארור; Gen 3:14).

---

7. "They must not remain in your land lest they cause you to sin against me, because you will serve their gods, because they will be a snare to you" (Exod 23:33; see also 34:12; Deut 7:1–5, 16; 12:30; Josh 23:12; Judg 2:2–3; Ps 106:36).

8. In other words, comments tying the final form Pentateuch to the end of Israel's biblical history.

9. Ps 106:34–37, 41a; see also Lev 26:32–33, 38; Deut 31:20.

10. In Job 5:12 and 15:5 ערום clearly has a negative connotation ("crafty, shrewd").

11. Job 5:12; 15:5; Prov 12:16, 23; 13:16; 14:8, 15, 18; 22:3; 27:12.

Although it is assumed by all the English versions that עָרוּם has the negative sense ("crafty") in Genesis 3:1, a literary analysis of Genesis 3 suggests otherwise. The description of the serpent commences with its being "more *prudent* than all the creatures of the field" (3:1) and, after having tempted Eve, concludes with its being "more *cursed* than all the creatures of the field" (3:14b). Verses 1 and 14 are nearly identical in the Hebrew, suggesting an intentional contrast between the two verses. The contrast suggests there is a negative reversal of the serpent's originally positive state.[12] Other reversals from a positive pre-Fall to a negative post-Fall state in Genesis 3 (i.e., the man's and the woman's), the contrasting parallelism in 3:1 and 3:14 with assonance between עָרוּם and אָרוּר, and the primarily positive connotations of עָרוּם throughout the remainder of Scripture all strongly suggest that עָרוּם should not be understood as a negative quality in 3:1. Not only does "prudent" make more sense in the narrative flow of events, it also distances God from any responsibility with respect to the origin of evil.[13] God did not make a "crafty" creature; he made a wise creature. The serpent's "prudence" may even be understood as a sign of God's special favor toward the serpent above the other animals before the Fall. The serpent's decision to use its prudence for evil intentions, however, resulted in a fall from divine favor to eternal humiliation (Gen 3:14–15). If I am correct in my assessment of the meaning of עָרוּם in 3:1, a possible solution to the age-old question about the timing of the serpent's (Satan's) fall is also provided. When did the serpent fall? It fell in Genesis 3.[14] Thus, Genesis 3 depicts the fall of Adam, Eve, *and* the serpent.

The misused prudence the original inhabitant of the land anticipates the cunning (עָרְמָה) of the Gibeonites who, like the serpent, also distinguish themselves from all the other inhabitants of Canaan (Josh 9:1–4). The purpose of the Gibeonite deception is the securing of a covenant of peace (vv. 6, 15), something explicitly forbidden in the Sinai

12. See Rashi's comments on Gen 3:1.

13. Not only do the ancient versions translate עָרוּם as "wise" or "prudent" (LXX, φρονιμώτατος; see Gen 41:33, 39; 1 Kgs 2:46a; 3:12 LXX; Tg. Neof., Tg. Ps.-J., חכים), but Jesus in the NT apparently understood the serpent's "prudence" as a positive quality (compare Matt 10:16 and Gen 3:1 [LXX]).

14. See Ezek 28:12–19. Though this passage obviously refers to the king of Tyre, it is quite probable that Ezekiel's description of the king is an intentional allusion to the story of the serpent in Gen 2–3, suggesting that the serpent's fall took place while it was in the Garden of Eden.

Covenant (Exod 23:32; Deut 7:2; see Josh 23:13). Just as the serpent's "cunning" results in the violation of God's word to Adam, so also the Gibeonites' cunning results in a violation of God's word to Joshua through Moses. The consequence for the Gibeonite deception is strikingly similar to Genesis 3:14, namely a curse (Josh 9:23; Gen 3:14) and perpetual humiliation (Josh 9:24, 27; Gen 3:14). Joshua's compromise of the "creation mandate," according to the pattern of Adam's compromise, plants a seed that eventually blossoms into total apostasy and exile (see Judg 2:1–3; 2 Kgs 17). The serpent, therefore, typifies and anticipates the native inhabitants who eventually lead the people of Israel astray.

It is also important to recall that the description of the serpent as one who "crawls on the belly" and the words of Eve "not to eat or touch" color the tempter, the temptation, and the Fall in terms of uncleanness, the state of which always results in separation in the Sinai Covenant (see Lev 11–15).[15] Concerning the serpent Wenham writes, "Furthermore, it may be noted that according to the classification of animals found in Leviticus 11 and Deuteronomy 14, the snake must count as an archetypal unclean animal. Its swarming, writhing locomotion puts it at the farthest point from those pure animals that can be offered in sacrifice. Within the world of OT animal symbolism a snake is an obvious candidate for an anti-God symbol, notwithstanding its creation by God."[16] In light of this background, the serpent's presence in the "land" represents a threat to Adam's ongoing proto-Sinaitic service to God in the prototypical sanctuary.

Prototypical Failure at Sinai and Subsequent Exile

Evidence presented thus far suggests that Genesis 1–3 was composed in view of key themes later on in the Pentateuch and also the Primary History. Prominent among these themes is God's relationship to Israel vis-à-vis the Sinai Covenant. A case has been made that Adam's relationship to God is depicted in Sinaitic terms. God prepares a special land for Adam and Eve. He entrusts them with the militaristic and royal responsibility for conquering it. God takes Adam from an "exilic" place, and causes him to rest in a Garden-Sanctuary, where Adam is given a priestly ministry. Adam is charged with a proto-Sinaitic commandment, one

15. Townsend, "Eve's Answer," 412–13, 420.

16. Wenham, *Genesis 1–15*, 73.

which anticipates the apodictic laws of the Decalogue, and one which bears proto-Sinaitic consequences for disobedience: curses, exile, and death. Adam and Eve's obedience is tested when they encounter an inhabitant of the land whose primary goal is to lead them away from their covenant-like relationship with God. In this section I argue that Adam and Eve's violation of the commandment foreshadows Israel's violation of the Sinai Covenant within the Sinai Narrative, and exemplifies Israel's experiences under the Sinai Covenant throughout the remainder of the Tanakh.

Earlier I noted that other exegetes, both ancient and modern, noticed parallels between the description of Adam and Eve's transgression of the commandment and Israel's transgression of Sinai. Ancient Jewish scholars argued that God's words to Adam, "Where are you (אַיֶּכָּה)?" foreshadowed the eventual mourning over Israel's exile in the book of Lamentations, a book whose Hebrew title, "How?" (אֵיכָה), shares the same Hebrew consonants.[17] Matthew Poole's *Synopsis Criticorum* and Jeffrey Niehaus draw a parallel between the theophanic appearance of the Lord in the garden (Gen 3:8), described as a "voice" (קוֹל) "walking" (הלך, *hithpael*), and the description of the theophanic appearance of God at Mount Sinai (see Exod 19:19).[18] Tvi Erlich, Sailhamer, and Niehaus all argue that Adam and Eve's fearful retreat from the "sound" of the Lord (Gen 3:8) anticipates Israel's fearful retreat from the Lord at Mount Sinai (Exod 20:18–21).[19] Sailhamer writes,

> The coming of the Lord at the mountain of Sinai is also foreshadowed in this scene of the Lord God's coming to the first disobedient couple. When the Lord came to Sinai (Deut 5:25; 18:16; cf. Exod 20:18–21), the people "heard the sound of the Lord God." The response of Adam in the Garden was much the same as that of Israel at the foot of Sinai. When the people heard the sound of the Lord at Sinai they were afraid "and fled and stood at a great distance and said . . . 'let not God speak with us lest we die'" (Exod 20:18–19). So also Adam and his wife fled at the first sound of the Lord in the Garden. Not only is the Fall a

17. *Gen. Rab.* 19.9

18. Niehaus, "Wind of Storm," 264; Poole, *Exegetical Labors*, 192.

19. Erlich, "Story of Garden," 22; Niehaus, "Wind of Storm," 264; Sailhamer, *Genesis*, 52.

prototype of all sins, but also the failure of Israel at Sinai is cast as a replica of this first sin.[20]

Erlich argues for the existence of several parallels between the sin in the garden and the sin of the Golden Calf.[21] Bovell, who understands the purpose of Genesis 1–3 to be a paradigmatic warning to the Israelites not to follow after the practices of the Canaanites and also a theological explanation for Israel's exile, cogently describes the sin in the garden in terms of Israel's covenantal violations when he writes, "[T]his verse [Gen 3:21] served as a prospective account, written in retrospect, of what became of Israel when they failed to keep the Torah of YHWH in the land that he had given them."[22]

A diversity of scholars representing various faith commitments from across the centuries have argued for a connection between Adam (in the Garden) and Israel's Fall (at Sinai). This lends credence to the thesis that Adam and Eve's failure is depicted as Israel's prototypical failure at Mount Sinai, and is also indicative of their failures throughout their history. In what follows, I examine inner- and intertextual evidence in support of viewing Adam's transgression as the prototypical violation of the Sinai Covenant.

ADAM'S TRANSGRESSION AND INNER-TEXTUALITY WITH THE SINAI NARRATIVE

Before discussing the parallels between the Fall in Genesis 3 and in the Sinai Narrative, it is necessary to discuss briefly what I mean by a "Fall" in the Sinai Narrative. Earlier I discussed Hans-Christoph Schmitt's study of the "faith theme" in the final redaction of the Pentateuch.[23] The faith theme not only provides the literary framework surrounding the Exodus Narrative (Exod 4:31; 14:31), but is also present in compositionally strategic places throughout the Pentateuch: the "Desert Tradition" (Num 14:11b; 20:12), the Patriarchal Narratives (Gen 15:6), Deuteronomy (Deut 1:32; 9:23), and the Sinai Narrative (Exod 19:9a).[24] Its presence in these structurally significant junctions in the Pentateuch strongly favors Schmitt's thesis, namely, that, among other things, faith is a primary

20. Sailhamer, *Pentateuch as Narrative*, 105.

21. Erlich, "Story of Garden," 25–27.

22. Bovell, "Genesis 3:21?" 361.

23. Schmitt, "Redaktion des Pentateuch," 170–89.

24. Exod 19:1—Num 10:11.

theological concern in the Pentateuch.[25] It is more than a curious detail that positive affirmations of faith in the Pentateuch disappear after the Exodus Narrative (Exod 14:31). Although the stated goal of God's appearance to Israel on Mount Sinai is faith (Exod 19:9a), no faith from Israel is forthcoming in the remainder of the Pentateuch.[26] The juxtaposition of the Wilderness Narrative (Num 10:11—21:25) with the Sinai Narrative (Exod 19:1—Num 10:11), and the parallel structures of Israel's grumblings moving toward and away from Mount Sinai,[27] strongly suggest that Israel's year-long sojourn at Mount Sinai did not achieve its stated purpose:

And the Lord said to Moses, behold I am coming to you in the thick of the cloud so that the people will hear when I speak with you and also believe (יאמינו) in you forever. (Exod 19:9a)	And the Lord said to Moses, "How long will this people spurn me, and how long will they not believe (לא יאמינו) in me, in all the signs which I did in their midst?" (Num 14:11)

In light of Schmitt's analysis, Exod 19:9a, strategically located in the introduction to the Sinai Narrative, must be regarded as a theological standard by which to measure the narrative logic of the Sinai Pericope (Exod 19–24), as well as the whole of the Sinai Narrative (Exod 19:1— Num 10:11). Reading the Sinai Pericope through this lens of faith suggests that Israel's fearful retreat from God and their plea for mediation at Mount Sinai was not the desired outcome, but rather a lack of faith (Exod 19:16b; 20:18–21). Sailhamer argues on the basis of the Hebrew of Exod 19:13b that God originally intended the people of Israel to ascend the mountain at the sound of the long blast of the trumpet. The people's fearful retreat, however, resulted in a rescinding of this offer and the need for Mosaic mediation.[28] Having directly heard the Decalogue from God himself (Exod 20:1–17), the people then beg Moses to stand in the gap so they will not die (20:18–21), and consequently, the Covenant

25. For a thorough analysis of the importance of the faith theme for the theology of the Pentateuch see Postell, "Where's the Faith?!"; Sailhamer, *The Pentateuch as Narrative*, 59–78.

26. The biblical writers themselves clearly noticed the disappearance of faith after Sinai as well (see Ps 78:22, 32; 106:12, 24; Heb 11:27–30). In compositional terms, one is forced to ask: Is Sinai presented in the Pentateuch as the solution to Israel's "faith" problem or as an illustration of it?

27. Sailhamer, *Meaning of Pentateuch*, 366; Sailhamer, "Parallel Structures."

28. Sailhamer, *Pentateuch as Narrative*, 51–55. See also Deut 5:5.

Code (20:22—23:33) is spoken through Moses rather than directly to the people. Commenting on Exod 20:18–21, Peter Enns writes,

> The people beg Moses not to have God speak to them again. It is apparently such a frightful experience that they fear for their lives. As we have seen in 19:16, this is not the reaction one might have expected. Certainly God's enemies should flee from his face, but his own people?
>
> Moses' answer to the people confirms that such fear and trembling in God's presence is an improper response: "Do not be afraid" (v. 20). Moses does not say, "Yes, O Israel, quake and tremble. You have met your God and he is to be feared."[29]

Evidence suggests that the author's depiction of Adam and Eve cowering in fear foreshadows Israel's fearful (faithless) retreat from the theophanic appearance of the Lord on Mount Sinai.[30] A few key linguistic and thematic links to Exodus 19–20 in Genesis 3 appear to support this. First, Eve's temptation is described as a violation of the tenth commandment not to covet (Gen 3:6; Exod 20:17). Second, the Lord's sudden appearance is described in terms elsewhere found only in Exod 19:19, for only in these two places does a "voice" or "sound" (קוֹל) "walk" (הלך; Gen 3:8 hithpael; Exod 19:19 qal). Third, the Lord's Sinai-like appearance causes Adam and Eve to retreat in fear, much like the people of Israel at Sinai (Gen 3:10; Exod 19:16; 20:18). Finally, in both narratives, a concern to cover nakedness attaches itself to the failure (Gen 3:7, 21; Exod 20:26).

In addition to foreshadowing Israel's fearful retreat at Mount Sinai, the structure of Genesis 1–3 anticipates the structure of the Sinai Narrative as well. The seven-day, Spirit-enabled "building project" of the land culminating in the Sabbath in Gen 1:1—2:3 anticipates the seven-speech, Spirit-enabled building project of the tabernacle culminating in the Sabbath in Exodus 25–31. It is likely not fortuitous, therefore, that each "building project" is quickly followed by a "Fall Narrative" (Gen 3; Exod 32–34). Thus, Adam and Eve's transgression is portrayed as the prototypical failure at Sinai.

The results of Adam's transgression—curses (Gen 3:14–19) and exile (Gen 3:23–24)—moreover, are painted in Sinaitic terms as well.

29. Enns, Exodus, 425. Chirichigno describes the request for mediation in Exod 20:18–21 as narrative "disequilibrium," see Chirichigno, "Narrative Structure," 475.

30. Sailhamer, Pentateuch as Narrative, 105.

Curses play a central role in the conditionality of the Sinai Covenant (Deut 28:15–68), the consequence of which is exile from the Promised Land (Deut 28: 64–68). As already noted, the pronouncement of the three-part curse (on serpent–woman–man) also anticipates the Purity Laws in Leviticus 11–15. Eve's dialogue with the serpent depicts the fruit from the Tree of the Knowledge of Good and Evil as "unclean," and thus, Adam and Eve's exile is depicted as two defiled Israelites driven outside the camp. Sailhamer writes, "The depiction of the man and woman being cast out of the Garden has an interesting parallel with the casting out of the one plagued with skin disease in Leviticus 13:46. This parallel is part of a larger strategy within the Pentateuch of depicting the Fall as a form of contamination that must be dealt with along lines similar to the cultic regulations described in Leviticus."[31]

Not only does Adam and Eve's expulsion closely align with the legislated banishment of the Purity Laws, but their expulsion eastward toward Babylon also anticipates Israel's eventual exile from the Promised Land to Babylon. Throughout Genesis 1–11 there is an easterly movement reaching its climax in the land of Babylon (2:8; 3:24; 10:30; 11:2).[32] Moreover, the compositional insertions into the genealogy of the Table of Nations regarding the establishment of Babylon and Assyria (10:8–11)—two significant kingdoms in the chastening of Israel's failure under the Sinai Covenant—infuse the final form Pentateuch with a retrospective acknowledgment that Adam's fate was their own. In Fretheim's words, "The expulsion mirrors later Israelite banishments from the land because of disloyalty to God (see Lev 26)."[33] Abram's call to leave Babylon and to return to the land of Canaan must be seen, therefore, as a reversal in the sinful directionality inaugurated with the disobedience of Adam and Eve. The story could be entitled, "From Paradise to Babylon and Back Again."

Adam's Transgression and Intertextuality with the Primary History

Not only is Israel's sin depicted as the prototypical failure *at* Sinai, it is also depicted as Israel's prototypical failure *under* Sinai. Adam and Eve's sin anticipates Israel's biblical-historical failures under the Sinai Covenant

31. Ibid., 110.
32. Ibid., 110–11.
33. Fretheim, *Pentateuch*, 79.

and their eventual exile to Babylon (2 Kgs 25). As I have already mentioned in an earlier chapter, numerous scholars see parallels between Genesis 1–3 and the Primary History. Blenkinsopp argues that the roles of the serpent, the woman, and the man all find their counterparts in the Deuteronomistic History.[34] The serpent is in some way tied to the seductive practices of the native inhabitants of Canaan (Deut 7:3–4). The woman's role looks forward to the women in the Deuteronomistic History who often provide the occasion for adopting these cults, and Adam finds his counterpart in the kings of Israel, like Solomon, who follow after these women and the practices of the inhabitants of the land (1 Kgs 11:1–8).[35] Anne Gardner is explicit on this point:

> Genesis 3 can be viewed as a mythological interpretation of Israelite religious history from the time of the settlement. 1 Kings 11:4f. clearly shows that in his old age Solomon's wives "turned away his heart after other gods . . . For Solomon went after Ashtoreth the goddess of the Sidonians, and after Milcom the abomination of the Ammonites." In fact both these gods were goddesses. At a later time King Ahab was seduced to the worship of Ba'al, the Canaanite god, by his wife Jezebel and he constructed an Asherah (1 Kgs 16:31–33). Examples of such disloyalty to Yahweh could be multiplied for there are numerous references to Asherah, the goddess or cult object, in the period of the monarchy, as well as four in the period of the Judges, however enough has been said to indicate the serious nature of the problem. Genesis 2:4b—3 can be viewed as a response to it.[36]

From the perspective of the final form Pentateuch, Genesis 1–3 contains Israel's story *en nuce*. I already discussed the parallel between the Gibeonites in Canaan and the serpent in the garden. Here it will be helpful to investigate other intentional allusions to Genesis 1–3 in the Primary History. In order to do so, it is necessary to look at Adam from another perspective as well. Not only is Adam depicted as prototypical Israel, he is also the embodiment of Israel's future kings, a prototypical king. Numerous scholars detect royal characteristics in the description of Adam.[37] The language of the creation mandate, namely to "rule" over

---

34. Blenkinsopp, *Pentateuch*, 66.

35. So also Schökel, "Motivos Sapienciales," 308.

36. Gardner, "Gen 2:4b—3," 15–16.

37. See for example Brueggemann, "From Dust to Kingship," 1–18; Fauth, "Garten," 57–84; Hutter, "Adam als Gärtner," 258–62; Reichenbach, "Genesis 1," 47–69; Van Seters,

creation (רדה; Gen 1:26, 28; see Num 24:19; 1 Kgs 5:4; Ps 72:8; 110:2) and to "conquer" the land (כבש; see Josh 18:1; 2 Sam 8:11; Ps 8:6–7), is clearly royal. Moreover, Adam's knowledge of the animals (Gen 2:19–20) in the context of other sapiential themes (see 3:6), suggests that he is a "wise-man" as well. Thus, Adam is depicted as a wise and royal figure, called to conquer the evil inhabitant of the Promised Land and to keep the commandments under threat of exile and death.

There are indications that the individual(s) responsible for the Primary History (Joshua—2 Kings) also looked to Genesis 1–3 as a para-digmatic presentation of Israel's failures. Joshua, for instance, is depicted as a wise and royal figure (Josh 1:7–8; see Deut 17:18; Ps 1:2) who is called to conquer (Josh 18:1) the same land originally given to Adam (compare Gen 2:10–14; Josh 1:4). While the successes of Joshua are impressive, two narratives in particular introduce an ominous tone into the first book of the Former Prophets. First, Achan, of the tribe of Judah, takes things that have been forbidden under the ban (Josh 7:1). According to Achan's confession, "he saw" a mantle from Shinar[38] (Babylon; Gen 11:1–9) and silver and gold, "coveted" (חמד) them, and "took" (לקח) them, a possible allusion to Eve's temptation in the garden (3:6).[39] Second, the Gibeonite deception of Joshua, parallel to the serpent's deception of Eve, results in an ongoing presence of "cunning" inhabitants in the Promised Land (Josh 9:3). These two incidents coupled with the portentous warnings about the seductive inhabitants (Josh 23) as well as Joshua's pessimistic certainty of Israel's failure (Josh 24:19–20), bolster the reader's expectations that the garden story will repeat itself. Joshua, another "Adam," failed to completely fulfill the creation mandate.

Another string of narratives with demonstrable intertextual ties to Genesis 1–3 is the story of Solomon's rise to success and subsequent failure.[40] Numerous allusions to and citations of Genesis 1–3 in the de-scription of Solomon's reign in 1 Kings lend credence to the likelihood that the author of the Torah portrayed Adam as a wise royal figure who,

---

"Creation of Man," 333–42; Waltke, *Old Testament Theology*, 218; Wifall, "Breath of His Nostrils," 237–40.

38. The mention of Babylon so early in the Former Prophets already anticipates Israel's eventual exilic fate at the end of the Former Prophets.

39. See also Schökel, "Motivos Sapienciales," 308.

40. For an insightful analysis of the subtleties of 1 Kgs 1–11, see Hays, "Narrator?" 149–74.

though called to conquer the land and take dominion over all the animals, follows the lead of his "royal" bride, is seduced by an inhabitant of the "Promised Land," and consequently, is cast into exile.

In 1 Kings 5, Solomon is described as a wise king (see 1 Kgs 5:9–11) who has "dominion over" (ב רדה; 1 Kgs 5:4; see Gen 1:26–28) a territory that is bounded by the same rivers originally surrounding the Garden of Eden (1 Kgs 5:1; Gen 2:10–14). Solomon's wisdom includes knowledge about "trees" (עצים), "cattle" (בהמה), "flying creatures" (עוף), "creeping things" (רמש), and "fish" (דגים). This language unmistakably echoes Genesis 1–2, where Adam is granted wisdom to name the animals (Gen 2:19–20) and given authority to rule over them (1 Kgs 5:13; Gen 1:26, 28, 29; see also Ps 8:7–9). In 1 Kgs 3:9 Solomon is also given the ability to discern between "good" (טוב) and "evil" (רע), again echoing key themes in the Garden Narrative (Gen 2:9, 17).[41] Solomon is depicted as a "new" Adam fulfilling the creation mandate.

There are parallels linking Solomon's construction of the temple to the creation account as well.[42] Solomon is filled with wisdom, understanding, and knowledge to do the work (1 Kgs 7:14), an allusion not only to Bezalel the Judahite, divinely gifted to build the tabernacle (Exod 31:3–5; 35:31–33), but also to the Spirit of God who facilitates the work of creation in Genesis 1:2. Solomon is described as one who "does all his labor" (ויעש את כל מלאכתו; 1 Kgs 7:14), likely an allusion to the divine completion of creation (Gen 2:1–3) and also to the completion of the tabernacle (Exod 39:43; see also 1 Kgs 9:1). The precious stones, gold, and cherubim in Solomon's temple serve as reminders of the precious stones and gold in Eden as well as in the tabernacle. Solomon completes the temple in the seventh month (1 Kgs 8:2), a possible allusion to the seventh day of creation (Gen 2:1–3). God's glory fills the temple, just as it did the tabernacle (1 Kgs 8:10–11; Exod 40:34–35). The temple's construction is consummated with the Solomonic blessing (1 Kgs 8:14–15), just as creation and the tabernacle were consummated with a blessing (Gen 2:3; Exod 39:43). Here, Solomon is described as a "new" Adam who has reestablished creation worship in an Eden-like sanctuary.

Once the author places Solomon's reign and building accomplishments in the context of the ancient glories of Genesis 1–2, the stage is set for the recapitulation of Adam's fall as well. First Kings 9:6–9 warns

41. See Ibid., 163–64, for the meaning of "good and evil" in 1 Kgs 1–11.

42. Townsend, "Eve's Answer," 407.

Solomon and his people about the dangers of being led astray by the worship of false gods, and the possibilities of being cast away from the land and the Lord's presence (1 Kgs 9:7; see Gen 3:23; 4:14). In light of what has been said, the description of Solomon's fall in 1 Kings 11 is likely patterned after Adam's fall in Genesis 3. Solomon's downfall commences with his love for foreign women, something not only forbidden in the Sinai Covenant (Deut 7:3), but also reminiscent of Eve's role in Genesis 3. Solomon "clings" (דבק) to foreign women (1 Kgs 11:2), a likely allusion to Adam's relationship with Eve (Gen 2:24). Solomon's love for foreign women results in his adoption of the idolatrous practices of the inhabitants of the land (1 Kgs 11:2). Just as Solomon had once enjoyed Adam's glories, he likewise repeats Adam's folly by passively following after the practices of his wives (1 Kgs 11:3, 5) and by adopting the practices of the evil inhabitants of the Promised Land. Solomon's sins initiate a downward spiral among the remainder of Israel's kings that eventually results in the same fate as Adam's: exile from the Promised Land to Babylon (2 Kgs 25). Solomon's failure is indicative of Israel's Primary History as a whole. Daniel Hays' comments are clear on this when he writes,

> The books of 1 and 2 Kings are books describing the history of Israel from a theological perspective. The central question driving the story in these two books is whether or not the monarchy, and thus also the people, will keep the law and follow Yahweh. The answer to this question is, of course, "no." The initial readers stand in the exile—the monarchy is gone, the land is lost, and the temple has been destroyed. Thus 1 Kings 1–11 must be read within the context of 2 Kings 25, where the final destruction of Jerusalem and the temple are described.[43]

Every "new Adam" in Israel's Primary History fails to fulfill Adam's mission. At the conclusion of the Primary History, the creation mandate remains unfinished business.

The literary relationship between Genesis 1–3 and the Primary History strongly suggests that Genesis 1–3 not only anticipates Israel's failure *at* Sinai, but as we have seen, it clearly foreshadows Israel's failure *under* Sinai throughout their biblical history. Moreover, when one considers the situationality in which the Pentateuch reached its final form, Hays' words about Kings just as easily apply to Genesis 1–3. To borrow Hays' words and apply them to the Pentateuch,

43. Hays, "Narrator?" 155.

> [The final form Pentateuch] is describing the history of Israel
> from a theological perspective. The central question driving the
> story in [this book] is whether or not the monarchy, and thus also
> the people, will keep the law and follow Yahweh. The answer to
> this question is, of course, "no." The initial readers stand in exile—
> the monarchy is gone, the land is lost, and the temple has been
> destroyed. Thus, [Gen 1–3] must be read within the context of
> [Deut 29–34], where the final destruction of Jerusalem and the
> temple are [prophetically described].[44]

PENTATEUCHAL BOOKENDS: FAILURE AND HOPE

Thus far I have argued that the intent of Genesis 1–3 is to introduce
(anticipate) key themes in the Pentateuch and prophetically to foreshadow Israel's biblically recorded historical experiences under the Sinai
Covenant. Because it is almost universally assumed, however, that the
intentionality of the Pentateuch in its final form is to call forth obedience
to the Sinai Covenant and its legislation, many interpret Genesis 1–3 as
a warning not to repeat Adam's transgression. Thus, Genesis 1–3 is regarded as an endorsement or prologue to the Sinai Covenant as a whole.
C. John Collins is representative of this commonly held assumption:

> It should not need any argument to show that the Pentateuch is
> about the Mosaic covenant. The events of the exodus lead up to
> Israel at Sinai receiving the covenant from God (Exod 19–20),
> and the rest of Exodus, Leviticus, and Numbers spell out the ob-
> ligations and privileges of the covenant. Deuteronomy presents
> itself as the speeches of Moses as Israel is on the verge of crossing
> the Jordan to take the Promised Land. The purpose of the Mosaic
> covenant is to constitute Israel, who are already the people of God
> and heirs of his promises to Abraham, as what Josephus called a
> "theocracy": that is, the covenant specified the operations of the
> civil and social as well as the religious spheres; we might call it a
> "church-state nexus." This will be the context in which the people
> of Israel are to live out their privilege as the people of God . . .
> Thematically, then, Genesis 1–11 set the stage for this mission
> of Israel to live as God's treasured people and thereby to be the
> vehicle of blessing to the rest of the world. There is one God, who
> made all that there is, and who made man in his own image (Gen

---

44. Ibid. All words in brackets are my own adaptation.

1); he entered into a special relationship with the first human beings, a relationship that was broken (Gen 2–3).[45]

It is clear from Collins' comments that "about the Mosaic covenant"
means "equivalent to" the Mosaic Covenant.

The purpose of this section is to challenge this assumption by inte-
grating what I have already argued about Genesis 1–3 with a closer look
at the Pentateuch's introduction and conclusion.[46] My purpose is to show
that reading Genesis 1–3 as a *warning* to the Israelites *to keep* the Sinai
Covenant rather than as a *prophecy* that the Israelites *would not keep* the
Sinai Covenant makes bad narrative sense of the final form Pentateuch.
I argue, instead, that Genesis 1–3 must be understood within the context
of the compositional strategy of the Pentateuch as a whole, which, as
I discussed earlier, is bound up with God's purposes for Israel and the
nations in "the last days" (Gen 49:1; Num 24:14; Deut 4:30; 31:28–29).
I have already discussed the introduction and conclusion to the Torah,
noting a pervasive prophetic pessimism about the human "inclination"
(יֵצֶר) and ability to keep the law.[47] The Torah's theology, however, is not
pessimistic. Rather, the candid honesty of Israel's failure to keep Sinai
serves as the backdrop for hope in God's faithfulness to fulfill his purposes. The second part argues, therefore, that Jacob and Moses serve as
paradigmatic Israelites waiting in exile for God to fulfill his promises
regarding "the last days."

---

45. Collins, *Genesis 1–4*, 33–35.

46. Narrative studies in recent years have confirmed the importance of introductions and conclusions for evaluating the strategy of any given biblical book. Miller
("Beginning of Psalter," 83) writes, "The beginning and end of a book are among the
chief indicators of its subject matter." Fretheim (*Pentateuch*, 43), concurs: "My approach is to take a close look at the beginning of the Pentateuch and its ending, and
the way they are related to each other." See also, ibid., 44, 53; Keiser, "Genesis 1–11,"
194–98, 201.

47. Although Childs and Fretheim do not agree on the exact parameters of the concluding chapters (Childs, *Introduction to Old Testament*, 31–34; Fretheim, *Pentateuch*,
29–34), both scholars recognize the strategic role these chapters play for the theology
of the final form Pentateuch (Childs, *Introduction to Old Testament*, 219–20; Fretheim,
Pentateuch, 53–56). Generally speaking we can say that Gen 1–11 forms an extended
beginning of the Pentateuch and Deut 29–34 its conclusion. Whether or not the conclusion begins in ch. 29 or 31 is inconsequential to my argument.

Inclusion of Failure in the Pentateuch

Introductions and conclusions[48] are important indicators about the intentions of a book. Since the Pentateuch is a unified composition, one expects to find certain compositional features, such as lexical and thematic links, in the introduction (Gen 1–3; also 4–11) and conclusion (Deut 29–34[49]) of the book.[50] The lexical evidence does in fact suggest that the Pentateuch's introduction and conclusion have been well thought out and carefully designed by the author. Lexical clusters in the introduction and conclusion of the Pentateuch provide textual coherence to the Pentateuch as a whole. Unique clusters of terms used in Genesis 1–3 and Deuteronomy 32–33 do not appear anywhere else in the Hebrew Bible.

To start, there are numerous lexical links in Genesis 1 and Deuteronomy 32.[51] Only in Genesis 1:1—2:4 and Deuteronomy 32 do the following cluster of terms all appear together in the Hebrew Bible: ארץ and שמים ("heaven" and "earth"),[52] תהו ("waste," Gen 1:2; Deut 32:10), רחף ("hover," Gen 1:2; Deut 32:11), עשב and דשא ("herbage" and "grass," Gen 1:11, 12; Deut 32:2), and תנין ("sea monster," Gen 1:21; Deut 32:33). The theme of God as creator in Deuteronomy 32:6 is also a likely reference to Genesis 1, and the use of אחרית ("end," Deut 32:20, 29) may be intentionally employed here for its semantic resonance with the first word of the Torah (ראשית, "beginning"). There are also likely links between Deuteronomy 32 and Genesis 2–3. Wisdom is an important theme in both Genesis 2–3 and Deuteronomy 32 (see Gen 3:18–20; 3:6; Deut 32:6, 15, 21, 28, 29).[53] "To be wise" (שכל, hiphal) is only used three times in the Pentateuch, namely, in the introduction (Gen 3:6) and the conclusion (Deut 29:8; 32:29). The root להט ("to flame") is only used twice in the Pentateuch (Gen 3:24; Deut 32:22) and the close juxtaposition of the root להט ("to flame") and חרב ("sword") only occurs in the

48. Childs (*Introduction to Old Testament*, 224) argues that Deuteronomy provides "the hermeneutical key for understanding the law of Moses, that is to say, the Pentateuch, in its role as the sacred scripture of Israel."

49. Fretheim, *Pentateuch*, 54.

50. For an example of the kinds of literary devices used to bring unity in the final composition of Isaiah, see Wong, *Text-Centered Approach*.

51. I am indebted to Yohanan Stanfield, PhD candidate at Hebrew University, for his observations regarding the lexical connections between Gen 1–3 and Deut 32.

52. Gen 1:1, 15, 17, 20, 26, 28, 30; 2:1, 4; Deut 32:1; see also 33:13.

53. Sailhamer, "Wisdom Composition," 15–35.

Hebrew Bible in these two places (Gen 3:24 and Deut 32:25), suggesting that the Song of Moses may be alluding to Adam's exile in Gen 3:23–24. The root מטר ("rain" as a noun or a verb), not a particularly common word in the Pentateuch,[54] also appears in Gen 2:3 and Deut 32:2. Finally, Deuteronomy 32 contains numerous references to serpents (זחלי עפר ["things that crawl on the dust"], v. 24; תנין ["sea monster"], v. 33; פתן ["asp"], v. 33). The other links to Genesis 1–3 in Deuteronomy 32 render it quite likely that זחלי עפר ("things that crawl on the dust") is an allusion both to the "serpent" in Gen 3:14 (see also Isa 65:25; Mic 7:17) and to the consequences of the curse on Adam in Gen 3:19.

Deuteronomy 33 also contains terms and clusters of terms that appear to be intentional links to Genesis 1–3. Deuteronomy 33:13 (see Gen 49:25) not only contains the juxtaposition of שמים and ארץ ("heaven" and "earth") but it includes the word תהום ("deep") as well (see Gen 1:1–2). Moreover, the *qal* feminine participle immediately following תהום ("deep"), namely, רֹבֶצֶת ("stretches out"), has strong assonance with the *piel* feminine participle for "hovers" in Genesis 1:2 (מְרַחֶפֶת). With the exception of Exodus 18:4, עֵזֶר ("help") only appears in the Pentateuch in Genesis 2:18, 20, and Deuteronomy 33:26, 29. Blessing is another prominent theme in Genesis 1:1—2:3 and Deuteronomy 33 (Gen 1:22, 28; 2:3; Deut 33:1 [2 x], 11, 13, 20, 23, 24). ראשית ("beginning") also appears in Gen 1:1 and Deut 33:21. Finally, the cluster of terms גרש ("thing put forth" [noun], "to drive out" [verb]), קדם, שכן, חרב, and איבה/איב ("east" or "ancient," "to dwell," "sword," and "to be hostile/enemy") is only found in the Hebrew Bible in Deuteronomy 33 and Genesis 3. These numerous lexical links, such as clusters of terms used together only in these two places, appear to warrant the conclusion that the introduction and the conclusion to the Pentateuch are carefully designed.

In addition to the lexical inclusions binding together the "beginning" (ראשית) and the "end" (אחרית) of the Pentateuch, the theological perspective of Genesis 1–11 is remarkably similar to the closing chapters of the Torah (Deut 29–34). It is necessary to take a more panoramic look at chs 1–11 in order to discern consistencies in the theological tone in the opening and closing chapters of the Pentateuch. In an essay on the literary relationship of "J" and "P" in Genesis 1–11, Blenkinsopp discerns a deep-rooted theological pessimism with respect to the human "incli-

---

54. See Gen 2:5; 7:4; 19:24; Exod 9:18, 23; 16:4 (as a verb); Exod 9:33–34; Deut 11:11, 14, 17; 28:12, 24; 32:2 (as a noun).

nation" (יצר) throughout Genesis 1–11 that is akin to the later prophets.[55] Blenkinsopp's primary thesis is that "J" represents the narrative expansion and commentary on the "P" material.[56] Blenkinsopp begins by isolating the supposed "J" material[57] and challenges the firmly rooted assumption that this source emanates from the enthusiastic optimism of the early monarchic period. Instead of optimism, a careful reading reveals a deep-seated pessimism, characteristic of a later time in Israel's history:

> The enthusiasm for agricultural life, nationalistic and religious optimism, idyllic pastoralism, humanism, and so on, deemed by these authors to be characteristic of J, are in fact conspicuously absent from these chapters, which speak of the curse on the soil, exile, and the vanity of human pretensions in general and in the political sphere in particular. One would imagine that this somber diagnosis of the human condition and pessimistic assessment of moral potential would fit much better a time of failure and disorientation than the heyday of the monarchy. The sense of the ineradicable human tendency to evil, expressed clearly before and after the deluge ([Gen] 6:5; 8:21), leaves little room for optimism. It finds its closest parallels in late prophecy, as in Jeremiah, who speaks of the desperate sickness of the human heart (Jer 17:9–10), and in some of the darker lucubrations of the later sages, as in the author of Job, who speaks of life as brief and full of trouble (Job 14:1–6).[58]

Blenkinsopp offers additional evidence for the pessimistic character of "J" in Genesis 1–11. He contends that Genesis 1–11 anticipates (or assumes) Israel's Primary History, evidence for him of a later dating of the "J" material.[59] It is worth quoting Blenkinsopp again at length:

> It is also worthy of note that Genesis 1–11 contains a kind of preview or foreshadowing of the history of the nation as a whole, a history that narrates repeated failures ending in disaster which is almost but not quite terminal. It may therefore not be pure

55. Blenkinsopp, "P and J," 1–15.

56. For a similar argument, see Wenham, "Priority of P," 240–58. Blenkinsopp's essay is a thorough literary analysis of the relationship of the hypothetical "J" and "P" material.

57. Gen 2:4b—3:24; 4:1–26; 6:1–8; 7:1–5, 7–10, 12, 16b, 17b, 22–23; 8:2b–3a, 6–12, 13b, 20–22; 9:18–27; 10:8–19, 21, 25–30; 11:1–9, 28–30.

58. Blenkinsopp, "P and J," 4.

59. By citing Blenkinsopp's observations about the content of the supposed "J" material, I am not endorsing his theory of sources and their dates.

coincidence that both the early history of humanity and the national history end with the forward thrust of events stalled in Mesopotamia (Gen 11:1–9; 2 Kgs 25:27–30). The parallelism is repeated on a different scale in the first incident of the primal history (Gen 2:4b—3:24). Like Israel, the Man is placed in a propitious environment, permanency in which is contingent on obedience to a commandment. Death is threatened as punishment for violation, but what follows at both the micro- and macrolevel is not death but exile.[60]

Thus far pessimism, wickedness, curse, and exile characterize the theological tenor of the supposed "J" source.

Having refuted the governing critical assumptions regarding the "J" material, Blenkinsopp proceeds to analyze the literary relationship of the "P"[61] and "J" material. The purpose for linking the creation narrative (Gen 1:1—2:4a, "P") with the subsequent "J" narratives (Gen 2:4b—4:26) in the "Generations of the Heavens and the Earth" (Gen 1:1—4:26), according to Blenkinsopp, is to explain why evil has entered into God's perfectly good creation,[62] evidence that "J" material is an explication of the "P" creation account. Looking at "the Generations of Adam" (Gen 5:1—6:8), Blenkinsopp argues that the "J" account of the spread of evil (Gen 6:1–8) has all the earmarks of being added to the ten-member genealogy of Gen 5:1-32 and appears to be a "somber and reflective meditation on the apparently ineradicable evil of the human heart (Gen 6:5–8), matched by a similar comment at the conclusion of the deluge story (Gen 8:21)."[63] Based on the fragmentary nature of the "J" account of the flood in "the Generations of Noah" (Gen 6:9—9:29), Blenkinsopp again concludes that the "J" material provides commentary on the "P" account. Consistent with the theological tenor of the earlier comments, the "J" perspective is morally bleak. Not only does Gen 8:21 correspond

60. Blenkinsopp, "P and J," 4.

61. The source division, according to Blenkinsopp, is as follows: 1:1—2:4a (P); 2:4b—4:26 (J); 5:1–32 (P); 6:1–8 (J); 9:28–29 (P *excipit*); 10:1–32 (P + J); 11:1–9 (J); 11:10–20 (P).

62. Compare, for instance, Gen 3:6 ("And the woman saw that the tree was good") to Gen 1:4, 10, 12, 18, 21, 25, 31 ("And God saw that it was good"). This rather obvious allusion back to Gen 1 (the seven-fold stamp of divine approval) in Gen 3:6 not only highlights the folly of Eve's pursuit of good apart from God (see also, Gen 6:2), but also strongly suggests that the author of Gen 3 was well aware of Gen 1 (contra Wellhausen). This allusion was pointed out to me by one of my Hebrew students, Alyson Dresner.

63. Blenkinsopp, "P and J," 9.

to the earlier reflections on the wickedness of the human inclination (Gen 6:5), but in Blenkinsopp's estimation, it is "quite modern" in that it corresponds to the post-biblical doctrine of the "evil inclination" (יצר הרע) and the postexilic theology of Chronicles concerning the human inclination (1 Chr 28:9; 29:18).[64] The doleful "J" comments about the spread of sin in prideful humanity are also inserted to the "P" material in "the Generations of the Sons of Noah" (Gen 10:1—11:9; see Gen 10:8–12, 13–14, 15–19, 25–30; 11:1–9).

Blenkinsopp's literary analysis of Genesis 1–11 leads him to the following conclusions. First, the pessimistic realism of the "J" commentary was intended to counterbalance the simple optimism of the "P" material: "For J moral incapacity, the sickness of the human heart, is ineradicably part of human nature, so much so that even God has to come to terms with it, as he does after the deluge (8:21)."[65]

Second, the coming to terms with Israel's moral and spiritual failures in the "J" commentary suggests a familiarity with later prophecy, such as Jeremiah and Ezekiel, as well as the outcome of Israel's national history.[66]

A text-centered approach provides another way to synthesize this data. First, rather than discussing Genesis 1–11 in terms of hypothetical sources, one can just as easily identify the "J" commentary as the work of the author. Second, the pervasive pessimistic realism of Genesis 1–11 and its close parallels with Israel's national history greatly undermine the common assumption that Genesis 1–3 serves as a prologue to the Sinai Covenant. It is difficult to see how a book that begins by recounting the story of the failure to keep the proto-Sinai covenant in the best of all worlds is intended to encourage the reader to keep Sinai in a post-Fall world.

A look at the conclusion to the Pentateuch is now in order. According to Fretheim, "The way in which a story ends is also important for the interpretation of the whole."[67] Remarkably, the Pentateuch ends with the same evaluation of the human "inclination" and pessimistic realism with which it begins: "And it will come to pass that many evils and distresses will find him. And this song will testify to him as a witness for it will not

64. Ibid., 10.

65. Ibid., 14.

66. Ibid., 15.

67. Fretheim, *Pentateuch*, 53.

be forgotten by his descendants. For I know his inclination (יֵצֶר), that which he is doing today, before I bring him into the land that I swore [to him]" (Deut 31:21).

Although Blenkinsopp mentions the references to the "inclination" in Genesis 6:5 and 8:21 and Chronicles, he fails to mention another key reference, namely, Deuteronomy 31:21. There are, in fact, three evaluations of the "intent" of the human heart in the Pentateuch: two times in the Flood Narrative (before, Gen 6:5, and after, Gen 8:21) and once again at the conclusion of the Pentateuch.[68] The evaluation of Israel's "inclination" in Deuteronomy 31:21 (see also vv. 28–29) is, in all likelihood, intended to be understood as an allusion to Genesis 6:5 and 8:21. This is evidenced by: (1) shared vocabulary (יֵצֶר ["inclination"], רַע ["evil"]) and; (2) the same theological perspective on the depravity of the human heart, one which leads Moses to conclude that failure in the future is inevitable (see especially Deut 31:20, 27–29). Commenting on this reference, Fretheim writes,

> But the same ending subverts that confidence with repeated drumbeats speaking of Israel's inclination to infidelity and warning of consequent disaster (28:15–68; 29:17–28; 30:17–19; 31:16–29; 32:15–35). The people are called to obey, and indeed they often can, but they are also so deeply inclined to disloyalty that they will not finally be able to control their own future or create the order the law suggests they can. Both law and liturgy will be an ongoing "witness against" their inability to do so (31:19, 21, 26, 28). Deuteronomy leaves readers wondering what might be in store for this inevitably disobedient people. These negative possibilities create an ending of no little ambivalence.[69]

Although Fretheim regards the Torah's ending as ambiguous, numerous statements suggest that it is anything but ambiguous. The closing chapters are riddled with the absolute certainty of Israel's violation of the Sinai Covenant and their impending exile. The blindness and rebellion that is indicative of the wilderness journey (Exod 15:22—17:7; Num 10:11—21:35; 25:1–19) and their sojourn at Sinai (Exod 20:18–21; 32:1—34:35) continues unabated at the end of Moses' life (Deut 9:7;

---

68. On the connections between Deut 31:27, Gen 6:6, and 8:21, see Ewald, *History of Israel*, 123–24.

69. Fretheim, *Pentateuch*, 54.

29:3[70]). Israel's future apostasy is inevitable (Deut 31:28–29).[71] Just as God destroyed Sodom and Gomorrah, so the land would be desolated (Deut 29:20–27). The future exile of Israel is taken for granted (Deut 30:1–6). Israel will repeat the prophetic events of the first three chapters of Genesis. The purpose of the Song of Moses is to serve as a continual witness against Israel's ongoing violations of the Sinai Covenant.[72]

The certainties of failure and the realities of the human proclivity to lawlessness, disobedience, and rebellion present in the introduction and conclusion to the Pentateuch undermine the belief that the purpose of the final form Pentateuch is to encourage its reader to keep the Sinai Covenant. How would the reader of the Pentateuch find any encouragement to keep the law if Adam and Eve failed to do it in the best of circumstances? Likewise, Israel violates the covenant at the foot of Mount Sinai, the great lawgiver falls short of the promise (Num 20:12), and Moses predicts with absolute certainty that Israel will fail and suffer Adam's fate in the distant future. If Moses is selling the law, he is a poor salesman. But, if he is not selling the law, then what is he selling?

Inclusion of Hope in the Pentateuch (Jacob and Moses)

Here I argue that the Pentateuch has been arranged in such a way that Jacob and Moses, two leaders in exile, serve as paradigmatic examples for the ideal readers of the final form Pentateuch to emulate. Although Israel's failure and exile are certain, hope is also assured; there are reasons to keep the faith alive.

To make the case that Jacob and Moses serve as paradigmatic exemplars of exilic faith, it is necessary to provide more evidence that the Pentateuch as a single composition is a well-designed work. The Pentateuch exhibits a high degree of symmetry as a five-fold book ex-

---

70. Isa 6:9–10 is likely an allusion to Deut 29:3 [4, EVVs].

71. The language here suggests that these verses allude to the Golden Calf Narrative. According to Freedman (Freedman et al, *Nine Commandments*, xi, 44–45), the Golden Calf, a violation of the first two commandments, serves as the paradigmatic prototype of all of Israel's future apostasies culminating in their eventual exile.

72. Childs, *Introduction to Old Testament*, 220, referring to Deuteronomy: "Moses is portrayed as offering a prophetic understanding of history in poetic dress which encompasses both past, present, and future. The song is addressed not to the contemporaries of Moses, but to later disobedient Israel, lying under the judgment of God. The great acts of redemption under Moses are described as belonging to the far distant past (32:7), and viewed from the perspective of the latter days' (31:29)."

tending from Genesis to Deuteronomy with Leviticus in the center, and Exodus/Numbers framing Leviticus, and Genesis/Deuteronomy framing Exodus/Numbers.

Figure 1. Symmetrical Structure of the Pentateuch

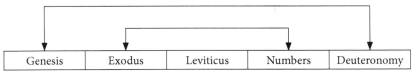

| Genesis | Exodus | Leviticus | Numbers | Deuteronomy |

Recent studies suggest that the five-fold arrangement of the "Pentateuch" accurately reflects the intentionality of the literary corpus and is not merely an artificial construct of later tradition.[73] Starting with the center, Leviticus, Christophe Nihan points to the nearly verbatim super- and subscriptions present in the introduction and conclusion to both Leviticus and Numbers (compare Lev 1 and Num 1:1, and Lev 27:34 and Num 36:13).[74] These super- and subscriptions point to intentional breaks in the narratives between Exodus and Leviticus on one side, and Numbers and Deuteronomy on the other. That being the case, Deuteronomy is necessarily set apart from Numbers by virtue of the subscription in Numbers. There is also a likely break between Genesis and Exodus since Genesis 50 serves as an epilogue to the Joseph Narrative.

In addition to the super- and subscriptions, there is evidence of a symmetrical design of the Pentateuch in the content of the "books" themselves.[75] Nihan's comments are insightful:

> On the level of the content, it was noted that there are several parallels between the books of Genesis and Deuteronomy on the one hand and of Exodus and Numbers on the other; obviously, those four books were intended by the Torah's editors to form a twofold frame around Leviticus. Genesis and Deuteronomy are both closed by a blessing of the 12 tribes (Gen 49//Deut 33) followed by the death of the main character who pronounced the blessing (Jacob and Moses respectively) and a notice of his burial (Gen 50//Deut 34). Besides, the parallel between Jacob and Moses is further highlighted by a series of devices. Exodus and Numbers

73. Nihan, *From Priestly Torah*, 69. See also Blenkinsopp, *Pentateuch*, 31–53.

74. Nihan, *From Priestly Torah*, 69–70. Clines, *Theme of Pentateuch*, 27–28.

75. To be clear, I am not arguing that the Pentateuch is five books; rather, I am making the case that these textual dividers coupled with the symmetry of the content provide powerful testimony to the unity of the Pentateuch in its final form.

similarly exemplify several parallels, particularly in the section on the wilderness wanderings and the rebellions of the Israelites, which stands at the center of both compositions. Furthermore, although the wilderness sojourn in Numbers is considerably more developed, virtually all the elements of the wilderness wandering of Exodus have a parallel in Numbers 10–21. The two sections also share some unique language, such as the motifs of the community's "murmurs" against Moses and Yahweh (לון Niphal or Hiphal), the accusation addressed to Moses of letting the community die in the desert (Exod 16:3; 17:3; Num 16:13; 20:4–5; 21:6), the nostalgia for Egypt expressed by the Israelites (cf. Exod 16:3; Num 11:5; 14:2–4; 20:5), etc. There are also obvious parallels between the so-called "legal" sections of the two books; Numbers 9:1–14, e.g., is clearly a complement to the Passover instruction in Exodus 12. Actually, E. Blum observed that most of the instructions in Numbers 1–10 are complements to Exodus 19–40 rather than to Leviticus.[76]

Although more evidence could be added to the "content" side of the argument for a symmetrical structure to the Pentateuch, enough has been said, in my opinion, to legitimize a more careful look at Jacob and Moses as strategically located paradigmatic figures in the Pentateuch.

There are numerous parallels between Jacob and Moses.[77] Jacob and Moses both find themselves in exile with God's people at the end of their lives. Although the circumstances clearly differ, each man's exile is connected with a statement of unbelief (Gen 45:26;[78] Num 20:12). Both figures are aware they will soon die and be "gathered to their people" (Gen 49:29; Deut 32:50) and "lie down with their fathers" (Gen 47:30; Deut 31:16).[79] Jean Pierre Sonnet and Nihan point to striking similarities between Gen 47:29 and Deut 31:14, where the "days of" (ימי) both men have "drawn near (ויקרבו) to die (למות)," an expression nowhere else attested in the Pentateuch.[80] Nihan and Sonnet fail to mention another parallel between Gen 47:29 and Deut 31:14: in both places, Jacob and Moses "call" (ויקרא) a new leader (Joseph/Joshua) to fill their places of

76. Nihan, *From Priestly Torah*, 71–72.

77. For a list of scholars who have commented on these many parallels, see Op, "Blessings in Genesis," 77–78.

78. This verse records Jacob's disbelief that Joseph was still alive, just prior to his departure into "exile."

79. Nihan, *From Priestly Torah*, 71–72 n. 11; Sonnet, *Book within Book*, 204.

80. Nihan, *From Priestly Torah*, 71–72 n. 11; Sonnet, *Book within Book*, 204–5.

leadership after their deaths.[81] Both men speak of or are spoken to about the "land of Canaan" just prior to their deaths (Gen 49:30; Deut 32:49).[82] Both men bless the tribes of Israel before their deaths in the form of lengthy, macro-structurally strategic poems (Gen 49:1; Deut 33:1). The content of these blessings relates to the "last days"[83] (Gen 49:1; Deut 31:29) and a coming king from the tribe of Judah (Gen 49:8–12; Deut 33:5,[84] 7). Both poems share an enormous amount of inner-textuality.[85] Both leaders are bitterly mourned at their deaths (Gen 50:10–11; Deut 34:8b) and are buried (Gen 50:5, 6, 7, 13, 14; Deut 34:6). Finally, Jacob is the first "Israelite" in the Pentateuch to die in exile and Moses is the last. Given the macro-structural significance of these "last day" poems in the

81. There are numerous parallels between the new leaders appointed by Jacob and Moses as well. Both are described as wise men (Gen 41:33; Deut 34:9), filled with God's Spirit (Gen 41:38; Deut 34:9), granted divine success (צלח) in all that they do (Gen 39:2–3, 23; Josh 1:8). Moreover, Joshua is from the tribe of Ephraim (a descendant of Joseph); he, like Joseph, dies at the age of 110 (Gen 50:22; Josh 24:29).

82. Nihan (*From Priestly Torah*, 23) also draws attention to the unique combination of words used together only in Deut 34:8b and in the Joseph Narrative (Gen 45:2; 50:10–11): בכי and אבל.

83. Gen 49:1 and Deut 31:29 are quite similar to one another and unlike Num 24:14 in that both verses speak about what will "happen" (קרא) in "the last days." Concerning the canonical function of Deut 33, Childs (*Introduction to Old Testament*, 220–21) writes, "The canonical function of ch. 33 serves to place the law fully within the perspective of divine sovereignty, shifting the focus from Israel's behaviour to God's ultimate purpose. The Mosaic legislation is thus subordinated to the overriding purpose of God for his people and the final eschatological realization of his will is attested in spite of the nation's failure."

84. There are minor differences in the vocalization of the Hebrew consonantal text between the MT and the LXX upon which rests a major theological point. The MT reads, "And there was (*wayyiqtol*) a king in Jeshurun, when he gathered to himself the heads of the people with the tribes of Israel" (see also Tg. Onq., Tg. Psa-J.). The king either refers to Moses (NRSV, Eben Ezra) or the Lord (ESV, GNT, HCSB, NET, NASB, NCV, NIV, NKJV, NLT, RSV). The *wayyiqtol* draws the reader's focus to the past. The LXX, however, differs markedly. Although the *Vorlage* of the LXX likely shares the same consonants with the MT (ויהי), the LXX translator vocalized this word as a future or jussive (see the Vulg., CG DD, Frg. Tg. VNL, Tg. Neof.), just as this verb appears in Deut 33:6b, the very next verse (וִיהִי). Thus, the reading of the LXX is eschatological: this is not a king from Israel's distant past, but rather, a king who will come in the future. Although a conclusive solution to this text-critical issue is beyond the scope of this book, suffice it to say, the LXX reading fits nicely with the overall compositional structure of the Pentateuch. In light of the content of the other macro-structural poems, one would expect to find a reference to an eschatological king here as well.

85. Op, "Blessings in Genesis," 71–89. Compare, for example, Deut 33:7 and Gen 49:10; Deut 33:13 and Gen 49:25; Deut 33:16 and Gen 49:26; Deut 33:20 and Gen 49:9.

Pentateuch,[86] given the degree of inner-textual links between Jacob and
Moses at the conclusions of Genesis and Deuteronomy, and given the
fact that Deuteronomy 33—a poetic blessing for the twelve tribes that
most clearly highlights the connection between Moses and Jacob—is a
post-Mosaic addition to the final form Pentateuch,[87] their importance
for discerning the intentionality of the Pentateuch should be regarded as
nothing less than programmatic in the final form Pentateuch.

A word about two more oblique parallels between these two figures
is necessary before I attempt to make some interpretative conclusions
about the role of Jacob and Moses. First, Genesis 1 and Deuteronomy 34
take up as a central concern the gift of the "land." Although Nihan does not
note a connection between the "land" in Genesis 1–3 and the Promised
Land, he recognizes the centrality of the land theme, calling attention to
its presence in the introduction and conclusion to Deuteronomy as well
as in the Patriarchal history. In his words,

"Among other parallels between Genesis and Deuteronomy, one
may note in particular that Deuteronomy is framed in 1:8 and 34:4 by
the reference to the promise of the land made by Yahweh to the patriarchs (Gen 12–50), with which the Patriarchal history in Genesis opens
(see Gen 12:1–3)."[88]

---

86. Sailhamer, *Pentateuch as Narrative*, 36: "At three macrostructural junctures in
the Pentateuch, the author has spliced a major poetic discourse onto the end of a large
unit of narrative (Gen 49; Num 24; Deut 31). A close look at the material lying between
and connecting the narrative and poetic sections reveals the presence of a homogenous
compositional stratum. It is most noticeably marked by the recurrence of the same
terminology and narrative motifs. In each of the three segments, the central narrative
figure (Jacob, Balaam, Moses) calls an audience together (imperative: Gen 49:1; Num
24:14; Deut 31:28) and proclaims (cohortative: Gen 49:1; Num 24:14; Deut 31:28) what
will happen (Gen 49:1; Num 24:14; Deut 31:29) in 'the end of days' (Gen 49:1; Num
24:14; Deut 31:29)."

87. Sailhamer, *Introduction*, 243: "It does not come as a surprise, then, that the poem
in Deut 33 is introduced with a specific and sudden reference to the death of Moses
. . . (33:1). All of a sudden, Moses is dead—even though his death has not yet been
recorded. It is immediately obvious that this small seam (33:1), which serves to attach
Deut 33 to the rest of the Pentateuch, follows abruptly on Deut 32:44–52. It does not
anticipate, but rather presupposes, the account of the death of Moses in Deut 34:5.
I venture to say, therefore, that viewed from the top down, the most natural closure to
the Pentateuch is Deut 32:52 and that Deut 33:1—34:12 is an addition to an already
completed composition." According to Op ("Blessings in Genesis," 82), Deut 33 is later
than Gen 49, the purpose of which is to portray Moses as a second Jacob.

88. Nihan, *From Priestly Torah*, 71–72 n. 12.

The Pentateuch, therefore, opens (Gen 1) and closes (Deut 34) with a focus on the unconquered land. Second, the Pentateuch opens and closes with the problem of exile (Gen 3:23–24; Deut 34:1–5).[89] Like Adam and Eve, Moses also must die outside the Promised Land (see Gen 5:5; Deut 34:5). The Pentateuch begins and ends with these two themes, land and exile, a longing look to the Promised Land from an exile, somewhere east of Eden. Op cogently captures the effect of a joint reading of the final chapter of Deuteronomy and the opening chapters of Genesis when he writes, "The Pentateuch bolts the entrance to the Promised Land through Moses' blessings and death. The reading cycle of the Pentateuch in the synagogue stops with Deuteronomy and begins with Genesis on the same day. There is perhaps a hint to eschatology. The fulfillment of God's promises is something still to come."[90]

What role do Jacob and Moses serve in the final form Pentateuch? First, both figures embody the collective identity of the people of Israel. Through Jacob/Israel comes Israel's name and its twelve tribes; through Moses comes national redemption and the gift of the Torah. Second, Jacob and Moses represent the collective experiences of a people in exile. Jacob and Moses remain steadfast in their hope about God's commitment to fulfill his promises about the land. For now, however, death in exile is a painful reality. Third, Jacob and Moses illustrate the need for a future-oriented faith (eschatology). Jacob dies in exile before the law, Moses dies in exile under the law. Answers for the human dilemma and the ongoing destructive forces of the evil "inclination" are neither in the past (before law) nor in the present (under law). Both men must look beyond the exile, knowing full well that God's purposes for his people will come to fruition in "the last days" (Gen 49:1; Deut 4:30; Deut 31:29) when the curse will finally be lifted (Deut 32:43), the enemy will be uprooted from the land and destroyed (Deut 33:24; Gen 3:15), and God will circumcise the hearts of his people (Deut 30:6). Finally, Jacob and Moses exemplify the eschatological hope in the coming of a conquering king (Gen 3:15) from the tribe of Judah (Gen 49:8–12; Deut 33:7) who will one day gather the people of Israel from exile (Deut 33:5; see

---

89. The final verses of the Blessing of Moses are likely an allusion to Adam's exile from the garden. Note the close juxtaposition of גרש and שכן in 33:27, 28 (elsewhere only in Ps 78:55) and the use of קדם in v. 27, a three-word cluster only found together in Gen 3:24 and Deut 33:27–28.

90. Op, "Blessings in Genesis," 79.

also 30:12–13); namely, a king who will fulfill Adam's mandate. For the reader of the final Pentateuch, all other royal figures in Israel's history (Adam, Noah, Moses, Joshua, Solomon, etc.) have failed to fulfill Adam's mandate to conquer the land. The ideal readers, like Jacob and Moses, find themselves in exile looking toward the unconquered land. The ideal readers recognize that the solution to sin, separation, and exile is not to be found in the past or in the present (namely, under the Sinai Covenant), but in the future. The ideal readers must trust God to fulfill his purposes through the coming-conquering king whom God will raise up in "the last days."

The Pentateuch begins and ends with a pessimistic realism about Israel's failure to keep the Sinai Covenant. "And they, like Adam, transgressed the covenant. There they acted treacherously against me" (Hos 6:7). The Torah in its final form is not, therefore, an endorsement of Sinai, that is to say, a motivational pep talk to keep the law. Rather, the final form Pentateuch candidly admits the problem of the human "inclination" (Deut 31:21) and the certainties of exile. However, this pessimism in no way undermines the Pentateuch's optimistic eschatology. The final form Pentateuch leaves the door open to a future work of God. The darkness of failure only provides the backdrop upon which the author points to the faithful God who will one day ensure the success of another "Adam" through whom he will accomplish all of his creation purposes. The final form Pentateuch, therefore, is both the diagnosis of the human condition, and the prescription for the cure. Until the cure comes the reader must wait in faith (see Gen 49:18).

7

Genesis 1–3: An Introduction to the Tanakh?

Although the intention of this chapter is to bring this study to a conclusion, I believe it would be fruitful to first consider Genesis 1–3 within the context of the canonical Tanakh. Since Brevard Childs forcefully argued for the importance of the canon for "doing" exegesis and biblical theology,[1] more scholars have been open to the possibility of there being a compositional strategy or governing theological concern behind the conscious assembly of the Tanakh into a single book.[2] William Horbury, for example, posits that the Tanakh was collected and edited on the basis of Israel's national aspiration for the coming of the Messiah.[3]

> The collection of the books, therefore, and the editing of the individual books, produce a series of what can properly be called messianic prophecies, envisaging the future—sometimes evidently the immediate future. This occurs within the period of the growth of the Old Testament, and accords with a major Old Testament theme, the eschatological interest of Deuteronomy and parts of the prophetic corpus. It was also momentous for the later development of messianism. The prominence of a coherent series of prophecies will have been among the factors which led to the interpretation of still further oracles as messianic, and to still greater specificity in conceptions of the work of the expected ruler or rulers.[4]

---

1. Childs, *Introduction to Old Testament*.

2. On a smaller scale, Hans-Christoph Schmitt argued for a programmatic and theologically motivated redaction of Gen 1—2 Kgs 25. See Schmitt, "Das spätdeuteronomistische Geschichtswerk," 261–79.

3. Horbury, *Jewish Messianism*, 25–31.

4. Ibid., 29.

If Horbury is correct, and if the canonical Tanakh was completed by the late Persian or early Greek period,[5] this would account for the explosive development of eschatological expectations among the Jewish people during the Second Temple period.

I will address two questions in this section. First, is there sufficient inner-biblical evidence for arguing for one particular shape of the Hebrew canon? Second, does Genesis 1–3 shed any light on the intentionality of the canonical Hebrew Bible or Tanakh as a single literary work? In other words, does the introduction to the Tanakh (Gen 1–3) provide any clues for discerning the theological intentions of those responsible for it?[6]

CANONICAL SEAMS AND THE INTENTION OF CHRONICLES

In a recent article on the shape of the Hebrew canon, Stephen Dempster calls attention to the battle currently being waged on the issue of the finalization of the Hebrew canon: "There are canons both blazing on the right and left and a veritable minefield of difficulties in front and behind including those of terminology, theology, history, and text."[7] Due to space restrictions, my purpose is admittedly not to provide an exhaustive treatment of the various positions in this canonical scuffle.[8] Dempster characterizes the debate in terms of the right and the left. Those on the right (the minority view) maintain that the OT canon was completed by the time the early church was born. Those on the left (the majority view) argue that the OT canon was not finalized until at least the second century AD. As a representative of the minority view, Dempster considers both external and internal evidence for his position in an effort to bolster his position.[9] Dempster's contribution to the debate comes by way

5. I concede that the dating of the tripartite Hebrew canon is hotly contested. In the following section, however, I investigate internal evidence for an early tripartite canon. The argument in this chapter, however, does not stand or fall with the dating of the finalization of the Hebrew canon. Whether early or late, my purpose is still the same: an attempt to understand the intentionality behind the arrangement of the Tanakh into a single book on the basis of internal evidence.

6. There are no plausible reasons for denying the possibility of a single "author" of the Tanakh as well.

7. Dempster, "Canons," 47.

8. Ibid., 47–50. Dempster's article offers the most up-to-date list of scholarly representation in this debate.

9. Ibid., 58–68. Dempster sifts through five areas of external evidence to support his thesis. He discusses the following data: (1) Ben Sira; (2) Q; (3) Josephus who speaks

of his analysis of inner-biblical evidence in support of an early canon, evidence that, according to Dempster, "has largely been ignored in the debate over the canons."[10]

Canonical Seams

According to Dempster, there are a growing number of scholars who point to the presence of inner-biblical stitches linking together the tripartite Tanakh into a unified whole,[11] as well as ubiquitous textual stitches throughout the Hebrew Bible linking the complexes of books together within each of the three major sections of the Tanakh.[12] Discussing these canonical seams, Sailhamer writes,

> The last two chapters of the Pentateuch, Deuteronomy 33–34 . . . for example, are apparent additions to an earlier version of the Pentateuch and serve to link it with Joshua 1:1–8 . . . and thus with the Former Prophets section of the Canon (Joshua–Kings). Moreover, the last section of Malachi, Malachi 4:4–6 . . . appears to be a redactional addition to the book of Malachi which links it to the Writings section of the Canon, specifically to Psalm 1, . . . the first textual unit of the Writings. Since the form and content of this material is strikingly similar (Deut 34:1–5 = Mal 4:4–6; Josh. 1:1–8 = Ps 1), it appears to be the work of a single person.[13]

Looking more carefully at the content of the seams, the Torah and the Prophets conclude with a focus on a "prophet like Moses." In Deuteronomy 34:10, there is an evaluative statement that never again had there arisen a prophet in Israel's biblical history like Moses (Deut 34:10; see Deut 18:15).[14] In Blenkinsopp's words, "The phrase in Deut

---

of a tripartite authoritative body of Scripture; (4) the New Testament; and (5) text and canon.

10. Ibid., 69.

11. Blenkinsopp, *Prophecy and Canon*; Sailhamer, *Introduction*; Shepherd, *Daniel*, 5–6.

12. See for example Shepherd, "Compositional Analysis," 184–93.

13. Sailhamer, *Introduction*, 101.

14. Blenkinsopp, *Prophecy and Canon*, 86. Although Blenkinsopp does not regard Deut 34:10 as an eschatological exegesis of Deut 18:15 based on his analysis of the Hebrew syntax, the syntax does not necessarily exclude the possibility of an eschatological reading of Deut 34:10. A counter argument is best illustrated with the parallel syntactical statement concerning Josiah in 2 Kgs 23:25 (see ibid., 176 n. 15), that "after him there never arose [another king] like him." This is simply the statement of one

34:10, therefore, implies an all-inclusive retrospective evaluation of the period from the death of Moses to the time of writing. It denies parity between Moses and the prophets and therefore puts the entire history of prophecy on a decisively lower level than the Mosaic epoch."[15]

Similarly, the Prophets conclude with a focus on the coming of the prophet Elijah (Mal 3:23 [4:5 English]), a prophet who in word and deed more closely parallels Moses than any other prophet in the Hebrew canon.[16] And as Shepherd notes, the correspondence of Malachi 3:23 with Malachi 3:1 suggests that this prophet is a "forerunner of sorts for the future work of God."[17] The congruence between the ending of the Torah and the Prophets is such that Blenkinsopp posits the possibility that Malachi 3:22–24 (English, 4:4–6) serves as the conclusion of "both the Law and the Prophets combined."[18]

Likewise, there is a remarkably similar portrait of a wise-royal figure poised to conquer the "land" in the introductions to the Prophets and the Writings. The Prophets commence with Joshua, Moses' "spirit-filled" protégé who is encouraged to keep the commandments so that he may "prosper" (שׂכל, hiphal) every place "he goes" (הלך; Josh 1:7). In addition, he is called to "meditate (הגה) on the Torah day and night (יומם ולילה)" so that he may be "successful" (צלח, hiphal) and "prosper" (שׂכל, hiphal; 1:8). The context makes it clear, moreover, that success

---

who could, from his vantage point in Israel's history, evaluate all of Israel's kings. Yet it is clear from the conclusion of Kings (2 Kgs 25:27–30) that this statement did not shut the door to the possibility and hope of the coming of another king like Josiah in the future. Similarly, Deut 34:10 may be interpreted as a critical appraisal of one who was able to evaluate all of Israel's biblical prophets on the basis of Deut 18:15. The past, however, by no means closes the door to the future. In other words, the door remains open to a future work of God. The fact that every other major section of the Tanakh concludes with an open door of eschatological expectation (2 Kgs 25:27–30; Mal 3:22–24; 2 Chr 36:22–23) strongly suggests that the same is the case for the conclusion of the Torah as well.

15. Ibid.

16. Ibid., 85, 121. Discussing the congruence between Elisha's endowment with Elijah's spirit and the seventy elders' endowment with Moses' spirit, Blenkinsopp (ibid., 85 n. 12) writes, "This is, therefore, one of several instances, of which the theophany at Horeb is the most obvious (1 Kgs 19:9–18; Exod 34:5–6), of the influence of Elijah on the developing Moses-tradition. It is not surprising then that Moses and Elijah are closely associated in Mal 3:22–24 and in subsequent Jewish and Christian tradition." A more conservative appraisal of the data reverses the directionality of this influence.

17. Shepherd, Daniel, 5.

18. Blenkinsopp, Prophecy and Canon, 121.

amounts to military triumph; namely, conquering the inhabitants of the Promised Land who are represented by their kings (Josh 1:2–6; 12:7–24). Likewise, the Writings open with a blessed man who does not "walk" (הלך) in the counsel of the wicked (Ps 1:1) but "meditates (הגה) day and night (יומם ולילה) on the Torah (1:2)" so that he "prospers" (צלח, *hiphal*) in everything he does (1:3). The editors of the BHS have correctly identified Psalm 1:3b as a gloss from Joshua 1:8, although "canonical gloss" would be a more appropriate designation. It is essential to point out, in addition, that the portrait of meditating day and night on the Torah so as not to turn to the left or to the right (see Josh 1:7) and to be successful finds its closest parallel in the law of the king in Deuteronomy 17:14–20.[19]

> And it shall come about when he sits upon the throne of his kingdom he shall write for himself a copy of this Torah upon a book before the priests, the Levites. And it shall be with him and he shall read it all the days of his life in order to learn to fear the LORD his God, to keep all the words of this Torah, and to do these statutes. So that his heart will not be lifted up over his brothers, so that he will not turn aside from the commandment to the right or to the left, so that [his] days will be lengthened upon his kingdom, he and his sons in the midst of Israel. (Deut 17:18–20)

Joshua and "the man" are both depicted as royal figures.[20]

More similarities between Joshua and "the man" emerge when one takes into account both the compositional function of Psalms 1–2 for the Psalter on the one hand, and the numerous lexical ties binding these two individual Psalms together on the other. In terms of the importance of Psalms 1–2 vis-à-vis the remainder of the Psalter, Robert Cole emphatically states, "Understanding the meaning of the first two psalms of the Psalter is essential in any attempt to describe the message of the book as a whole. In their role as introduction to the Psalter, one's reading of them should be determinative for the interpretation of subsequent psalms."[21]

19. Cole, "Integrated Reading," 91.

20. Ibid., 78–79: "[A] comparison between Josh 1:8 and Deut 17:18–19 reveals that the otherwise military leader was commanded much as a king to read daily in the Torah. Support for this is found in the resemblances noticed by scholars between Joshua and later monarchs in the book of Kings. Consequently, the figure described in Ps 1 also carries royal trappings."

21. Ibid., 75. See also Miller, "Beginning of Psalter," 91.

Regarding Psalms 1 and 2 and their lexical links,[22] Cole notes, "They have been fully integrated with each other and, functioning together as an introduction to the entire book, they expound a uniform message."[23]

Throughout the remainder of the article Cole argues that an integrated reading, one which is fully in line with the authorial intent, is merited by the high degree of mutual inner-textuality as well as the fact that both Psalms together function as the introduction to the Psalter. The intended effect of this reading is to identify the primary character in both Psalms as one and the same individual. The "man" of Psalm 1 is the "anointed one," the "son of God" in Psalm 2. "Transplanting upon streams of water" in 1:3 is "establishing" God's king upon Zion in 2:6. The wicked people of Psalm 1 are those who oppose the Lord and his anointed in Psalm 2 (vv. 1–3). If Cole has successfully argued his case, then the man's "success" in 1:3 is spelled out more clearly in Psalm 2. "Success" is portrayed as military success against the enemies of God whereby the "land" is given as a possession to the king and to his people (Ps 2:8; see Josh 22:4). When read as an integrated unity, Psalms 1–2 depicts a royal, conquering figure who, in essence, is a Joshua *redivivus*.

Other lexical links between Psalm 2 and Joshua 1 support Cole's thesis. In both places, God's enemies futilely "take their stand" (התיצב) against this conquering royal figure (Josh 1:5; Ps 2:2).[24] What is more, success in the book of Joshua and Psalm 2 is portrayed as a defeat of the "kings of the land" (Josh 12:7–24; Ps 2:2). In both places, individuals are enjoined to "be wise" or "successful" (שׂכל, hiphal; Josh 1:7–8; Ps 2:10).[25] In light of what has already been said, Cole's comments on Psalm 1:3 and Psalm 2 are helpful.

> Psalm 1:3c in recalling the words to Joshua is defining success as military victories. Joshua was portrayed as enjoying complete (almost) triumph over his enemies and the same is now stated without qualification of the new Joshua in Psalm 1. As a result, a picture emerges from Psalm 1 by itself of a ruler triumphing militarily over his enemies and Psalm 2 will simply expand fur-

22. Cole, "Integrated Reading," 76–77. Links noted by Cole are: (1) נתן (1:3; 2:8); (2) הגה (1:2; 2:1); (3) "destruction" (אבד) of the "way" (דרך; 1:6; 2:12); (4) ישׁב/מושׁב (1:1; 2:4), the conspicuous absence of superscriptions; (5) and the inclusio with the word אשרי binding together these psalms into an integrated unity (1:1; 2:12).

23. Ibid., 76.

24. Ibid., 78.

25. For a list of other lexicial links between Josh 1 and Ps 2, see ibid., n. 8.

ther on the same theme . . . Such a reading of Psalm 1 undoubt-
edly explains the reason for its pairing with Psalm 2. Psalm 2
likewise portrays a monarch who enjoys unqualified success on
the battlefield against his enemies . . . Both psalms speak of the
same judgment through military force of the wicked, the latter
identified more specifically as rebellious rulers, accomplished by
the ideal and divinely chosen king.[26]

For emphasis it is worth quoting Cole once more:

It becomes increasingly clear that Psalms 1 and 2 at the head of
the Psalter do not present two different themes of wisdom and/or
Torah and kingship respectively, but rather *both* depict the ideal
kingly warrior who enjoys complete domination of his enemies.
His meditation in the Torah (1:2) simply means complete adher-
ence to the Deuteronomic command for the king (Deut 17:18–
20), which was also repeated to Joshua. The royal characteristics
of the figure in Psalm 1 are based implicitly on these references to
Deuteronomy and Joshua, while in Psalm 2 such characteristics
are explicit (2:6, מלכי). As noted above, links to Joshua are also
evident in Psalm 2 itself.[27]

Cole's comments are all the more striking when one considers the
canonical location of these links. This inner-biblical evidence, namely
the homogenous material on the seams of the Tanakh, commends itself
to the acceptance of a compositionally designed tripartite Hebrew Bible.
It is essential to note, moreover, that the canonical stitching in Psalms
1–2 strongly suggests that the third and final section of the canon rightly
begins with the book of Psalms (see Luke 24:44) rather than Ruth. The
homogenous nature of the material linking the Law to Prophets and
Prophets to Writings suggests it is possible to discern a theological intentionality of the Tanakh as a unified book of sacred books. In Sailhamer's
words, "The Hebrew Bible as we now have it comes to us with a particular
shape: the TaNaK (the Law, the Prophets, and the Writings). It appears
that this shape was not an historical accident, but rather the result of a
deliberate attempt to establish certain fundamental notions about the
Hebrew Bible."[28]

---

26. Ibid., 78–79.
27. Ibid., 80.
28. Sailhamer, *Introduction*, 249.

What can these links tell us about the intentionality of the Tanakh? Why do the Law, the Prophets, and the Writings all conclude with an open door of possibility toward the eschatological future? Furthermore, why do the Prophets and the Writings both begin with a royal figure poised to conquer the "land?"

Attempts to discern the theological intentionality of the Tanakh as a unified composition primarily have been limited to the content of the seams alone. Although there are marked differences between Blenkinsopp and Sailhamer's interpretations, both scholars infer from the seams that the author/editor is extolling the virtues of Torah observance and/or meditation while maintaining an expectant posture to the eschatological future.[29] For Sailhamer, Joshua and "the man" portray the ideal "wise man" who must seek God's will in the written word until the time prophecy is restored in the future.[30] They serve as paradigmatic examples for every subsequent reader of the Tanakh who also must meditate day and night on the Torah until the coming of the prophet like Moses.[31] Blenkinsopp, however, does not incorporate Joshua 1 and Psalm 1 into his equation. And Sailhamer does not address an important piece of the interpretive puzzle, namely Psalm 2.[32] What is more, neither scholar incorporates the introduction to the Torah (Gen 1–3) into their analyses. Yet the remarkable similarities of the introductions to the Torah, the Prophets, and the Writings warrant further investigation. Before factoring the introduction of the Torah into my discussion, it is necessary to discuss the role of Chronicles within the Hebrew canon.

Chronicles and the Hebrew Canon

Scholars are beginning to recognize the role played by Chronicles in the finalization of the Hebrew canon. According to Zipora Talshir, a "canonical consciousness" is evident throughout the book of Chronicles. Based on a careful reading of Chronicles, Talshir argues that the "the Torah, Sam–Reg [Kings], probably also the classical Prophets and the Psalms, as well as other books, constitute an existing, authoritative literary

29. Blenkinsopp, *Prophecy and Canon*, 122–23; Sailhamer, *Introduction*, 249.

30. Sailhamer, *Introduction*, 249.

31. Dempster, "Canons," 73.

32. See Sailhamer, *Meaning of Pentateuch*, 56. Although Sailhamer refers to Pss 1–2 as one of the seams, he does not discuss the role of Ps 2 in his analysis of the intentionality of the canonical seams.

tradition"[33] for the Chronicler. Talshir regards the book of Chronicles as a vital clue for understanding the process of the origination of canon-related concepts of biblical literature.

Hendrik J. Koorevaar goes a step beyond Talshir by arguing that Chronicles was more than simply a part of the "origination of canon-related concepts"; rather, it was intentionally composed as the conclusion to the Old Testament canon itself.[34] Koorevaar first adduces evidence for the priority of the Palestinian Canon over the Alexandrian Canon in order to demonstrate the antiquity of the Hebrew canon.[35] Koorevaar contends that the Protestant adoption of the Hebrew books of the Bible, on the one hand, while maintaining the traditionally later canonical order of the Vulgate, on the other, represents a theologically costly compromise.[36] Next, Koorevaar convincingly demonstrates that Chronicles should not be regarded as the introduction to a larger Chronistic work (Chronicles-Ezra-Nehemiah).[37] Finally, Koorevaar shows that in all four

33. Talshir, "Canon-Related Concepts," 403 (words in brackets provided). In her words (ibid., 401), "The reference to written lamentations, the way Ps 106 is quoted together with the adjacent doxology which closes a collection of psalms, the total devotion to the prophets' teaching resulting in an overall revision of the history of Judah, the awareness of a large scale history ranging from Gen to Reg, the perception of Sam–Reg as the work of contemporary prophets and their use as the base and framework for a newly interpreted history, and the handling of the Torah by standards characteristic of later Midrash in an attempt to turn its variegated laws into one harmonious and obligatory way of life, all form internal indications which may point out the accepted literary tradition in the milieu of the Chronicler, or, alternatively, to his contribution to its formation."

34. Koorevaar, "Die Chronik," 42–76.

35. Ibid., 43–45. The following arguments are offered in support of the priority of the Palestinian Canon: (1) Judaism knows only the Tanakh as Holy Scripture; (2) the Greek version of the Apocrypha exists with only fragmentary Hebrew or Aramaic originals; (3) the extent of the LXX manuscripts is not consistent; and (4) thus, the concept of the Alexandrian Canon as an originally Jewish canon (i.e., pre-Christian), must be rejected.

36. Ibid., 45: "Das Ergebnis ist auf jeden Fall eine Veränderung des kanonischen Aufbaus des Alten Testaments, die nicht ohne Auswirkungen auf das Gesamtbild im Mosaik der alttestamentlichen Theologie bleiben kann." Translation: "The effect, in any case, is an alteration of the canonical configuration of the Old Testament which cannot remain without consequences to the overall picture in the mosaic of Old Testament theology."

37. Ibid., 45–50. According to Koorevaar, 2 Chr 36:22–33, is not only a secondary adaption of Ezra 1:1–4, but also forms a strategic conclusion to the Book of Chronicles as a whole. Moreover, literary and theological similarities between Chronicles and Ezra-Nehemiah have often been amplified at the expense of the differences. Finally,

categories of the Palestinian canonical arrangement (literary, chronological, abnormal, and liturgical), the majority arrangement attests to the
position of Chronicles as the final book in the Writings.[38]

A final argument in favor of Chronicles-last could also be added
to the list. Earlier I mentioned the affinities between the conclusions to
both the Primary History and to the book of Chronicles (2 Kgs 25; 2 Chr
36). Both books end with the description of the Babylonian captivity.
Likewise, in both conclusions a reference to a specific date indicates a
marked shift in Israel's exilic situation (2 Kgs 25:27; 2 Chr 36:22). In both
cases, a foreign king's favorable intentions toward the Israelites signify
the open-ended possibility of a future work of God (2 Kgs 25:27–30;
2 Chr 36:23). Moreover, in different ways, both endings possibly allude to
the end of Genesis where Israel's first exile from the Promised Land com-
menced. The description of Jehoiachin's release from prison and change
of clothes (2 Kgs 25:27, 29) may be an allusion to Joseph's similarly unexpected turn of events (Gen 41:14).[39] Likewise, Nahum Sarna contends
that behind the chronological framework of Chronicles (from Adam to
exile) is a conscious attempt to parallel Genesis. He writes, "Genesis and
Chronicles both begin with the origin and development of the human
race and both end with the promise of redemption and return to the
land of Israel. The two books actually employ the same key verb in this
connection (Gen 50:24–25; 2 Chr 36:23; פקד, עלה; *pkd*, *'lh*)."[40]

Thus, in different ways, 2 Kings 25 and 2 Chronicles 36 portray
a Joseph-like situation, whereby hope for a future return is extended
beyond the adverse circumstances of the Babylonian exile. One should
note, moreover, if in fact Kings and Chronicles end with an intentional
allusion to Joseph and his circumstances in exile, such an ending is re-

---

Chronicles' separation from Ezra-Nehemiah in the Hebrew canon strongly undermines
the notion of a single Chronistic composition.

38. Ibid., 50–51. Nahum Sarna ("Bible: Canon, Texts, Editions," 830) writes: "The
final position of Chronicles is most remarkable since Ezra-Nehemiah follows naturally
in continuation of the narrative. The anomaly is emphasized by the widespread support
it received in the manuscripts and early printed editions."

39. Commenting on Jeremiah's synoptic passage of Jehoiachin's release (Jer 52:31),
the editors of the BHS suggest that Codex Vaticanus' additional reference to Jehoiachin's
haircut likely originated from the translator's perception of an allusion to the Joseph
story in Gen 41:14. Although this variant is likely not the original reading, it does suggest that the similarities between Jehoiachin and Joseph may not be fortuitous.

40. Sarna, "Bible: Canon, Texts, Editions," 831.

markably well suited to the anticipation of a prophet like Moses in the canonical seams (Deut 34:10; Mal 3:22–23). Just as Israel's exilic situation in the final chapters of Genesis sets the stage for the coming of Israel's prophet and redeemer, Moses, so the conclusion of Kings and Chronicles reinforces the expectation of another prophet and redeemer like Moses (a second Moses) who will lead Israel out of exile once again. Finally it should be noted that the endings of Kings and Chronicles are similar in that both intimate the ongoing importance of the house of David in God's plan for the people of Israel.[41] These similarities suggest that the author of Chronicles intentionally modeled the conclusion of his book after Kings. Thus, it would ultimately undermine the compositional strategy of Chronicles to place it anywhere other than the final position in the Hebrew canon.

What purpose does Chronicles serve in the canon? According to Koorevaar, the Chronicler's primary purpose in composing Chronicles is to provide a canonical conclusion to, and sealing of, the Old Testament, such that it provides a unifying theological summary of the content and message of all the individual books of the Old Testament.[42] Koorevaar points out that Chronicles consciously begins with a reference to Adam (1 Chr 1:1; Gen 1–3) and ends with a citation of the introduction to the penultimate book (Ezra–Nehemiah) in the Hebrew Canon (2 Chr 36:22–23; Ezra 1:1–4), thereby sealing the OT into a single meta-narrative by means of the principle of "beginning and end." It is worth quoting Koorevaar at length:

41. Ibid. The raising up of Jehoiachin at the conclusion of Kings is only explicable from the standpoint of God's intention to raise up a future king from the house of David. Likewise, Cyrus' commissioning of one from among God's people who would "build a house" (2 Chr 36:23) can be none other than the eschatological scion of David (see 1 Chr 17:12). Sarna is clear on this point when he writes, "Indeed, the messianic theme of the return to Zion as an appropriate conclusion to the Scriptures was probably the paramount consideration in the positioning of Chronicles."

42. Koorevaar, "Die Chronik," 61. In Koorevaar's words (ibid., 68–69), "In that the Chronicler writes his book with the intention thereby to close and seal the Old Testament canon, the Old Testament finally emerges as a book. According to Childs, perhaps the most important discovery of the latest research of Chronicles is the recognition that the Chronicler attempted to interpret the history of Israel in the context of a unity of authoritative scripture. The theme of writing is at the same time relatively frequently mentioned in the book itself. The Chronicler collects genealogies, writings, and letters. It corresponds to his perception to definitively order the existing writings of the Old Testament." (Translation my own).

The books that precede Chronicles start with Genesis and end with Ezra-Nehemiah. By also starting with Adam and ending with Cyrus' edict, the Chronicler picks up introductorily the beginning of the *first* book of the canon (Genesis) and concludes with the beginning of the *last* book of the canon (Ezra/Nehemiah). Thereby it is expressed that he overviews the entire preceding Old Testament and is thinking from that perspective. He works with the recapitulating method of "beginning and end." He offers therefore a concluding interpretive key for the entire preceding Old Testament. The method of "beginning and end" assumes an already existing sequence of Old Testament books in Chronicles. He must begin with Genesis and end with Ezra-Nehemiah. It is possible that this sequence is already available to him as authoritative tradition at the moment of writing Chronicles, or that he himself determined it.[43]

By consciously arranging and commenting on the principal themes of the entire Old Testament, the Chronicler has, thereby, provided a key to understanding the Old Testament itself.[44] Further reflecting on the principle of "beginning and end," Koorevaar draws a parallel between Adam and Cyrus. Koorevaar writes, "It [Chronicles] begins with Adam, the man to whom YHWH, the God of Heaven, subjected the entire earth, and ends with Cyrus, to whom YHWH had given all the kingdoms of the earth."[45] Relating the three principal themes of Chronicles—David, the

---

43. Ibid., 66–67. (Translation mine.) "Die Bücher, die der Chronik vorangehen, fangen mit 1 Moses an und enden mit Esra/Nehemia. Dadurch, daß der Chronist ebenfalls mit Adam beginnt und mit dem Edikt des Cyrus endet, greift er einleitend den Anfang des *ersten* Kanonbuches (Genesis) und abschließend den Anfang des *letzten* Kanonbuches (Esra/Nehemia) wieder auf. Dadurch ist zum Ausdruck gebracht, daß der das ganze vorangehende Alte Testament überblickt und von daher denkt. Er arbeitet mit der zusammenfassenden Methodik von 'Anfang und Ende'. Er bietet somit einen abschließenden interpretativen Schlüssel für das ganze vorangehende Alte Testament. Die Methodik von 'Anfang und Ende' setzt eine bereits vorhandene Reihenfolge der alttestamentlichen Bücher beim Chronisten voraus. Er muß mit 1 Mose anfangen und mit Esra–Nehemia enden. Es ist möglich, daß diese Reihenfolge ihm schon im Moment des Schreibens der Chronik als verbindliche Tradition vorgelegen hat, oder daß er sie selbst festlegte."

44. Ibid., 71: "Der Chronist hat mit der in seinem Buch vorgenommenen theologischen Ausrichtung einen Schlüssel zum Verständnis des Alten Testaments gegeben."

45. Ibid., 67. "Sie beginnt mit Adam, dem Menschen, dem Jhwh, der Gott des Himmels, die ganze Erde unterworfen hat, und endet mit Cyrus, dem Jhwh alle Königreiche der Erde gegeben hat."

Temple, and Mount Zion—to the personalities of Adam and Cyrus at the "beginning and end," Koorevaar writes:

> Chronicles begins with Adam and ends with Cyrus, the king of Persia. Israel is rooted to the world in the beginning of the book, into humanity, in Adam with his mandate to rule over the whole world. At the end of the book, Israel is finally weaved into all the kingdoms of the earth, over which YHWH has given Cyrus dominion. To him belongs the mandate of YHWH in it, to build the temple in Jerusalem. For that reason Cyrus summons Israel to come to Jerusalem. The history of Israel is fixed between the non-Israelite and universal ruler, Adam, and the non-Israelite and world ruler, Cyrus. Such a frame makes it clear that Chronicles did not pursue the goal of understanding Israel with its Davidic King and its temple as the final goal; rather both are understood as the center. Israel as the people of Yahweh, with David and the Temple, has a function of universal significance, all of humanity is its horizon, and it is true for all the nations.[46]

By means of the genealogies linking Adam to David (1 Chron 1–10), David, the temple, and Jerusalem all stand under the long shadow of God's original mandate to Adam in Genesis 1:26–28. This mandate, however, is left hanging in the balance under the interim authority of the figure of a Gentile, Cyrus. Dempster, who incorporates an awareness of the significance of the canonical seams into his discussion, concurs with Koorevaar's understanding of Chronicles when he writes:

> Read in conjunction with the canonical seams it brings the Bible to an end, by noting that the Scriptures had a goal and that goal was not only to establish a people in the world to worship God properly but move history toward its divine goal, in which

---

46. Ibid., 58. (Translation mine.) "Die Chronik beginnt mit Adam und endet mit Cyrus, dem Perserkönig. Israel wurzelt am Anfang des Buches in der Welt, in der Menschheit, in Adam mit seinem Herrschaftsauftrag über die ganze Welt. Am ende des Buches ist Israel schließlich eingeflochten in alle Königreiche der Erde, über die Cyrus von Jhwh die herrschaft gegeben ist. Zu ihr gehört der Auftrag Jhwhs an ihn, den Tempel in Jerusalem zu bauen. Darum fordert Cyrus Israel auf, nach Jerusalem zu ziehen. Israels Geschichte ist damit eingespannt zwischen dem Nichtisraeliten und universalen Herrscher Adam und dem Nichtisraeliten und Weltmachtsherrscher Cyrus. Ein solcher Rahmen verdeutlicht, daß die Chronik nicht das Ziel verfolgte, Israel mit seinem davidischen Könighaus und seinem Tempel als Endziel zu begreifen, beides ist vielmehr als Zentrum verstanden. Israel hat als Volk Jahwes mit David und dem Tempel eine Funktion von universaler Bedeutung, ihr Horizont ist die ganze Menschheit, sie gilt für alle Völker."

a Davidic descendant would play a part. Thus the genealogies, which start in Genesis with Adam and move the narrative forward to the people of Israel and a royal leader, are now resumed in the genealogies of Chronicles to lead the people of Israel, but beyond them to David. David and his reign become virtually the center stage of Chronicles after nine chapters of genealogies, so that von Rad can remark about chapter 11 and what follows: "The Chronicler's account starts with David. This at the same time gives the keynote of the most important theme in the whole work, for what does it contain apart from David?"[47] What is Chronicles but one long, loving, and lingering meditation on Scripture by recapitulating it again and bringing out many of its central points? As a final book in the canon, it is an appropriate, concrete demonstration of the consequence of meditating on the Scriptures.[48]

If Koorevaar and Dempster have correctly perceived the theological and canonical function of Chronicles, then this points to the singular significance that the Chronicler attributed to the introduction to the Torah in his theological summary of the message of the OT in its entirety. Thus, Genesis 1–3 simply cannot be ignored if one is attempting to understand the intentionality behind the final arrangement of the Tanakh.

THE CONQUERING KING IN GENESIS 1–3 AND THE SEAMS OF THE TANAKH

Earlier I noted how Sailhamer did not include Genesis 1–3 and Psalm 2 as part of his interpretation of the intentionality of the seams of the Tanakh. Thus, Joshua and "the man" (Ps 1:1) merely symbolize and exemplify the ideal reader of the Tanakh, who, like the individuals on the seams, must meditate on the Scriptures until the dawning of the eschatological age, namely, the coming of the prophet like Moses. When Genesis 1–3, Psalm 2, and the beginning and end of Chronicles are all factored into the canonical equation, however, Adam, Joshua, and the "man" embody and exemplify the figure of the ideal reader's aspirations, namely, the coming of a king, who, like the prophet Moses (Deut 34:10; Mal 3:22–23), will rescue God's people from exile, and who, like Joshua, will conquer the land and reestablish the Edenic sanctuary in the Promised Land.

47. Von Rad, *Old Testament Theology*, 350, as cited in Dempster, "Canons," 75–76.
48. Dempster, "Canons," 75–76.

Summing up my analysis of Genesis 1–3 in earlier chapters I argued that Adam is presented as a wise, royal-priestly figure who has been given the mandate to conquer the Promised Land and to worship and enjoy God in an Edenic sanctuary. God's mandate to Adam embodies and anticipates God's mandate to all Israel's future rulers and kings. Adam is called to rule over the creatures of the Promised Land and to conquer the seditious inhabitant within it. The Edenic sanctuary anticipates, or better, provides the template for Israel's future sanctuary. It comes as no surprise, therefore, that subsequent biblical authors depicted Israel's kings/rulers (e.g., Solomon in 1 Kgs 1–11) and their successes and failures in light of the description of Adam in the early chapters of Genesis. Thus, in the introduction to the Torah we see the first failed attempt of a wise, royal figure to conquer the Promised Land. Adam, Israel's first prototypical king, failed. He must live somewhere east of Eden. Genesis 3:15, however, when interpreted both within the context of the Pentateuch and the canonical Tanakh as a whole, must be regarded as the promise of a royal seed from the tribe of Judah,[49] a future "Adam" who defeats, not only the wicked inhabitants of the Promised Land, but the serpent itself, in the last days and takes up Adam's rule (see Gen 1:26–28; Num 24:19; Ps 72:8; 110:2).[50] Israel's eschatological hope for the attainment of the promise of the "land," therefore, is presented in royal terms (Gen 49:1, 8–12; Num 24:5–9, 17–24; Deut 31:28–29; 33:5, 7), and this hope is already introduced in the opening chapters of the Torah. Adam is the type set for this coming conquering king. The "king" of the ראשית ("beginning") provides the job description for the king of the אחרית ("end").

It cannot be fortuitous, therefore, that a royal-conquering individual appears in the seams of the Tanakh as well. Joshua, a prophet who is similar to Moses on a much lesser degree (Deut 34:10),[51] is presented as another Adam who is also called to conquer the Promised Land and to establish a center for Eden-like worship in the land. Due to Joshua's incomplete success, however, the crafty Gibeonites remain in the land

49. The link between Adam and David is already established in the Pentateuch. The Chronicler simply makes this link explicit.

50. For an excellent treatment of Gen 3:15 within its Pentateuchal and canonical context, see Hamilton, "Seed of Woman," 253–73.

51. Deut 34:9b ("and the sons of Israel listened to him") is also a likely allusion to Deut 18:15b ("you must listen to him").

with disastrous consequences. The seeds for exile and destruction have been planted. Thus the Primary History ends where the Torah's Primeval History ended—Babylon (Gen 11; 2 Kgs 25). Yet the conclusion of the Primary History, by alluding to the final chapters of Genesis, leaves the door open for the coming of a prophet-redeemer like Moses. This prophet like Moses is once again featured at the conclusion of the Prophets (Mal 3:22–24 [English, 4:4–6]). The marked similarities between Malachi 3:23 (English, 4:5) and 3:1, and significantly, Exodus 23:20,[52] color the role of this coming messenger in the shades of a future exodus and the coming of a prophet like Moses.

Finally, the Writings begin with a Joshua-like (Adam-like) figure called to conquer the Promised Land (Ps 2:8–9) and establish an Edenic sanctuary (Ps 1:3;[53] 2:6). This individual, however, is quite unlike Adam and Joshua. His success and victory are assured. Cole insightfully writes,

> However, there exists a notable difference of grammatical mood between Psalm 1:2 and Joshua 1:8. The latter is precative and the former is indicative. In other words, Joshua is enjoined to meditate continually in the Torah, while for the figure of Psalm 1 it is an accomplished fact. The same can be said comparing the conditional promise to Joshua of success (אז תצליח, Josh 1:8) with Psalm 1:3 where success is absolute and unqualified (וכל אשר יעשה יצליח). Consequently, the blessed individual of Psalm 1 is portrayed as an ideal royal figure greater than Joshua in his unswerving devotion to Yahweh's Torah and enjoying consequent success.[54]

Interestingly, Cole refers to those particular times in Joshua's life that, as I argued elsewhere, intentionally depict Joshua's failures as recapitulations of Eve's sin of coveting (Achan and the defeat at Ai) and her

---

52. Exod 23:20 is a reference to a messenger whom God will send to prepare the way to the Promised Land.

53. Creach ("Like a Tree," 36.) writes the following comments on Ps 1:3a: "Although Ps 1:3a borrows from Jer 17:8, the psalm deviates significantly from Jeremiah at points. Furthermore, when Ps 1:3a departs from Jer 17:8, it consistently includes vocabulary drawn from other texts in which Zion or the temple is depicted as a garden paradise. Thus, the writer of Ps 1:3a transforms the simile of the tree (as it appears in Jer 17:8) into a comparison of the righteous to trees planted in the temple precincts." See Ezek 47:12; Ps 46:5; 52:10; 65:10; 92:13–15.

54. Cole, "Integrated Reading," 79.

deception by the serpent (the Gibeonites, Josh 11:21–23).[55] It is essential to note, moreover, that this coming conquering king, according to Psalm 2:7, fulfills God's promises to David in 2 Samual 7:14.[56] Chronicles, as the conclusion of the canon, frames Israel's mission in terms of two individuals who have been given authority to rule the land. However, Cyrus' authority is presented more in terms of an interim lordship until an individual should arise whose "LORD his God is with him. And let him go up!" (2 Chr 36:23). The similarities between the final chapters of Kings and Chronicles in light of possible allusions to the conclusion of Genesis infuse the canonical conclusion with an eschatological aura.

Two more things must be noted about the language used in 2 Chronicles 36:23. First, the phrase "to build me a house" is, in light of the importance of David and the Davidic Covenant for the Chronicler, an unmistakable reference to 1 Chronicles 17:12 and 2 Samuel 7:13. Remarkably, but not unsurprisingly, the final section of the tripartite canon (the Writings) opens and concludes with a reference to the Davidic Covenant. Thus, Cyrus must merely be regarded as the individual God calls to pass the baton of Adam's mandate to the coming Davidic king. Secondly, and as a reinforcement of the first point, the phrase "the Lord his God is with him" is only used two other times in Chronicles, both of which refer to a Davidic king (2 Chr 1:1; 15:9). The only other place this phrase is used outside of Chronicles is in Numbers 23:21, in the context of Balaam's eschatological oracles (see Num 24:14). There it is written, "He did not regard wickedness in Jacob, nor did he see trouble in Israel, the LORD his God is with him, and the war cry of a *king* is with him." Thus, Cyrus' final words, within the canonical Tanakh, cannot be understood as a validation of the accomplishment of Ezra and Nehemiah's work (contra Koorevaar[57]), but as a confession that their work did not result in the eschatological fruition of the promises of the Torah, the Prophets, and the Writings. Sarna cogently frames the significance of this last statement within the book of Chronicles when he writes, "Indeed, the messianic theme of the return to Zion as an appropriate conclusion

---

55. Ibid., 79, n. 11: "[T]he short description of the leader in Ps 1 is one of unqualified success, without any hints of failure such as the defeat at Ai, succumbing to the deception of the Gibeonites, or Joshua's qualified success in the summary statement of Josh 11:21–23."

56. Dempster, "Canons," 73.

57. Koorevaar, "Die Chronik," 67.

to the Scriptures was probably the paramount consideration in the positioning of Chronicles."[58]

How does Genesis 1–3 contribute to my understanding of the theological intentions of the canonical Tanakh? I suggest that these intentions become clear, particularly when one interprets Genesis 1–3 in light of the introductions and conclusions to every major division within the canonical Tanakh.[59] The Tanakh in its final form is an expression of faith and longing expectation for the coming of the conquering king. Meanwhile, God's people, much like Moses and Jacob before them, must trust God to accomplish his "last day" purposes somewhere east of Eden.

CONCLUSION

This book represents a sustained attempt to treat Genesis 1–3 as a text specifically and strategically designed with the end in sight. I have argued that Genesis 1–3 foreshadows Israel's failure to keep the stipulations of the Sinai Covenant, their seduction by the native inhabitants of the Promised Land, and their exile to Babylon. The certitude of failure with which the Pentateuch opens is likewise present in the conclusion. Moses emphatically states, "For I know his *intention* (יצר) which he is doing today *before I bring him to the Land which I swore*" (Deut 31:21b). Israel's failure to keep the commandments, their spiritual compromises with the native inhabitants, and their eventual exile were already known to Moses and, therefore, anticipated throughout the book that bears his name. The "inclination" is such that even in the best of all worlds, human beings have a proclivity towards evil and rebellion against their Maker. Neither the waters of the Flood nor the stipulations of Sinai could rectify the predicament of the human inclination (Gen 6:5; 8:21; Deut 31:21). Yet this framework of pessimism serves an important purpose within the compositional strategy of the Pentateuch. It drives the sincerely seeking reader to the realization that only the "compassionate, gracious, longsuffering" God who is "abounding in lovingkindness and truth" (Exod 34:6) is able to rectify the vicious cycle of sin, unbelief, exile, and death. Moses

58. Sarna, "Bible: Canon, Texts, Editions," 831.

59. The author(s) responsible for the final form Pentateuch is, most likely, the same individual responsible for the final form of the Tanakh. This thesis is warranted from the fact that Deut 34, which is part and parcel of the final form Pentateuch, also serves as one of the canonical seams to the final form Tanakh.

was not only certain about Israel's failure: he was certain about Israel's future. The final-form Pentateuch's confirmation of Moses' predictions about exile and death merely reinforces and validates his predictions about regathering and life in "the last days" (Deut 4:31). God himself will circumcise the hearts of his people so that they will love the LORD their God with all their heart and with all their soul so that they *may live* (Deut 30:6). Thus, the final form Pentateuch serves as an apologetic for a new and necessary covenant in light of the experiences of the past.

Moreover, I argued that Adam not only typifies Israel, but also embodies Israel's king. Adam, the wise, royal figure failed to conquer the land, thus initiating a pattern emulated by all of Israel's subsequent kings, eventually leading to lives lived somewhere east of Eden. When Genesis 1–3 is interpreted in light of the strategically positioned "end time" poems about Israel's coming king (Gen 49:8–12; Num 24:17–24; Deut 33:5, 7), Adam's creation mandate is understood as the *telos* of all biblical eschatology and the motivating factor behind the arrangement and canonization of the Hebrew Bible: the establishment of God's kingdom through the regency of God's coming, conquering king (see Exod 15:18; Num 24:17–24).

If I have successfully defended my thesis, important implications for biblical theology entail. First, I challenged the nearly universal perspective among Jews and Christians that to "keep the Torah" is to follow the stipulations of the Sinai Covenant. I have made a case that Jesus' words in John 5:46 do in fact have an exegetically verifiable foundation from within the Torah itself: "For if you believed Moses you would believe in me, for he wrote about me." Thus, if I am correct in my interpretation of the intentionality of the final-form Pentateuch, then the very notion of "Torah observance" is fundamentally redefined. The meaning of Torah observance must be aligned with the compositional intentionality of the final form Pentateuch: to observe the Torah, therefore, is to believe in the one about whom Moses testified and through him, to experience the realities of a circumcised heart.

A second implication is the remarkable explanatory powers a textual understanding of Genesis 1–3 offers for the theology of the New Testament. If Adam is a royal figure, as a corollary, Eve is depicted as a bride divinely prepared for her husband. When read in this light, it is easy to see how the NT writers interpreted the story of Adam and Eve as the biblical template for the Messiah and his ekklesia. While there may not be a one-to-one correspondence between Genesis 2:24 and Paul's interpretation of it in Ephesians 5:29–33, it is clear that the trajectory for such an interpretation is deeply rooted within the confines of the intentionality of the text itself.

Moreover, the hope expressed in the Tanakh for the coming of a conquering king is equally represented in the NT. One could go so far as to say that the book of Revelation, much like the book of Chronicles, is a prolonged reflection and summarization of the contents of all the Scriptures, whose message he reduces to the theme of the coming, conquering king who will successfully fulfill the creation mandate and enjoy a bride who is, thanks be to God, compatible to him in every way (Rev 22:1–5).

Bibliography

Alexander, T. D. *From Paradise to the Promised Land*. 2nd ed. Grand Rapids: Baker Academic, 2002.

Alter, Robert. *The Art of Biblical Narrative*. New York: Basic, 1981.

———. *The Five Books of Moses: A Translation with Commentary*. New York: Norton, 2004.

Anderson, Bernhard. *From Creation to New Creation*. Minneapolis: Fortress, 1994.

Ashley, Timothy R. *The Book of Numbers*. The New International Commentary on the Old Testament. Grand Rapids: Eerdmans, 1993.

Astruc, Jean. *Conjectures sur la Genèse*. Brussels: Chez Fricx, 1753.

Atwell, James E. "An Egyptian Source for Genesis 1." *JTS* 51 (2000) 441–77.

Auld, A. Graeme. "Imago Dei in Genesis: Speaking in the Image of God." *Expository Times* 116 (2005) 259–62.

Austin, J. L. *How to Do Things with Words: The William James Lectures Delivered at Harvard University*. Cambridge: Harvard University Press, 1962.

Baker, Douglas P. "The Image of God: According to Their Kinds." *Reformation & Revival* 12 (2003) 97–109.

Bar-Efrat, Shimeon. *Narrative Art in the Bible*. JSOTSup 70. Sheffield: Almond, 1989.

Barr, James. "Hebrew Lexicography: Informal Thoughts." In *Linguistics and Biblical Hebrew*, edited by Walter R. Bodine, 137–51. Winona Lake, IN: Eisenbrauns, 1992.

Barth, Karl. *Church Dogmatics*. Translated by J. W. Edwards. Vol. 3.1. The Doctrine of Creation, edited by G. W. Bromiley and T. F. Torrance. Edinburgh: T. & T. Clark, 1958.

Barthes, Roland. "The Death of an Author." In *Image, Music, Text*, edited by Stephen Heath, 142–48. New York: Hill & Wang, 1977.

Bartholomew, Craig G., et al., editors. *Canon and Biblical Interpretation*. The Scripture and Hermeneutics Series 7. Grand Rapids: Zondervan, 2006.

Barton, John. *Reading the Old Testament: Method in Biblical Study*. London: Darton, Longman & Todd, 1996.

Bauks, Michaela. "Genesis 1 als Programmschrift der Priesterschrift (Pg)." In *Studies in the Book of Genesis*, edited by A. Wénin, 333–45. Sterling, VA: Leuven University Press, 2001.

Beauchamp, Paul. "L'analyse Structurale et L'exégèse Biblique." In *Congress Volume. Uppsala 1971*. VTSup 22. Edited by G. W. Anderson, et al. 113–28. Leiden: Brill, 1972.

Bechtel, Lyn M. "Genesis 2.4b—3.24: A Myth About Human Maturation." *JSOT* 67 (1995) 3–26.

———. "Rethinking the Interpretation of Genesis 2:4b—3:24." In *Feminist Companion to Genesis*, edited by Athalya Brenner, 77–117. Sheffield: Sheffield Academic, 1993.

Begrich, J. "Die Paradieserzählung: Eine Literargeschichtliche Studie." *ZAW* 50 (1932) 93–116.

Ben-Porat, Ziva. "The Poetics of Literary Allusion." *PTL: A Journal for Descriptive Poetics and Theory of Literature* 1 (1976) 105–28.

Bergey, Ronald. "The Song of Moses (Deuteronomy 32.1–43) and Isaianic Prophecies: A Case of Early Intertextuality?" *JSOT* 28.1 (2003) 33–54.

Bernard, Jacques. "Genèse 1 à 3: Lecture et Traditions de Lecture, Pt. 1." *Mélanges de Science Religieuse* 41.3–4 (1984) 109–28.

Beaugrande, Robert-Alain de, and Wolfgang Ulrich Dressler. *Introduction to Text Linguistics.* New York: Longman, 1981.

Biblia Hebraica. Edited by K. Elliger and W. Rudolph. Stuttgart, 1983.

Biblia Hebraica. Edited by Rudolf Kittel. Stuttgart: Württembergische Bibelanstalt Stuttgart, 1937.

Biddle, Mark E. "Ancestral Motifs in 1 Samuel 25: Intertextuality and Characterization." *JBL* 121 (2002) 617–38.

Blenkinsopp, Joseph. "P and J in Genesis 1:1—11:26: An Alternative Hypothesis." In *Fortunate the Eyes That See*, edited by Astrid B. Beck, et al., 1–15. Grand Rapids: Eerdmans, 1995.

———. *The Pentateuch: An Introduction to the First Five Books of the Bible.* Garden City, NY: Doubleday, 1992.

———. *Prophecy and Canon: A Contribution to the Study of Jewish Origins.* London: University of Notre Dame Press, 1977.

Blokland, A. F. den Exter. *In Search of Text Syntax.* Amsterdam: Vrije Universiteit Press, 1995.

Boda, Mark J. "Reading Between the Lines: Zechariah 11.4–16 in Its Literary Contexts." In *Bringing Out the Treasure: Inner Biblical Allusion in Zechariah 9–15*, edited by Mark J. Boda and Michael H. Floyd, 277–91. New York: Sheffield Academic, 2003.

Borsch, Frederick Houk. "The Eclipse of Biblical Narrative: A Study in Eighteenth and Nineteenth Century Hermeneutics." *Religious Education* 70 (1975) 571–72.

Bovell, Carlos. "Genesis 3:21: The History of Israel in a Nutshell?" *Expository Times* 115 (2004) 361–66.

Bozung, Douglas C. "An Evaluation of the Biosphere Model of Genesis 1." *Bibliotheca Sacra* 162.648 (2005) 406–23.

Broich, Ulrich. "Formen der Markierung von Intertextualität." In *Intertextualität: Formen, Funktionen, anglistische Fallstudien*, edited by Ulrich Broich and M. Pfister, 31–47. Konzepte der Sprachund Literaturwissenschaft 35. Tübingen: Niemeyer, 1985.

Broyles, Craig C. "Traditions, Intertextuality, and Canon." In *Interpreting the Old Testament: A Guide for Exegesis*, edited by Craig C. Broyles, 157–75. Grand Rapids: Baker, 2001.

Brueggemann, Walter. "From Dust to Kingship." *ZAW* 84 (1972) 1–18.

———. "Kerygma of the Priestly Writers." *ZAW* 84 (1972) 397–414.

———. "Of the Same Flesh and Bone, Gen 2:23a." *CBQ* 32 (1970) 532–42.

Budde, Karl. *Die biblische Urgeschichte: Gen 1—12, 5.* Giessen: Ricker, 1883.

Calvin, John. *Commentaries on the First Book of Moses Called Genesis.* Vol. 1. Translated by John King. Grand Rapids: Eerdmans, 1948.

Cassuto, Moshe D. *A Commentary on the Book of Genesis: Part 1: From Adam to Noah*, 3rd ed. Jerusalem: Magnes, 1961.

Childs, Brevard S. *Biblical Theology in Crisis.* Philadelphia: Westminister, 1970.

———. *Introduction to the Old Testament as Scripture.* Philadelphia: Fortress, 1979.

Chirichigno, Gregory C. "The Narrative Structure of Exod 19–24." *Bib* 68 (1987) 457–79.

Claassens, L. Juliana M. "And the Moon Spoke Up: Genesis 1 and Feminist Theology." *Review & Expositor* 103 (2006) 325–42.

Clines, David J. A. *The Theme of the Pentateuch.* JSOTSup 10. Sheffield, UK: JSOT, 1982.

Coccejus, Johannes. *Opera omina theologica, exegetica, didactica, polemica, philologica, LXX circiter tractatibus post prafationem enumber atis, absoluta. Quibus Vereris ac Novi Instrumenti; Veritas Religionis Christianae; Lites Recentes atque Veteres; Infucatae denique Pietatis Exercitia.* Vol. 1. Fracofurti ad Moenum: Typis & Impensis Balthasaris Christophori Wustii, 1689.

Cole, Robert. "An Integrated Reading of Psalms 1 and 2." *JSOT* 98 (2002) 75–88.

———. "Translation of Schneider, W. Grammatik des Biblischen Hebräisch." Wake Forest, NC: Southeastern Baptist Theological Seminary, n.d.

Collins, C. John. *Genesis 1–4: A Linguistic, Literary, and Theological Commentary.* Phillipsburg, NJ: P&R, 2006.

———. "What happened to Adam and Eve? A Literary-Theological Approach to Genesis 3." *Presbyterion* 27 (2001) 12–44.

Creach, Jerome F. D. "Like a Tree Planted by the Temple Stream: The Portrait of the Righteous in Psalm 1:3." *CBQ* 61 (1999) 34–46.

Culley, Robert C. "Action Sequences in Genesis 2–3." *Semeia* 18 (1980) 25–33.

D'Angelo, Mary Rose. "Gender Refusers in the Early Christian Mission: Gal 3:28 as an Interpretation of Gen 1:27b." In *Reading in Christian Communities*, edited by Charles A. Bobertz and David Brakke, 149–73. Notre Dame: University of Notre Dame Press, 2002.

DeClaissé-Walford, Nancy L. "An Intertextual Reading of Psalms 22, 23, and 24." In *Book of Psalms*, edited by Peter W. Flint, et al., 139–52. Boston: Brill, 2005.

Dempster, Stephen. "Canons on the Right and Canons on the Left: Finding a Resolution in the Canon Debate." *JETS* 52 (2009) 47–77.

Dumbrell, William J. *The Faith of Israel: A Theological Survey of the Old Testament.* Grand Rapids: Baker, 2002.

———. "Genesis 2:1–3: Biblical Theology of Creation Covenant." *ERT* 25 (2001) 219–30.

———. "Genesis 2:1–17: A Foreshadowing of the New Creation." In *Biblical Theology: Retrospect and Prospect*, edited by Scott J. Hafemann, 53–65. Downers Grove, IL: InterVarsity; 2002.

Eichrodt, Walther. "In the Beginning." In *Israel's Prophetic Heritage: Essays in Honor of James Muilenburg*, edited by Bernhard W. Anderson and Walter Harrelson, 1–10. New York: Harper & Brothers, 1962.

Eisenstein, Sergei. *The Film Sense.* Translated by Jay Leyda. London: Harcourt Brace, 1947.

Elbert, Paul. "Genesis 1 and the Spirit: A Narrative-Rhetorical Ancient Near Eastern Reading in Light of Modern Science." *Journal of Pentecostal Theology* 15.1 (2006) 23–72.

Emmrich, Martin. "The Temptation Narrative of Genesis 3:1–6: A Prelude to the Pentateuch and the History of Israel." *Evangelical Quarterly* 73 (2001) 3–20.

Engnell, Ivan. "'Knowledge' and 'Life' in the Creation Story." In *Wisdom in Israel and in the Ancient Near East: Presented to Professor Harold Henry Rowley in Celebration of*

His Sixty-Fifth Birthday, edited by Martin Noth and D. Winton Thomas, 103–19. VTSup 3. Leiden: Brill, 1955.

Enns, Peter. *Exodus*. NIV Application Commentary. Grand Rapids: Zondervan, 2000.

Erlich, Tvi. "The Story of the Garden of Eden in Comparison to the Position of Mount Sinai and the Tabernacle." *Alon Shvut for Graduates of the Har Eztion Yeshiva* 11 (1998) 17–35.

Ewald, Heinrich. *The History of Israel to the Death of Moses*. Translated by Russell Martineau. London: Longmans, Green, & Co, 1867.

Fauth, Wolfgang. "Der Garten des Königs von Tyros bei Hesekiel vor dem Hintergrund vorderorientalischer und frühjüdischer Paradiesvorstellungen." *Kairos* 29.1–2 (1987) 57–84.

Firmage, Edwin B. "Genesis 1 and the Priestly Agenda." *JSOT* 82 (1999) 97–114.

Fishbane, Michael A. *Biblical Interpretation in Ancient Israel*. Oxford: Oxford University Press, 1985.

———. *Biblical Text and Texture: A Literary Reading of Selected Texts*. Oxford: Oneworld, 1998.

Fohrer, Georg, et al., eds. *Exegese des Alten Testments: Einführung in die Methodik*. Heidelberg, Germany: Quelle & Meyer, 1983.

Fokkelman, J. P. *Narrative Art in Genesis: Specimens of Stylistic and Structural Analysis*. Assen: Van Gorcum, 1975.

———. *Reading Biblical Narrative: An Introductory Guide*. Translated by Ineke Smith. Louisville: Westminster John Knox, 1999.

Freedman, David Noel, et al. *The Nine Commandments: Uncovering a Hidden Pattern of Crime and Punishment in the Hebrew Bible*. New York: Doubleday, 2000.

Frei, Hans W. *The Eclipse of Biblical Narrative: A Study in Eighteenth and Nineteenth Century Hermeneutics*. New Haven: Yale University Press, 1975.

———. Review of *The Eclipse of Biblical Narrative: A Study in Eighteenth and Nineteenth Century Hermeneutics* by John Thomas Fitzgerald Jr. *Restoration Quarterly* 18 (1975) 238–40.

———. "Response to [C. F. H. Henry] 'Narrative Theology, an Evangelical Appraisal.'" *Trinity Journal* 8 (1987) 21–24.

Fretheim, Terence E. "Is Genesis 3 a Fall Story?" *Word and World* 14 (1994) 144–53.

———. *The Pentateuch*. Nashville, TN: Abingdon, 1996.

Gadamer, Hans-Georg. *Truth and Method*. Translated by Garrett Barden and John Cumming. New York: Seabury, 1975.

———. *Wahrheit und Methode*. 2nd ed. Tübingen: Mohr, 1965.

Gardner, Anne. "Genesis 2:4b--3: A Mythological Paradigm of Sexual Equality or of the Religious History of Pre-exilic Israel?" *SJT* 43 (1990) 1–18.

Gesenius' Hebrew Grammar. 2nd ed. Edited by E. Kautzsch. Revised by A. E. Cowley. Oxford: Clarendon, 1910.

Gillingham, Susan E. *The Image, the Depths and the Surface: Multivalent Approaches to Biblical Study*. JSOTSup 354. London: Sheffield Academic, 2002.

Gray, Gorman. *The Age of the Universe: What Are the Biblical Limits?* Washougal, WA: Morningstar, 2000.

Greenspoon, Leonard J. "From Dominion to Stewardship? The Ecology of Biblical Translation." *Journal of Religion & Society* 3 (2008) 159–83.

Grenz, Stanley J. "The Social God and the Relational Self: Toward a Trinitarian Theology of the Imago Dei." In *Trinitarian Soundings in Systematic Theology*, edited by Paul Louis Metzger, 87–100. London: T. & T. Clark, 2005.

Gunkel, Hermann. *Genesis übersetzt und erklärt.* 2nd ed. Handkommentar zum Alten Testament, edited by D. W. Nowack. Göttingen: Vandenhoeck und Ruprecht, 1902.

———. *The Legends of Genesis.* Translated by W. H. Carruth. New York: Schocken, 1964.

Hailperin, Herman. *Rashi and the Christian Scholars.* Pittsburgh: University of Pittsburgh Press, 1963.

Halliday, M. A. K., and Ruqaiya Hasan. *Cohesion in English.* London: Longman, 1976.

Hamilton, James M., Jr. "The Seed of the Woman and the Blessing of Abraham." *TynBul* 58 (2007) 253–73.

Harris, Bill K. "Symbolism in Creation: Ancient Near Eastern Influence upon the Genesis Creation Accounts and Philosophical Implications." MA thesis, California State University, 2007.

Harrison, R. K. *Introduction to the Old Testament: With a Comprehensive Review of Old Testament Studies and a Special Supplement on the Apocrypha.* Grand Rapids: Eerdmans, 1969.

Hart, Ian. "Genesis 1:1––2:3 as a Prologue to the Book of Genesis." *TynBul* 46 (1995) 315–36.

Hasel, Gerhard F. "Recent Translations of Genesis 1:1, A Critical Look." *The Bible Translator* 22 (1971) 154–67.

Hays, J. Daniel. "Has the Narrator Come to Praise Solomon or to Bury Him? Narrative Subtlety in 1 Kings 1–11." *JSOT* 28 (2003) 149–74.

Hays, Richard B. *Echoes of Scripture in the Letters of Paul.* New Haven: Yale University Press, 1993.

———. "'Who Has Believed Our Message?' Paul's Reading of Isaiah." In *The Conversion of the Imagination: Paul as Interpreter of Israel's Scripture*, 25–49. Grand Rapids: Eerdmans, 2005.

Hengstenberg, Ernst Wilhelm. *Dissertations on the Genuineness of the Pentateuch.* Translated by J. E. Ryland. Edinburgh: Lowe, 1847.

Henry, Carl F. H. "Narrative Theology: An Evangelical Appraisal." *Trinity Journal* 8 (1987) 3–19.

Hepner, Gershon. "Verbal Resonance in the Bible and Intertextuality." *JSOT* 96 (2001) 3–27.

Hess, Richard S. "Genesis 1–2 in Its Literary Context." *TynBul* 41 (1990) 143–53.

Hirsch, E. D. *Validity in Interpretation.* New Haven: Yale University Press, 1965.

Horbury, William. *Jewish Messianism and the Cult of Christ.* London: SCM, 1998.

Hurowitz, Victor. "The Genesis of Genesis: Is the Creation Story Babylonian?" *Bible Review* 21 (2005) 36–48, 52–54.

———. "P—Understanding the Priestly Source." *Bible Review* 12 (1996) 30–37, 44–47.

Hutter, Manfred. "Adam als Gärtner und König (Gen 2:8,15)." *Biblische Zeitschrift* 30 (1986) 258–62.

Japhet, Sara. "Periodization between History and Ideology II: Chronology and Ideology in Ezra-Nehemiah." In *Judah and the Judeans in the Persian Period*, edited by Oded Lipschits and Manfred Oeming, 491–508. Winona Lake, IN: Eisenbrauns, 2006.

Jastram, Nathan, and William C. Weinrich. "Man as Male and Female: Created in the Image of God." *Concordia Theological Quarterly* 68 (2004) 3–96.

Jenson, Robert W. "The Bible and the Trinity." *Pro Ecclesia* 11 (2002) 329–39.

Jerome. *Saint Jerome's Hebrew Questions on Genesis.* Translated by C. T. R. Hayward. Oxford Early Christian Studies, edited by Henry Chadwick and Andrew Louth. Oxford: Clarendon, 1995.

Jervis, L. Ann. "The Story that Shaped Paul's Way with Women." In *Loving God with Our Minds*, edited by Michael Welker and Cynthia A. Jarvis, 265–79. Grand Rapids: Eerdmans, 2004.

Jobling, David. "The Myth Semantics of Genesis 2:4b--3:24." *Semeia* 18 (1980) 41–49.

Johnston, Gordon H. "Genesis 1 and Ancient Egyptian Creation Myths." *Bibliotheca Sacra* 165.658 (2008) 178–94.

Kantrowitz, David. *Judaic Classics Library*. CD ROM Version 2.2. Skokie, IL: Davka Corporation, 2001.

Kearney, Peter J. "Creation and Liturgy: The P Redaction of Ex 25–40." *ZAW* 89 (1977) 375–87.

Keil, C. F., and F. Delitzsch. *The Pentateuch*. Vol. 1, *Commentary on the Old Testament*. Reprint. Peabody, MA: Hendrickson, 1989.

Keiser, Thomas A. "Genesis 1–11: Its literary Coherence and Theological Message." PhD diss., Dallas Theological Seminary, 2007.

Kim, Hyun Chul Paul. "Jonah Read Intertextually." *JBL* 126 (2007) 497–528.

Kiuchi, Nobuyoshi. *Leviticus*. Apollos Old Testament Commentary 3. Downers Grove, IL: InterVarsity, 2007.

Kofoed, Jens Bruun. *Text and History: Historiography and the Study of the Biblical Text*. Winona Lake, IN: Eisenbrauns, 2005.

König, Eduard. *Die Genesis: Eingeleitet, Übersetzt und Erklärt*. Gütersloh: Bertelsmann, 1925.

Koorevaar, Hendrik J. "Die Chronik als intendierter Abschluß des alttestamentlichen Kanons." *Jahrbuch für Evangelische Theologie* 11 (1997) 42–76.

Kovacs, Brian W. "Structure and Narrative Rhetoric in Genesis 2–3: Reflections on the Problem of Non-Convergent Structuralist Exegetical Methodologies." *Semeia* 18 (1980) 139–47.

Kutsch, E. "Die Paradieserzählung Genesis 2–3 und ihr Verfasser." In *Studien zum Pentateuch*, edited by Georg Braulik, 9–24. Vienna: Herder, 1977.

Leonard, Jeffery M. "Identifying Inner-Biblical Allusions: Psalm 78 as a Test Case." *Journal of Biblical Literature* 127 (2008) 241–65.

Levenson, Jon D. *Creation and the Persistence of Evil: The Jewish Drama of Divine Omnipotence*. San Francisco: Harper & Row, 1988.

Levin, Christoph. "Die Redaktion RJP in der Urgeschichte." In *Auf dem Weg zur Endgestalt von Genesis bis II Regum*, aufl. Martin Beck und Ulrike Schorn, 15–34. New York: de Gruyter, 2006.

Levine, Nachman. "The Curse and the Blessing: Narrative Discourse Syntax and Literary Form." *JSOT* 27 (2002) 189–99.

Lim, Johnson Teng Kok. *Grace in the Midst of Judgment: Grappling with Genesis 1–11*. Beihefte zur ZAW 314. Berlin: de Gruyter, 2002.

Lode, Lars. "The Two Creation Stories in Genesis Chapters 1 to 3." *Journal of Translation and Textlinguistics* 14 (2001) 1–52.

Lohfink, Norbert. "Die Erzählung von Sündenfall." In *Das Siegeslied am Schilfmeer: Christliche Auseinandersetzungen mit dem Alten Testament*, 81–101. Frankfurt: Knecht, 1965.

———. "Subdue the Earth? (Genesis 1:28)." In *Theology of the Pentateuch*, edited by Linda M. Maloney, 1–17. Edinburgh: T. & T. Clark, 1994.

Long, V. Philips. "History and Fiction: What is History?" In *Israel's Past in Present Research*, edited by V. Philips Long, 232–54. Winona Lake, IN: Eisenbrauns, 1999.

Longacre, Robert E. "Texts and Text Linguistics." In *Text versus Sentence: Basic Questions in Text Linguistics*, edited by Janos Petofi. Hamburg: Buske, 1979.

Lyons, Michael A. "Marking Innerbiblical Allusion in the Book of Ezekiel." *Bib* 88 (2007) 245–50.

Lyra, Nicholas von. *Postilla super totam Bibliam*. Vol. 1. Unveränd. Nachdr. [d. Ausg.] Strassburg 1492 ed. Frankfurt: Minerva, 1971.

MacDonald, Nathan. "The Imago Dei and Election: Reading Genesis 1:26–28 and Old Testament Scholarship with Karl Barth." *International Journal of Systematic Theology* 10 (2008) 303–27.

Magnuson, K. T. "Marriage, Procreation and Infertility: Reflections on Genesis." *Southern Baptist Journal of Theology* 4 (2000) 26–42.

Markl, Dominik. "Hab 3 in intertextueller und kontextueller Sicht." *Bib* 85 (2004) 99–108.

Mathews, Kenneth A. *Genesis 1—11:26*. In New American Commentary, edited by E. Ray Clendenen. Vol. 1A. Nashville: Broadman & Holman, 1996.

Mays, James Luther. "The Self in the Psalms and the Image of God." In *God and Human Dignity*, edited by R. Kendall Soulen and Linda Woodhead, 27–43. Grand Rapids: Eerdmans, 2006.

McConnell, Walter, III. "In His Image: A Christian's Place in Creation." *Asia Journal of Theology* 20 (2006) 114–27.

McFall, Leslie. *The Enigma of the Hebrew Verbal System: Solutions from Ewald to the Present Day*. Historic Texts and Interpreters in Biblical Scholarship 2. Sheffield: Almond, 1982.

Merrill, Eugene H. "Rashi, Nicholas de Lyra, and Christian Exegesis." *Westminster Theological Journal* 38 (1975) 66–79.

Miller, Patrick D. "The Beginning of the Psalter." In *Shape and Shaping of the Psalter*, edited by J. Clinton McCann Jr., 83–92, JSOTSup 159. Sheffield: JSOT, 1993.

Miqraoth Gedoloth. *Berayshit*. Tel Aviv: Pardes, 1969.

Morris, Paul. "Exiled from Eden: Jewish Interpretations of Genesis." In *Walk in the Garden*, edited by Paul Morris and Deborah Sawyer, 117–66. Sheffield: JSOT, 1992.

Muilenburg, James. "Form Criticism and Beyond." *JBL* 88 (1969) 1–18.

Niccacci, Alviero. *The Syntax of the Verb in Classical Hebrew Prose*. Translated by W. G. E. Watson. Sheffield: JSOT, 1990.

Nicholson, Ernest W. *The Pentateuch in the Twentieth Century: The Legacy of Julius Wellhausen*. New York: Oxford University Press, 1998.

Niehaus, Jeffrey. "In the Wind of the Storm: Another Look at Genesis III 8." *VT* 44 (1994) 263–67.

Nihan, Christophe. *From Priestly Torah to Pentateuch: A Study in the Composition of the Book of Leviticus*. Forschungen zum Alten Testament. Tübingen: Mohr Siebeck, 2007.

Noble, Paul R. "Esau, Tamar, and Joseph: Criteria for Identifying Inner-Biblical Allusions." *VT* 52 (2002) 219–52.

Ong, Walter J. "The Jinnee in the Well-Wrought Urn." *Essays in Criticism* (1954) 309–20.

Op, Hans Ulrich Steymans. "The Blessings in Genesis 49 and Deuteronomy 33: Awareness of Intertextuality." In *South African Perspectives on the Pentateuch Between Synchrony and Diachrony*, edited by Jurie le Roux and Eckart Otto, 71–89. London: T. & T. Clark, 2007.

Ortlund, Eric. "An Intertextual Reading of the Theophany of Psalm 97." *Scandanavian Journal of the Old Testament* 20 (2006) 273–85.

Otto, Eckart. "Die Paradieserzählung Genesis 2–3: Eine nachpriesterschriftliche Lehrerzählung in ihrem religionshistorischen Kontext." In *Jedes Ding hat seine Zeit*, edited by Otto Kaiser, 167–92. BZAW 241. Berlin: de Gruyter, 1996.

Ouro, Roberto. "The Garden of Eden Account: the Chiastic Structure of Genesis 2–3." *Andrews University Seminary Studies* 40 (2002) 219–43.

———. "Linguistic and Thematic Parallels Between Genesis 1 and 3." *Journal of the Adventist Theological Society* 13 (2002) 44–54.

Packer, James I. "Reflected Glory: What Does Genesis Mean by Man Being Made in the Image of God?" *Christianity Today* 47.12 (2003) 56.

Parker, Judson F., and Daniel Patte. "Structural Exegesis of Genesis 2 and 3." In *Society of Biblical Literature Seminar Papers* 13, edited by Paul J. Achtmeier, 141–59. Missoula, MT: Scholars, 1978.

Patte, Daniel. "Genesis 2 and 3: Kaleidoscopic Structural Readings." *Semeia* 18 (1980) 1–164.

———. "One Text: Several Structures." *Semeia* 18 (1980) 3–22.

———. "Speech Act Theory and Biblical Exegesis." *Semeia* 41 (1988) 85–102.

Plank, Karl A. "By the Water of a Death Camp: An Intertextual Reading of Psalm 137." *Literature and Theology* 22 (2008) 180–94.

Poole, Matthew. *The Exegetical Labors of the Reverend Matthew Poole*. Translated by Steven Dilday. Culpeper, VA: Master Poole, 2007.

———. *Synopsis criticorum aliorumque Sacrae Scripturae interpretum et commentatorum: summo studio et fide adornata, indicibusque necessariis instructa*. vol. 1. London: Ribbii, van de Water, & Halma, 1684.

Postell, Seth. "An Eschatological Reading of Genesis 1:1." Unpublished doctoral seminar paper presented at Southeastern Baptist Theological Seminary, Wake Forest, NC, 2006.

———. "Treating Biblical Hebrew as a 'Living' or a 'Dead' Language? A Summary and Evaluation of Two Modern Linguistic Approaches to the Biblical Hebrew Verbal System." Unpublished doctoral seminar paper presented at Golden Gate Baptist Theological Seminary, Mill Valley, CA., 2007.

———. "Where's the Faith?! A Reappraisal of Exodus 20:18–21 from a Compositional Perspective." Unpublished doctoral seminar paper presented at Golden Gate Baptist Theological Seminary, Mill Valley, CA., 2007.

Provan, Iain W. "Creation and Holistic Ministry: A Study of Genesis 1:1 to 2:3." *ERT* 25 (2001) 292–303.

Rad, Gerhard von. "The Form Critical Problem of the Hexateuch and Other Essays," In *The Problem of the Hexateuch and Other Essays*, 1–78. London: Oliver & Boyd, 1966.

———. *Genesis*. Translated by John H. Marks. The Old Testament Library, edited by G. Ernest Wright, et al. Philadelphia: Westminster, 1961.

———. *Old Testament Theology*. 2 vols. Translated by D. G. M. Stalker. New York: Harper & Row, 1962.

Raj, J. R. John Samuel. "Yahweh's Earth Our Abode: Towards Making Peace with the Creation." *Bangalore Theological Forum* 37.2 (2005) 40–60.

Reichenbach, Bruce R. "Genesis 1 as a Theological-Political Narrative of Kingdom Establishment." *Bulletin for Biblical Research* 13 (2003) 47–69.

Richter, Wolfgang. *Grundlagen einer althebäischen Grammatik.* Vol. 1. St. Otilien: Eos Verlag, 1978.

Ronan, Marian. "The Stewardship Model of Christian Environmentalism." *Living Pulpit* 15.3 (2006) 18–19.

Rosenberg, Joel. *King and Kin: Political Allegory in the Hebrew Bible.* Indiana Studies in Biblical Literature. Bloomington, IN: Indiana University Press, 1986.

Rowe, Robert D. *God's Kingdom and God's Son: The Background to Mark's Christology from Concepts of Kingship in the Psalms.* Arbeiten zur Geschichte des antiken Judentums und des Urchristentums 50. Leiden: Brill, 2002.

Sailhamer, John H. "Creation, Genesis 1–11, and the Canon." *Bulletin of Biblical Research* 10 (2000) 89–106.

———. "Exegesis of the Old Testament as a Text." In *A Tribute to Gleason Archer,* edited by Walter C. Kaiser and Ronald Youngblood, 279–96. Chicago: Moody, 1986.

———. "Genesis." In *Genesis, Exodus, Leviticus, Numbers,* Expositor's Bible Commentary, edited by Frank E. Gaebelein, 2:1–284. Grand Rapids: Zondervan, 1990.

———. *Genesis Unbound: A Provocative New Look at the Creation Account.* Sisters, OR: Multnomah, 1996.

———. *Introduction to Old Testament Theology: A Canonical Approach.* Grand Rapids: Zondervan, 1995.

———. *The Meaning of the Pentateuch: Revelation, Composition and Interpretation.* Downers Grove, IL: InterVarsity, 2009.

———. "Notes on Biblical Hebrew Syntax." Unpublished class notes, Southeastern Baptist Theological Seminary, 2004.

———. "Parallel Structures in the Center of the Pentateuch." Unpublished paper presented at Golden Gate Baptist Theological Seminary. Mill Valley, CA, 2007.

———. *The Pentateuch as Narrative.* Grand Rapids: Zondervan, 1992.

———. "A Wisdom Composition of the Pentateuch?" In *Way of Wisdom,* edited by James I. Packer and Sven K. Soderlund, 15–35. Grand Rapids: Zondervan, 2000.

Sarna, Nahum. "The Bible: The Canon, Texts, and Editions." In *Encyclopedia Judaica,* 4:816–36. Jerusalem: Keter, 1971.

Schmidt W. H. S.v. "ברא *br'*." In *Theological Lexicon of the Old Testament,* edited by Ernst Jenni and Claus Westermann, 1:253–56. Peabody, MA: Hendrickson, 1997.

Schmitt, Hans-Christoph. "Redaktion des Pentateuch im Geiste der Prophetie." *VT* 32 (1982) 170–89.

———. "Das spätdeuteronomistische Geschichtswerk Genesis 1—2 Regum 25 und seine theologische Intention." In *Congress Volume,* edited by J. A. Emerton, 261–79. Leiden: Brill, 1997.

Schmutzer, Andrew J. "The Creation Mandate to 'be fruitful and multiply': A Crux of Thematic Repetition in Genesis 1–11." PhD diss., Trinity Evangelical Divinity School, 2005.

Schneider, Michael. "Texte—Intertexte—Schrift: Perspektiven intertextueller Bibellektüre." In *Kontexte der Schrift Band 2, Kultur, Politik, Religion, Sprache-Text,* 361–76. Stuttgart: Kohlhammer, 2005.

Schneider, Wolfgang. *Grammatik des biblischen Hebräish.* Munich: Claudius, 1974.

Schökel, Alonso Luis. "Motivos Sapienciales y de Alianza en Gn 2–3." *Bib* 43 (1962) 295–316.

Schüle, Andreas. "Die Würde des Bildes: eine Re-Lektüre der priesterlichen Urgeschichte." *Evangelische Theologie* 66 (2006) 440–54.

Scotchmer, Paul F. "Lessons from Paradise on Work, Marriage, and Freedom: A Study of Genesis 2:4—3:24." *ERT* 28 (2004) 80–85.

Searle, John R. *Speech Acts: An Essay in the Philosophy of Language.* London: Cambridge University Press, 1969.

Searle, John R., and Daniel Vanderveken. *Foundations of Illocutionary Logic.* New York: Cambridge University Press, 1985.

Seeligmann, Isac Leo. "Voraussetzungen der Midrashexegese." *VT* 1 (1953) 150–81.

Shea, William H. "The Unity of the Creation Account." *Origins* 5 (1978) 9–39.

Shepherd, Michael B. "Compositional Analysis of the Twelve." *ZAW* 120 (2008) 184–93.

———. *Daniel in the Context of the Hebrew Bible.* Studies in Biblical Literature 123. New York: Lang, 2009.

Ska, Jean Louis. "Genesi 2–3: qualche domanda di fondo." *Protestantesimo* 63 (2008) 1–27.

Sommer, Benjamin D. "New Light on the Composition of Jeremiah." *CBQ* 61 (1999) 646–66.

———. *A Prophet Reads Scripture: Allusion in Isaiah 40-66.* Stanford, CA: Stanford University Press, 1998.

Sonnet, Jean Pierre. *The Book within the Book: Writing in Deuteronomy.* Biblical Interpretation. Leiden: Brill, 1997.

Sousan, André. "The Woman in the Garden of Eden: A Rhetorical-Critical Study of Genesis 2:4b—3:24." PhD diss., Vanderbilt University, 2006.

Sparks, Kent. "Enuma Elish and Priestly Mimesis: Elite Emulation in Nascent Judaism." *JBL* 126 (2007) 625–48.

Stark, Judith Chelius. "Augustine on Women: In God's Image, But Less So." In *Feminist Interpretations of Augustine,* edited by Judith Chelius Stark, 215–41. University Park: Pennsylvania State University Press, 2007.

Sternberg, Meir. *The Poetics of Biblical Narrative: Ideological Literature and the Drama of Reading.* Indiana Literary Biblical Series. Bloomington: Indiana University Press, 1985.

Steymans, Hans Ulrich. "The Blessings in Genesis 49 and Deuteronomy 33: Awareness of Intertextuality." In *South African Perspectives on the Pentateuch between Synchrony and Diachrony,* edited by Jurie Le Roux and Eckart Otto 71–89. New York: T. & T. Clark, 2007.

Stordalen, Terje. *Echoes of Eden: Genesis 2-3 and Symbolism of the Eden Garden in Biblical Hebrew Literature.* Contributions to Biblical Exegesis and Theology 25. Edited by T. Baarda, et al. Leuven: Peeters, 2000.

———. "Genesis 2,4: Restudying a Locus Classicus." *ZAW* 104 (1992) 163–77.

Talshir, Zipora. "Several Canon-Related Concepts Originating in Chronicles." *ZAW* 113 (2001) 386–403.

Talstra, Eep. "From the 'Eclipse' to the 'Art' of Biblical Narrative: Reflections on Methods of Biblical Exegesis." In *Perspectives in the Study of the Old Testament and Early Judaism: A Symposium in Honour of Adams S. van der Woude on the Occasion of His 70th Birthday,* edited by A. S. van der Woude, et al, 1–41. Leiden: Brill, 1998.

———. "Syntax and Composition: the Use of Yiqtol in Narrative Sections in the Book of Exodus." In *Studies in the Book of Exodus: Redaction, Reception, Interpretation,* 225–36. Leuven: Peeters, 2006.

———. "Text Grammar and Hebrew Bible. I: Elements of a Theory." *Bibliotheca Orientalis* 35 (1978) 169–74.

————. "Text Grammar and Hebrew Bible. II: Syntax and Semantics." *Bibliotheca Orientalis* 39 (1982) 26–38.

Tarwater, John K. "The Covenantal Nature of Marriage in the Order of Creation in Genesis 1 and 2." PhD diss., Southwestern Baptist Theological Seminary, 2002.

Toews, Brian G. "Genesis 1–4: The Genesis of Old Testament Instruction." In *Biblical Theology: Retrospect & Prospect*, edited by Scott J. Hafemann, 38–52. Downers Grove, IL: InterVarsity, 2002.

Towner, W. Sibley. "Clones of God: Genesis 1:26–28 and the Image of God in the Hebrew Bible." *Interpretation* 59 (2005) 341–56.

Townsend, P. Wayne. "Eve's Answer to the Serpent: An Alternative Paradigm for Sin and Some Implications in Theology." *Calvin Theological Journal* 33 (1998) 399–420.

Trible, Phyllis. *Rhetorical Criticism: Context, Method, and the Book of Jonah*. Minneapolis: Fortress, 1994.

Trimpe, Birgit. *Von der Schöpfung bis zur Zerstreuung: Intertextuelle Interpretationen der biblischen Urgeschichte (Gen 1–11)*. Vol. 1. Osnabrücker Studien zur jüdischen und christlichen Bibel. Osnabrück: Universitätverlag Rasch, 2000.

Valiyapparambil, Sebastian. "The Power of the Powerless: A Study of the Feminist Concepts of Edith Stein in the Light of Gen 1:26–27, 'in his own image … male and female he created them.'" *Sevartham* 30 (2005) 163–64.

Van Dijk, Teun. *Some Aspects of Text Grammar: A Study in Theoretical Linguistics and Poetics*. Paris: Mouton, 1972.

Van Seters, John. "The Creation of Man and the Creation of the King." *ZAW* 101 (1989) 333–42.

Vanhoozer, Kevin J. *Is There a Meaning in This Text? The Bible, the Reader, and the Morality of Literary Knowledge*. Grand Rapids: Zondervan, 1998.

Vervenne, Marc. "Genesis 1,1—2,4: The Compositional Texture of the Priestly Overture to the Pentateuch." In *Studies in the Book of Genesis*, edited by A. Wénin, 35–79. Leuven: Leuven University Press, 2001.

Vollmer, J. S.v., "עשׂה *śh*." In *Theological Lexicon of the Old Testament*, edited by Ernst Jenni and Claus Westermann, 2:944–51. Peabody, MA: Hendrickson, 1997.

Wall, John. "Imitatio Creatoris: The Hermeneutical Primordiality of Creativity in Moral Life." *Journal of Religion* 87 (2007) 21–42.

Waltke, Bruce K., and Charles Yu. *An Old Testament Theology*. Grand Rapids: Zondervan, 2007.

Walton, John H. "Creation in Genesis 1:1—2:3 and the Ancient Near East: Order Out of Disorder after Chaoskampf." *Calvin Theological Journal* 43 (2008) 48–63.

————. *The Lost World of Genesis One: Ancient Cosmology and the Origins Debate*. Downers Grove, IL: InterVarsity, 2009.

Weimar, Peter. "Struktur und Komposition der priesterschriftlichen Schöpfungserzählung (Gen 1,1—2,4a)." In *Ex Mesopotamia et Syria Lux*, 803–43. Münster: Ugarit-Verlag, 2002.

Weinrich, Harald. *Tempus: besprochene und erzählte Welt*. Stuttgart: Kohlhammer, 1971.

Wellhausen, Julius. *Prolegomena zur Geschichte Israels*. 2nd ed. Berlin: Reimer, 1883.

Wenham, Gordon J. *Genesis 1–15*. Word Biblical Commentary 1. Waco, TX: Word, 1987.

————. "The Priority of P." *VT* 49 (1999) 240–58.

————. "Sanctuary Symbolism in the Garden of Eden Story." In *I Studied Inscriptions before the Flood*, edited by Richard Hess and David Toshio Tsumura, 399–404, Sources for Biblical and Theological Study 4. Winona Lake, IN: Eisenbrauns, 1994.

Westermann, Claus. *Genesis 1–11*. Translated by John J. Scullion. A Continental Commentary. Minneapolis: Fortress, 1994.

Weyde, Karl William. "Inner-Biblical Interpretation: Methodological Reflections on the Relationship Between Texts in the Hebrew Bible." *Svensk exegetisk årsbok* 70 (2005) 287–300.

White, Hugh C. "Introduction: Speech Act Theory and Literary Criticism." *Semeia* 41 (1988) 1–24.

———. "The Value of Speech Act Theory for Old Testament Hermeneutics." *Semeia* 41 (1988) 41–63.

Whybray, R. N. *The Making of the Pentateuch: A Methodological Study.* JSOTSup 53. Sheffield: JSOT, 1987.

Wifall, Walter R. "Breath of His Nostrils: Gen 2:7b." *CBQ* 36 (1974) 237–40.

Williamson, H. G. M. "Isaiah 62:4 and the Problem of Inner-Biblical Allusions." *JBL* 119 (2000) 734–39.

Wimsatt, William K., and Monroe C. Beardsley. "The Intentional Fallacy." *Sewanee Review* 54 (1946) 468–88.

Witte, Markus. *Die biblische Urgeschichte: redaktions- und theologiegeschichtliche Beobachtungen zu Genesis 1:1—11:26.* BZAW 265. Berlin: de Gruyter, 1998.

Wolde, E. J. van. "The Creation of Coherence." *Semeia* 81 (1998) 159–74.

———. "A Reader-Oriented Exegesis Illustrated by a Study of the Serpent in Genesis 2–3." In *Pentateuchal and Deuteronomistic Studies: Papers Read at the XIIIth IOSOT Congress Leuven 1989*, edited by Christian H. W. Brekelmans and Johan Lust, 11–21. Leuven: Leuven University Press, 1990.

Wong, Yee-Cheung. *A Text-Centered Approach to Old Testament Exegesis and Theology and Its Application to the Book of Isaiah.* Jian Dao Dissertation Series 9, Bible and Literature Series 6. Hong Kong: Alliance Bible Seminary, 2001.

Zakovitch, Yair. *An Introduction to Inner-Biblical Interpretation.* Even-Yehuda, Israel: Reches, 1992.

Zimmer, J. Raymond. "The Creation of Man and the Evolutionary Record." *Perspectives on Science and Christian Faith* 48 (1996) 16–26.

———. "The Creation Story and Evolution." *Journal of Interdisciplinary Studies* 5.1–2 (1993) 77–92.

———. "Genesis 1 as a Sign of the Evolutionary Record: Art and Implications." *Perspectives on Science and Christian Faith* 56.3 (2004) 172–80.

Scripture Index*

---

* Page numbers in italics denote figures and tables

181

Subject and Name Index*

---

* Page numbers in italics denote figures and tables

Sailhamer, John (*cont.*)
  text *vs.* event interpretation,
    62n84
  on text vs event interpretation,
    55–56, 62n84
  thema terms, 63, 63n91
  on the Torah, 156
Sarna, Nahum, on Chronicles, 158,
  158n38, 165–66
Satan. *See also* serpent
  fall of, 84
  serpent as, 103–4, 121n5
Schmitt, Hans-Christoph, 20–22
Schökel, Alonso, 32n32, 114–15
Scripture, unity of, 11–13
Second Temple Judaism, 1, 19, 76
seduction and exile, 120–34
Seeligmann, Leo, 5
serpent. *See also* Satan
  Adam's fall and, 3, 104–5, 163
  Blenkinsopp on, 130
  Canaanites and, 33n35, 104,
    104n108, 105–6, 121–24
  as cult symbol, 104n110
  dietary laws and, 109n131
  Emmrich on, 33n36
  Eve and, 109n131, 117, 129, 131,
    164–65
  Gibeonites and, 106–7
  God's mandate to conquer, 100,
    102
  Noah's fall and, 104–5
  Poole on, 3, 12–13, 13n35
  as prudent, 122–24
  role of, 121, 121n5, 130
  as Satan, 103–4, 121n5
  sexual perversity and, 114, 121n6
  Sousan on, 103
  victory over, 120
  Wenham on, 121, 124
sexuality
  Eve and the serpent, 105n112
  human, 104–5

sexual immorality, of the
  Canaanites, 104–5, 121n6
sexual perversity, 114, 121n6
Shepherd, Michael B.
  on author's compositional strat-
    egy, 71n132
  on Elijah, 152
sin, 38, 104–5, 114, 120–24, 126. *See
  also* transgression
Sinai Covenant. *See also* Mosaic
  Covenant; Pentateuch
  curses in, 129
  disobedience, consequences for,
    118–19
  Fall Narrative, 124, 126
  Genesis, role in, 22, 108–19
  between God and Adam, 115–19
  Israelites, as warning to, 135, 166
  Israel's failure and, 3–4, 114–19,
    120, 124–30, 141–42
  Pentateuch and, 39–40, 88–89
  Pentateuch and, Sailhamer on,
    39–40, 69–70, 87–88n54
  as prototypical, 114–19
  Song of Moses and, 142
  Sousan on, 29
  text-centered approach to
    Genesis, 108–20
Sinai Narrative
  Erlich, analysis of, 38–39
  interpretation of, 3–4, 21, 25, 28,
    115n146, 116, 125, 126–29
  Wilderness Narrative and, 21,
    127
Ska, Jean Louis, 16n59
Solomon
  Adam and, parallels between,
    32n32, 130
  as Israel failure, 131–33
Sommer, Benjamin D.
  on inner-biblical exegesis, 72
  on intertextuality, 64n102,
    65–66, 65n104

30595287R00120

Printed in Great Britain
by Amazon